TALES OF EMPIRE

0. Humphrey Bowman (Director of Education in Palestine, 1920–36) and friends (Bowman accompanied Prince Faisal of Arabia to Britain in 1919).

Tales of Empire

THE BRITISH IN
THE MIDDLE EAST
1880–1952

Derek Hopwood

I. B. TAURIS & CO LTD
Publishers
LONDON

Published by
I. B. Tauris & Co Ltd
110 Gloucester Avenue
London NW1 8JA

British Library Cataloguing in Publication Data

Hopwood, Derek, *1933–*
   Tales of Empire: the British in the Middle
   East
   1. Middle East. Britons, history
   I. Title
   956′.00421

   ISBN 1–85043–129–9

Printed and Bound in Great Britain by
T. J. Press (Padstow) Ltd, Padstow, Cornwall

Dedicated to the memory of Elizabeth Monroe

CONTENTS

LIST OF PLATES

ACKNOWLEDGEMENTS

Permission to quote or to reproduce photographs is gratefully acknowledged to the Imperial War Museum, Mrs Colin Hope-Gill, John Murray (for 'Egyptian Service' by Russell Pasha), Mrs Kim Rowland (Gorst photograph), the Jerusalem and East Mission.

PREFACE

The wave of nostalgia for times imperial has beaten mainly on the shores of India. There have, too, been many stories out of Africa, perhaps fewer from the Middle East, although the British were just as busy there for well over a century and a half. During this period (1798–1971) many hundreds of British soldiers, diplomats, civil servants, teachers and missionaries served in the Middle East. At the height of Britain's 'moment' there was a British presence (in addition to diplomats) in fourteen Arab states. Britons worked and played, lived, loved and died there and left behind them many traces. There remain universities and schools, dams, railways, bridges, churches and cathedrals, and the more intangible influences of education, manners, methods of administration and memories in people's minds.

The men and women who actually worked on the ground were drawn to the Middle East by a mixture of motives – good old-fashioned imperialism, the urge to convert and civilize, to educate, or the desire for a different life in exotic surroundings. They ranged from the avowed missionary to merchant and trader and the great pro-consuls. During their stay in the area many of them wrote unofficially about their lives and work, reporting incidents, details and reactions not to be found in the official documents. They also left diaries and sent letters home. All these are full of life, humour, tragedy, boredom – the factors that make up expatriate existence.

As the empire was drawing to a close it was realized that many of these documents must be lying around in trunks and attics, in danger of disintegration. My late colleague, Elizabeth Monroe, the author of 'Britain's Moment in the Middle East', began a breathless search for such papers (and photographs) before it was too late. She was extremely successful and now St Antony's College has a substantial and unique collection. Many serious researchers have used the material for academic monographs, but reading through the collection it occurred to me that much information was being ignored that threw light on the more informal aspects of life in the Middle East.

Accordingly I started a search through thousands of papers for those anecdotes, personal stories, humourous moments, neglected by others, which often underlined the real enjoyment of working in the Middle East. Of course there were darker moments, and these have also been included. It would have been unfortunate for so much human material to have remained unknown, so I collected what I thought the most interesting and put it into some sort of order – hence the present book. I hope the reader gains at least some of the enjoyment I experienced in preparing it. The photographs are also largely from the same archive.

Since I wished to include in this book only unpublished material and only material in St Antony's, the shape has been determined by what was available in the archives. Most of the papers were deposited by men and women who had served in Palestine and Egypt. There are very large individual collections, for example that of St John Philby who worked in Arabia and kept every word he wrote – invoices, letters, diaries – but much of this has been published and a lot is boring. The papers dealing with other areas of British interest – Turkey, Iran, Iraq – are not so comprehensive. I have tried to find interesting extracts on as wide an area as possible although, inevitably, coverage is uneven.

The book is dedicated to Elizabeth Monroe who began it all. My thanks also to Diana Grimwood-Jones and Gillian Grant, the two archivists of the collection who guided me to and through the choicest items.

Derek Hopwood

ONE

OUT TO EGYPT

The imperial highway

8.15 on a grey Friday night in London before the Great War. In Charing Cross station the Peninsular & Orient Brindisi Express stands ready to pull out for Dover. After five short days its passengers will be enjoying the clear blue skies and sunshine of Egypt. In the Pullman coaches of the South Eastern Railway men and women about imperial business are beginning the first leg of a journey which will take them on to Calais, Paris, Turin, Brindisi and Port Said. Such events occurred many hundreds of times and in different places – Britons leaving home for service in the far corners of the British empire.

The Brindisi Express was the quickest way to reach Egypt in those days. From the early part of the nineteenth century the P & O had been engaged in transporting Britons throughout the Empire – onward from Egypt to Aden, India, Hongkong and Australia. The overland route to the Mediterranean, besides being quick, avoided the dreaded crossing of the Bay of Biscay. The more hardy joined their ship in London's Royal Albert Dock. In 1900 the first-class fare to Egypt via Brindisi was £21.0.0d. Travellers could take other routes: to Marseilles for a Messageries Maritimes vessel to Alexandria, or to Naples for the Florio-Rubattino line also to Alexandria – with fares rising to £21.8.0d.

Joining the train in London was the first step in a great adventure, sometimes lasting forty years or more, for those Britons who had chosen to live and work in the Middle East. On the journey they would meet other colleagues bound for Egypt, often fellow graduates from Oxford or Cambridge, new recruits or old hands returning from home leave. A camaraderie and spirit of adventure drew together all those who were devoting their lives to the great cause of serving England abroad. An eyewitness account from G.W. Steevens in

December 1898 recreates the atmosphere of that train journey to Brindisi:

The P and O express offered an experience with its own peculiar flavour. There was nothing externally in the three long sleeping and dining cars and three luggage-vans to mark it off from any of the other 'Grand European Expresses' purveyed by the Sleeping-Car Company. The beds were the same – the food was the same – and when I say that it was Wagons-Lits food, I say all. It is a class of nourishment wholly by itself, whether you come on it in France, or Hungary, or Turkey. Some like it and some don't.

The brown-uniformed attentive attendants were the same as everywhere – except it suddenly struck you that they all talked English – and there you got the clue to the peculiar character of the train. It was altogether an English train. So far it had not embarked a single passenger who was not a Briton. And their trade it was not difficult to see. Fair-haired and blue-eyed, square-shouldered and square-jawed, with puckered brows and steadfast eyes that seemed to look outwards and inwards at the same time, self-contained, self-controlled, and self-reliant, they were unmistakably builders – British empire-builders. The faces of the women were serene with the imperturbable serenity of those who have seen too many strange sights to be surprised now at anything; and in their patient aspect was a hint of the tragic heroism that sends its children to be brought up by strangers and forget their mothers.

The empire-builders were going forth to their long work again. To every point of the remotest East were returning, quite uncomplaining, the obscure makers of the British empire. It was a geography lesson in itself – and remember that this train leaves London every Friday night, and that its freight is always the same. Thinking this, you saw that the two engines, three cars, and three vans were no ordinary train after all. They were a very vital link in that band of scarlet that grips the world – the British empire. Thinking of the load of heavy hearts it bore, of self-sacrifice, of single-eyed, unquestioning duty-doing, you began for the hundredth time to say that you never before had quite realised what 'British empire' means.

The travellers began to feel more at ease as the train took them away from dowdy, wet, northern Europe to the warmth and blue skies of Italy – into the welcoming sun:

To the imperial Englishmen in the train, the sun was welcome; it has become a second climate. Not that it dispels care for them. But no sun or storm can shake the steady independence of the British character when you get it at its best. This was to be seen in little things during the long day's run down Italy. When you see men of other nations on the third day of a railway journey, they are generally unkempt to look at and unwholesome to sit by. The precise, imperturbable, Imperial Englishman takes off all his clothes, and goes to bed cleanly in his pyjamas: he bathes standing up, and shaves religiously each morning, and carefully brushes his clothes. He talks little, although there is a freemasonry about the smoking-room of the P and O Express which melts down great parts of his native reserve. When he does talk, it is not of money, like the travelling American, nor of beer and time-tables, like the travelling German, but of sport.

As the sun slanted down we were obviously drawing near Brindisi; the whole population of the Express with one accord began to write home. The letters did not appear to run very fluently, and were probably not masterpieces of literature. But they were letters home – the first letters home, the first, it was pathetic to think, of how many! It was pathetic to wonder how many of these taciturn, decidedly uninspired, all but commonplace men had made themselves widowers and childless in the interest of the British empire. It was their business, and they were doing it. Duty has got to be done in the proper place, at the proper time, in spite of all things. Just as at the proper time and in spite of all things – a standing rebuke to the kingdom of Italy, where it alone is certain and punctual – the Imperial Express clanked into Brindisi.

In this small southern Italian port the passengers left the train and joined their ship. Once aboard they settled down to their respective journeys – some for only a few days to Port Said, others for weeks to India or the Far East. The ships were not very impressive although they improved over time. Steevens continues his account of the journey:

I had always imagined a liner of the P and O as something peculiarly stately and luxurious – the lawful heir of the old East Indiaman. There is something in the very name 'Peninsular and Oriental' that fills the ear and imagination. I was a trifle disappointed at first to find the *Britannia* only a ship after all. It was rather painful to find the smoking-room about half the size of an Atlantic liner's and decorated with green tiles that recalled bedroom suites in Tottenham Court Road. The table, again, was not what the letters P and O had seemed to promise. That, at least, is the way I put it: older travellers gloomily said it was just what they expected. Brawn is a very difficult viand to get really bad; but such musty brawn as exists on the world's markets seemed to have been cornered by the cook of the *Britannia*.

Yet the P and O grows on you; even in two days it grows on you. There is something stately about it, after all; and it is very English, to boot, and very picturesque. The ship is not a ferry-boat, like an Atlantic liner, but something between a hotel and a home. It is even more miraculously clean than other ships. The officers are point device in their smartness and courtesy; the very stewards have something of the grand manner of good servants. You dress decorously for dinner, and your cabin gives you plenty of room to dress in. You begin to realise that you are going to a part of the world where your people are sahibs, to be treated as such, and to behave as such.

Then there is the family aspect of the ship, which conveys an impression of stability. There are babies with nurses – not in themselves objects of delight, but interesting because of the wonderful destiny that makes them at home half round the world before they know right hand from left. When the mothers bring the babies up on to the promenade-deck you get an illustration of the continuity of the British empire – continuity in space, and continuity in time. These toddling nuisances are quite at home at sea. With many it is not their first voyage, nor their second. They are quite at home; their home from birth up is the world, wherever there may be work to do.

Each day the sun has shed himself upon us more lavishly. We have let him soak in and in, till today English winter is already cleansed from the system. For, by now, we are well in the south of the Levant; we are already within touch of Egypt. At noon, and by lunchtime we could hardly be more then eight or nine miles away – and yet no sign of it. Three-quarters of an hour for lunch, and we must be tumbling over it – yet still no sign. But, yes, there on the starboard bow! There is a group of dust-coloured houses, with a light tower, quite close, not a mile away.

Only it seems to be standing on nothing, in the middle of the sea. To port and starboard is still blue sea – nothing else at all. We are getting much closer now, and we see two low dust-coloured breakwaters pushing their snouts through the same blue sea. Then some shipping near the houses – only still no coast-line. The houses are Port Said; the breakwaters are the Suez Canal; and the land which you cannot see is ancient Egypt. You seem to have arrived at nowhere.

To first-time travellers in Egypt impressions were overwhelming – the dense mass of humanity, porters, hawkers, guides, small boys all clamouring for custom, and particularly the innumerable, half-naked coal carriers who refuelled the ship during its stay in Port Said. There seemed to be no order and little decorum. To some of those who already knew Egypt it was more of a homecoming, a reacquaintance with the familiar. John Young, once a government official, remembers his time in Egypt:

A quarter of a century takes up a large portion of one's existence and I look back upon the Near East as part of my being. When I return to Cairo, which I have done at intervals until the world ceased to be at peace, I have felt as if I were returning home. Between visits I have read disturbing accounts of change and so-called progress and I wonder if I will find next time that the nature of the Egyptian too has altered. I leave England with a sense of uneasiness, as the ship comes alongside I stand on deck in feverish anxiety but when the gangway goes down I breathe a sigh of relief for up surges the same un-disciplined crowd of porters and there on the quay is the same rabble of carriage and car drivers who hail me with deafening shouts. Then a few words of explanation, a joke, an Arabic proverb and I am once more with old friends.

Returning home aroused different emotions. The 'Egyptian' hands joining Far Eastern boats at Port Said immediately felt the superior glare of the real sahibs and memsahibs returning from India. In the hierarchy of empire the 'Indians' were clearly on top. Humphrey Bowman, working as a teacher in Egypt, was not even in the first rank of Britons in Cairo and had to suffer the torment of travelling second class home. He took the Austrian Lloyd line from Port Said:

We left Cairo after an early dinner and slept that night at Ismailia. It is a deserted place, and the hotel we stayed at was about ¾ mile from the station – our luggage was carried by 3 porters, one of whom took all the heavy baggage and staggered along slowly after us. We only arrived at 12 midnight, and were glad to get to bed after a glass of beer and some biscuits. We rose early to catch the train to Port Said. Before leaving, we had rather a row with the manager, as he charged us very heavily for baths, which we kicked at. After a short dispute, Brown said: 'Oh it doesn't matter – we simply won't pay.' At this, the manager said: 'Shut all the doors! I am the proprietor and you don't leave the hotel until you have paid.' We saw it was no use making any more fuss: so we paid up, promising to tell all our friends in Cairo never to come there. The whole thing was very absurd, as there was only a servant (a native) in evidence and he did not attempt to shut the doors as there were at least 6 in the hall alone!

We reached Port Said by about 11, and went on board the S.S. *Bohemia* with our luggage, to see over cabins and then went and had our lunch at the Eastern Exchange Hotel. Brown and I shared a cabin with 2 others: colonials from South Africa, rather rough diamonds, but not bad fellows. We were 2nd class; but in the 1st class we had several friends. We sat on the 1st class deck with them for the first 2 days and no one seemed to raise any objection. It was a trifle choppy as we left Port Said at 4 pm: but not really rough, and the sun was warm, and the sky blue: so nothing seemed to matter – and best of all! we were really on our way home. Last night we got expelled from the 1st class: it was quite our own fault, as some young ladies, whom we named the 'Flowers of the Veldt' had asked us to join them in a small dance. We were dressed in flannels, while they were all in evening dress and the result was that we were very conspicuous. The Captain came up to Brown first and hinting that he was a 2nd class passenger, requested him to return to his own quarters. Then before we could warn him the Captain went to MacKintosh, though at the moment he was sitting with one of the 'flowers', and sent him about his business. I saw what was up, and returned to the 'East End' of my own accord and for the rest of the voyage we remained there, occasionally visited by our 1st class friends.

The quality of the ships plying across the Mediterranean began to improve and passengers (particularly in the 1st class) travelled in the greatest luxury. By the 1920s the surroundings appropriate for 'Indians' began to overwhelm some of the more humble from Egypt. Harry Boyle, an old Egypt hand who had first gone out in 1885, reported in 1921:

At 3 we got to the quay and had only to get out of the train and walk on board this gigantic ship. At 3.30 we sat down to lunch and the ship sailed. Oh! The divine coolness and freshness of the sea-air again. It is life. For the first time for six weeks I am not streaming with perspiration. I know a lot of other people on board, and we are a curious company. The Chief Steward told me before dinner that we represent nine different nationalities. It is the most gorgeous ship one can imagine – absurdly so. Enormously large, with satin-furnished saloons, library, lounges hung with pictures, great carpeted staircases – all like some splendid palace. All the passengers are dressed into fits; tea is served in a winter-garden of palms and flowers; the beds have heavy silk curtains, hot and cold water laid on in each cabin, etc., etc.

We are a mixed company. English, Jews – of the highest class – French, Italians, Egyptians, Greeks and others. We have a most magnificent Italian Cardinal, superb in his red hat and white silk robes – a most charming old gentleman. The only English ladies are our Lady Bernard and the wife of one of the officers from Khartoum. But the others!! For beauty and costume they really do take the cake and they are most sparkling and agreeable. Of course, they are all residents of Egypt, so there is a mixture of languages which is quite confusing, though I am fairly used to it now. I had tea today with a party where we spoke indifferently Arabic, French, Italian and English.

Another passenger, Herbert Addison, noted the remarkable variety of ships available:

During vacation times, too, we could enjoy the widest range of international advantages. With virtually no competition – as yet – from the aeroplane, the steamship companies by competing among themselves had provided for us an almost unparalleled choice of routes across the Mediterranean. The old stagers among the expatriates could still travel by P & O, climbing up the accommodation ladder at Port Said beneath the unsympathetic gaze of the Anglo-Indians leaning over the rail and looking down upon the lesser breeds without the law. On the Dutch liners from Batavia you were most lavishly fed: the Japanese ships of the N.Y.K. company were, as Baedeker might have said, 'well spoken of'. Of the other ships coming through the Suez Canal, the Bibby liners from Rangoon had developed a kind of special relationship with their British passengers: this was because on the homeward trip through the Red Sea the *Cheshire* or the *Warwickshire* would call at Port Sudan and there embark its quota of *fool sudani* (the Arabic name for monkey nuts). The title was applied to the Anglo-Sudanese officials by their opposite numbers the Anglo-Egyptian officials who came aboard at Port Said. A healthy rivalry between opposing teams at deck games was thereby encouraged.

It was the Orient ships from Australia that offered a unique sporting facility: the captain would raise a cricket team to meet the passengers in a match on a netted enclosure on the boat deck. Then of course from Alexandria we had our own Lloyd Triestino and Sitmar ships to Italy, and the Messageries liners to Marseilles: or, if you were quick to use them, the Khedivial Mail line ran express liners to Athens and Constantinople. Our own Italian ships? Why, yes. On our homeward or outwards journeys we had grown so used to seeing friends or colleagues for us the ship had become a kind of club. And the oddest thing of all was – that as the ships got better and better and faster and faster, offering still better service, the passenger fares grew *less* and *less*. When I first went to Egypt in 1921, I paid £28 for a 2nd class passage in a 4-berth cabin. Twelve years later, when travelling in the reverse direction from Alexandria to Venice, a berth in a 1st class single-berth cabin only cost me £16.

Homes away from home: Cairo

Cairo, the greatest city in the Middle East, was home for most Britons in Egypt, whether it was a life in the barracks, the British residency, school or university, or government department. It was the centre of social activity, of exclusive clubs, restaurants and churches, and for many expatriates an unusually pleasant place. It had many of the advantages that a European city offered, together with cheap servants and a high standard of living. To one long-time expatriate Cairo was 'quite as civilised as Paris'. The drawbacks of the city included the stiflingly hot weather during the summer, the din and the smells. Harry Boyle (who worked in the residency for many years and of whom more later) wrote feelingly to his mother:

Cairo 28th July 1909

Dearest Mother,
Ugh! we are getting through some nasty weather just now. The Nile is dawdling on his grandfatherly way down and we are having some still windless nights. I am most fit and don't mind much, though it is tiresome

not thinking of sleep before about 3.30 a.m. which is always the case, but I shall be pleased when it is over. Last night I dined out in the desert, where it seemed a different world, and tonight I am going out there to sleep. But this state of things never lasts long and by the time you get this it will be long over. I was thinking yesterday – but not, as you know, in any hostile spirit – what a very uncomfortable condition one is always in here, from an English point of view, in the warm weather. One is never what *you* would call comfortable. What with the unholy odours all over the place; the fact of being always moist, if not dripping; the legions of biting mosquitoes and sand-flies; the – to me pleasant, but to others hateful – everlasting brazen glare and blaze of dusty sunshine; all these considerations properly considered make me understand why some people get so cross when any one like myself says that he enjoys a Cairo summer.

About 3.30 comes the dawn and with it a blessed coolth. Don't regard the above as a personal jeremiad; it would be a quaint thing if it came to that! but it is a local picture of circumstances. Last night I smoked a pipe about 2, leaning out of the window; suddenly from the house opposite issued a lady's voice saying (in French): 'Mr Boyle, would it annoy you at all if we were to make a little music? We can none of us go to sleep in this H..l and the more we try the worse it gets.' I of course agreed with enthusiasm - though rather objecting inwardly – so we had musical outbursts till about 3. Such is summerlife in Grand Cairo.

Even out of the summer period the weather could be extremely trying and enervating – Boyle again:

We have had some snorting hot days, one being up to 100 in the shade; but I am extremely fit. I also sleep well at nights, which is the main point. I don't believe anyone else could sleep in my present house. My rooms have big windows opening right over the street which is about the noisiest in Cairo. All night troops of camels are passing to the markets (they have to go at night when the streets are clear, as sometimes there are 300 or 400 in one gang); at day-break the people begin to pour out to their work, and about 5 there is the beginning of a constant stream of electric trams which pass right under my bedroom window with amazing rows. Besides this, there are all the occasional sounds; natives squabbling and roaring at each other, gentlemen going home drunk with hashish at all hours – my house is on the main road to one of the largest Arab quarters – the sentries at the Museum in front changing guard, barking dogs, squealing of ladies who are having feminine tiffs, every sort of fruit-sellers cries, in short a real pandemonium. However nothing of it all disturbs me, and I sleep like six, with my window wide open and the sun pouring in most gaily.

Others less eccentric than Boyle also stayed on in the Cairo summer but when Vice-Consul Thomas Rapp arrived there one August everyone who could had fled the heat – the wealthy to Europe and the government, the residency and the less privileged to Alexandria:

The heat of the Cairo summer for those obliged to remain behind was mitigated by local habits. The pace of life slackened and all offices were closed in the afternoon. Everyone, except the Englishmen who played cricket, or who, like the Anglican Bishop Gwynn, played golf immediately after lunch, then took a siesta, only to become mobile again towards evening. This was then spent in open-air restaurants or cafes until well after midnight to give the overheated houses a chance to cool down.

John Young was devoted to the city:

Cairo in the early years of the century was indeed a pleasant place. The high buildings of modern times had not yet been constructed and many of the houses in the European quarter were two storeyed villas standing in their own gardens. The streets, bordered by tall acacia trees gave a welcome shade. Their sweet scented flowers in spring being succeeded by long dry seed pods which rattled in the summer breezes, known by the Egyptians as 'women's tongues'. Pedestrians, leisurely moving *arabias* (small open carriages), donkeys and camels shared the traffic and the hoot of the motor car had not yet been heard. There were donkeys for hire at the principal corners of the streets and though still ridden by the general public they had only just come to be patronized by British residents. Electric trams had lately commenced to run and the tramway to the Pyramids was opened early in 1900. Before that to get there, a distance of 8 miles, one took a donkey or *arabia* unless a visitor to the Mena House Hotel was lucky enough to engage a seat in the daily 'Mena Ra', a four in hand coach which left Shepheards Hotel at midday. The leading residential district was around Kasr al Dubara.

The Gezira suburb now covering a large portion of that island hardly existed. It had, however, recently become fashionable to drive in the late afternoon in Gezira where along the river road which passes round the Sporting Club could be seen an hour before sunset Egyptian Pashas in their open carriages and veiled ladies of the harem in closed Broughams 'taking the air', the picturesquely dressed running syces who cleared the way for them stopping to rest at the Kasr al Nil bridge while the procession continued round the island without them. No other road bridge spanned the Nile and visitors to the Gezira Palace Hotel and members of the Sporting Club who wished for a shorter route to or from the town crossed the river by the Bulaq ferry, an ancient paddle steamer with a jovial Egyptian effendi at the wheel who was always addressed by the passengers as 'Captain'.

We lived in Cairo in an atmosphere of stability and security. In winter visitors thronged to the country when the hotels of Shepheards, the Continental, the Savoy in Cairo and the Grand at Helouan were full. Dances took place nearly every night and since by Army regulations British officers in both the Army of occupation and the Egyptian Army wore mess kit in the evening their bright uniforms gave colour and variety to all meetings whether in clubs, private houses, or the opera.

The well known Turf Club founded soon after the British occupation had, after several starts and setbacks, settled in a small house with garden in the Sharia Manakh. Then, the British Agency moving from Sharia Maghraby to their present building, the committee took over their premises on lease and settled into a long occupation of some 40 years. The lease has terminated, the site has been rebuilt with tall blocks of flats while the Turf Club is now owner of its own property on the other side of the street, constructed as a club, more suitable and certainly more sanitary. But it has not the atmosphere of the old building with the huge ilex tree in its untidy garden, the terrace for dinner laid at small tables in summer, lit by shammadan candles (now never seen) and the famous character the steward Alphonse, not to speak of Harry Aspinall, beloved of all, who had been secretary almost since the beginning. There was the Sporting Club in its many acred grounds at Gezira with the usual recreations including polo and golf where a terrified caddy once reported that a player's ball had landed in a nest of young cobra snakes. There was golf at Helouan, a nice hotel course in the desert much patronized by the hotel visitors as well as by residents of Cairo in spite of the rather uncomfortable train journey, in which to insure the inspection of tickets the collector walked the whole length of the train clinging to the outside bars and handles of carriage doors. Many a nervous passenger when travelling alone at night has been startled when the door has suddenly been opened from without and the compartment was entered by a tarboushed effendi. There was riding in the desert or round Gezira race course: there were trips on camels from the Pyramids to the Fayum, now a motor road.

Boyle's affection for Cairo life soon evaporated after he left and on a return visit in 1921 he found none of his old pleasure:

15 April

Here I am, in a Cairo I hardly recognize! To me, its charm is entirely gone, and I seem to breathe a totally different atmosphere. We got to Port Said at 11 a.m. yesterday. I have all I want at this old Club [the Turf Club] – I am now writing at the exact spot where my table stood in the old Chancery thirty-six years ago – under a huge portrait of Lord Cromer.

This place – Cairo – is so fearfully changed that I can hardly find my way about in streets I passed along every day for twenty-four years. All the glorious avenues of trees are cut down; great gardens swallowed up by

enormous European buildings, and the beauty is gone. I could cry over it.
One whole quarter, which was acres of blooming orange groves, is all
hideous semi-detached villas; and town houses, which when I left were two
storeys high, surrounded by large gardens, are now immense boulevard
shops, five or six storeys of flats over them . . .

24 April

It is curious that Egypt no longer appeals to me in the least. I don't say I
dislike it, but it has no charm for me now, and it is with joy that I shall turn
my foolish face towards Eller How [his home in the Lake District] and my
own darling one.

To those newly arrived residents who had not known Cairo before
the war there was still much to relish. Even the greater freedom for
Egyptians to express their demands was welcome. A sympathetic
attitude could make life enjoyable, as Herbert Addison, a university
teacher, found:

Trivial annoyances were only a small price to pay for the privilege of
watching a cultural and national renaissance. Within our own university
grounds at Giza there were visible symbols – a new library, new lecture
rooms, new laboratories. In the city of Cairo itself, it was odd – odd in the
inconsequent manner which was so delightedly Egyptian – to observe that
one of the effects of nationalist fervour was to make still more manifest the
fact that the people living in the kingdom of Egypt constituted in reality a
multi-racial society. The conditions that idealists dream about today were
visible for all to see in Cairo. Egyptian Moslems and Egyptian Copts lived
more or less amicably together. Berberines – Egyptian subjects from Nubia
whose native language was not even Arabic – were welcomed in principle
and were doubly welcome in particular because as domestic servants they
made the expatriates so comfortable in our homes. Wealthy Jews or
entrepreneurs of Jewish origin ran the big department stores in Cairo –
Cicurel's, Sednaoui's, Orosdi-Back's. Friendly Greek grocers would deliver
groceries, act as temporary bankers and serve as information bureaux. At
Italian shops such as Buccellati's you could buy drawing instruments and
material. Armenians handled jewellery. As for ironmongery, there was only
one instruction you got if in need of any item out of the ordinary: it was
'Vous le trouverez chez Gerard.' Joseph Gerard, in Ataba el Khadra, would
sell it to you. At the Cairo Opera House Italian opera companies were
presenting *Tosca* or *La Traviata*: or, during other weeks of the Cairo winter
season, Sybil Thorndike and Lewis Casson would stage *Milestones*, sure of
full houses because at that time the Egyptian secondary school pupils were
reading it as a set book. In April it would accommodate the members of the
Cairo Amateur Dramatic and Musical Society for their presentation of *The
Mikado* or *The Gondoliers* or *When Knights were Bold*.

The British presence in the post-war era was still very obvious, however. The Union Jack flew over the residency and the nearby Kasr el Nil barracks, British owned shops and banks and commercial concerns such as ICI and Shell were inescapably present. To Addison this did not (at the time) lead to intolerance:

'Observe and enjoy'? At least we had the sense to do that, we British expatriates. It was quite a long time later that I really came to understand how lucky we were. Once in South Africa a new engineering acquaintance suddenly asked me 'And what do you do about your colour problem in Egypt, Professor Addison?' I was astonished. I was quite taken aback. I could only murmur 'But we haven't got a colour problem.' Nor had we. Anyone could go into Shepheard's Hotel if he seemed to be appropriately dressed: in a summer suit, in a dark suit, in white tie and tails, in the uniform of an Egyptian or a British officer, or what was then beginning to be described as National dress – cloak and turban, *aqal* and *kuffieh*.

Equally free from any taint of racial discrimination were the little Cairo trams and the motor-buses that we often found convenient; and if some of the compartments were debarred to males – the *harem* compartments marked DAMES – this was natural enough in a Moslem country.

In a morning in early April the warmth of the sun would still be pleasant after the cold winter days. In the streets the blossoms of the camel-foot trees might not quite have disappeared, and at any moment the first burgeoning of the jacaranda might be noticed. If you wanted shade, you could find it in Groppi's garden. Some acquaintance or a friend was sure to be there, to talk to or drink with. If a newsboy had offered you *La Bourse Egyptienne* he had lost points because he ought to have known that as an Englishman you would want *The Egyptian Gazette*.

Commuters

In the nineteenth century Britons lived in the modern sectors of central Cairo. In the next century Cairo began its inexorable growth into surrounding areas and expansion in already overcrowded ones. After the First World War migrants flooded into the city and some expatriates chose to live further out from the centre. It was possible to commute into the city from the suburbs, three purpose built satellite towns. Heliopolis to the north east designed and built by the Belgians in 1905, Helouan, a spa on the Nile or Maadi, a garden city developed after the war, also on the river. Herbert Addison, the university teacher, chose to live in Helouan which was much frequented at the turn of the century by Europeans seeking the cure and warm dry Egyptian air. During the season the grand hotels provided dances and bands, the town and surrounds offered swimming, golf, shooting and racing – all these in addition to the multitude of treatments to which the patients subjected themselves – the electric light bath, the Berthe vapour bath, the Vichy bath and douches, column, rain and needle. Although Helouan was fading after the First World War Addison felt that this was the right environment for him and decided to live there:

Of course it was foolish of me to have called on anyone at three o'clock on an October afternoon in 1921. But Helouan seemed such an odd, attractive kind of town, and I was so anxious to get myself settled there, that I took no notice of the heat and of the inhabitants slumbering in the shade: I walked straight up to Carton House and rang the bell. The door opened and a formidable unwelcoming figure appeared – a large lady in a wrap who, as I ought to have known, had been aroused from her siesta. No, she said, Carton House did not accept strangers. But, I just had time to say before the door closed, I am not a stranger: Mr Bolland told me to come to you. The door opened wide: I was admitted to a cool, shady hall. Bolland, whose name had served as an open sesame, was an official in the Sudan Agency in Cairo to whom my brother had given me an introduction. He had evidently made himself very popular in Carton House. The large lady, now completely mollified, introduced herself as Madame Carton de Wiart, one of the joint proprietresses of the *pension*. Certainly I could become a *pensionnaire*, and a room would be waiting for me on Saturday.

Addison commuted daily by train from the town with its fading elegance into Cairo:

So here was a design for living – a pattern of existence – that was based at one extreme on Carton House at Helouan and at the other extreme, on the Sultanieh School of Engineering at Giza. In between was the daily commuter journey in the trains of the Egyptian State Railways from Bab el Luk station in Cairo to the station at Helouan. Walking about the little town, observing the forlorn hotels and shuttered villas, sensing the air of stagnation and decline that in itself had a hint of nostalgic charm, one could of course understand that in any event the Helouan season had not begun in October, and that elsewhere in the world in this autumn of 1921 other health resorts had hardly got back on their feet after the end of the 1914 war. The former visitors from Europe were no longer in evidence; the remaining British, able-bodied or not, still had some of the attractions left for them, particularly the golf-course. The hard desert hereabouts could be rolled to give a smooth surface on which the golf-ball would run – especially with a following wind – for scores and scores of yards. On the area technically serving as putting-greens, the groundsmen could sprinkle sand

which, watered and brushed, encouraged players to putt quite confidently.
It was to protect these greens that a particular local rule had been framed,
which read: 'Ladies are particularly requested not to wear long skirts, as by
so doing the surface of the greens is destroyed.' Notwithstanding this
consideration, though, I found that when I myself tried to play golf on the
Helouan course, the exercise amounted to no more than a good walk
spoiled. In the end I had to say to myself that if I could not play desert golf
properly I would make a machine that would. And so I did. With the help
of my colleague Baker, I built an apparatus in which a revolving arm
actuated by a strong spring was intended to simulate the motions of a golfer.
Before an interested audience of local caddie-boys, we set up the tripod
mounting, clamped a club to the arm, adjusted it into the correct attitude
for addressing the golf ball, wound up the spring, and released it. To the
delight of the onlookers, the ball trickled for a few yards only and came to
rest.

Despite the attractions of golf and climate the English inhabitants
gradually began to drift away from Helouan:

Yet the ebb-tide that seemed to carry away the British residents from
Helouan, one by one, did occasionally fall slack and reverse its flow. Up on
the hill near the Observatory some newcomers were preparing for other
kinds of patients. They were Murdoch and Helen Rodger. When Murdoch
Rodger had completed his term of service as a medical officer at the big
Egyptian asylum at Abbassia and had drawn the indemnity to which he was
entitled, he decided to invest the money in an enterprise that he hoped
might be serviceable to his compatriots. As at that time, there was no
suitable retreat in Egypt for Europeans who suffered mental illness, Rodger
decided to build one and run it himself. Whether in fact the hill above
Helouan was the best locality for such an enterprise, who can decide now?
What unfeeling critics said at the time was that if patients were sane when
they arrived at the new mental home, the bare desert surroundings would
soon drive them off balance.

Some of those who left Helouan, including Addison, moved to
Maadi:

. . . a flourishing villa colony about half-way between Cairo and Helouan,
with a sporting club, a swimming bath, another golf course and altogether a
more congenial social life than Helouan could offer us. So that is why in
1926 I too deserted Helouan and set up house in Maadi, called derisively by
those who remained Tooting-by-the-Nile. It was the creation of the
Egyptian Delta Land and Investment Company, who had reclaimed the
desert, built the road and the club-house and some of the villas and had

planted the avenues of lebbakhs and jacaranda and poincianas. It was a waxing oasis, too. You could see reclamation actually in progress.

Living in Maadi soon showed me how wrong it was to imagine that sub-tropical countries had no seasons but only climate. We had clearly-marked seasons, both social and natural. Coming back from leave in September each year we could never cease to be astonished by the sight of the Nile in full flood. After we had all settled down for the autumn and winter, the social season began. We had golf competitions and flower shows, where zinnias and cinerarias would compete with roses and chrysanthemums. Just a month before Christmas, the poinsettias began to flame. Later, children would assemble outside the club-house, each carrying a lantern, ready to sing Christmas carols.

By the end of February, the cold weather would be nearly over. On a still, silent night, the approaching warmth would be heralded by one single sound. A frog would croak. The frogs in the irrigation ditches were coming back to life, and within a few weeks their clamour would keep us awake at night. After the frogs, the flowering trees. In March the camel-foot came into flower; in April, the jacaranda. By now it was warm enough to sit out on our balconies or in our gardens after dinner – or at least it might be warm enough, for an untimely return of a cold spell might ruin an outdoor dinner-party, set the table-cloth flapping dismally in the breeze, and induce the guests to look longingly at the solid warm house their hostess had so imprudently deserted. But on the right night, warm and still, you could listen to the ghostly sound of the dry lebbakh pods as an occasional light air set them tapping one against the other.

Within a few more days, all the pods would have fallen and the new green leaves have appeared. From the lebbakhs that lined the road to Cairo, the delicate scent of the new flowers woud descend, so that especially at night-time you seemed to be driving along a continuous avenue of fragrance. At the same time, the mud-banks between the road and the river had sprung into life. The melon-growers had come to harvest their crop: their hand-barrows and donkey-carts, piled high with splendid melons on their way to market, nearly blocked the roadway.

At last, in mid-May, the flaming red poincianas gave the signal that the leave season was near. Not that the families who remained behind need necessarily be envious of those who would soon be setting out for England or Scotland or the Alps. The summer months in Maadi might be the gayest of the year. Boys and girls from their schools in England would spend their own holidays with their parents in Egypt. There would be endless hours in the swimming bath, and competitions: parents versus children: on the cricket pitch and elsewhere.

The cricket ostensibly reached a slightly higher level on one memorable occasion. Donald Bradman's test-match team, on its way from Australia to England, stopped off in 1934 for a week in Egypt and played a few games against local teams. According to legend, the reason why the Maadi team won was that the matting pitch had stretched since it was last used, its length had not been checked, and thus the visiting team had to bowl and bat on a pitch a yard longer than usual. Not quite cricket? Or not quite true?

The den of vice

If Maadi was the essence of bourgeois respectability, Port Said had the reputation of being the den of vice of the Middle East. It was often the entry point for travellers to Egypt and a port of call for those journeying further east. Travellers went ashore perhaps in the hope of a slightly naughty experience, but often were only shown a few dog-eared dirty postcards. Thomas Rapp was vice-consul there just after the Great War:

Port Said had not yet shed the evil reputation it had gained for itself before the war, when every kind of vice was openly flaunted and when it was a notorious transit centre for the White Slave traffic between Europe and the East. It had then fully merited to be called a sink of iniquity and a hell on earth. No one had had any power to deal with the situation, even if the will existed, for the traffickers in vice were mostly protected by the Capitulations and the privileges they gave to foreigners. But now, in 1920, it was a very different place, if not yet so in the public mind.

Outwardly at least the European quarter, in the immediate vicinity of the Canal, seemed as orderly and moral as an ordinary European provincial town. The change had come about through the overriding powers of martial law. Drastic action had become imperative when Egypt was full of troops during the war and venereal disease was proving as great a menace as the enemy. The Port Said police under Colonel Grant had then combined with the military authorities to undertake a vigorous cleansing operation. All the established haunts of vice had been suppressed or banished to a remote part of the Arab Town. Even the more respectable night clubs had been closed, not a single one remaining. Virtue had been enforced on the soldiery, where admonitions and purity committees had failed. Now, if no passenger ships were in port, the European quarter was entirely dead after dark, but when passengers came ashore cafes and shops sprang to life and there was a certain animation centering on Simon Artz and the Eastern Exchange Hotel. Then, too, pimps made their appearance offering 'nice ladies' or obscene postcards. But the company of a 'nice lady' meant a long drive in a gharry into Arab town. There was never any question of direct solicitation.

On several occasions, however, we had to deal with the results of these visits to Arab town, where passports, money and watches were very liable to disappear, the victim usually feeling that his pleasures had been bought too dearly. That they were dubious seemed confirmed by a couple of visits I made late at night with the Provost Marshal who was in search of British soldiers who might be there in disobedience to orders. Accompanied by a patrol of well-armed military police we visited each 'maison de tolerance' in turn and flimsy doors not immediately opened were forced by a well placed kick. One felt that 'fille de joie' was an entire misnomer for the slatternly inmates, who well matched the squalor of their sordid surroundings. Sometimes the Benevolent Fund was called upon to help the victims; but it is a commentary on human nature that the advances of money we made were rarely repaid by those who preferred to forget the whole incident. I remember only one exception to this rule: a parson, to whom we had given £5 for his fare to Jerusalem, honorably refunded it.

Only one known lady of easy virtue remained in the European quarter. She was a Frenchwoman who went by the name of Lilly, with whom the police were powerless to deal because of her protection by the Consul. In outward appearance and conduct when in the town there was nothing to indicate her profession, but her private clientele during the war had been numerous and profitable. She had consequently amassed a small fortune, believed to amount to £7,000, with which she intended to retire to France and acquire a husband. This she actually did, spurred to action by the shock of an Italian client dying in her embrace from heart failure.

Historical interlude

To fit the following memories of Egypt into a framework a short historical excursion may help. The British occupied Egypt in 1882 and finally left in 1954 during which time the occupation and the Anglo-Egyptian relationship underwent several changes. These affected the lives of the many Britons working in the country. In 1882 Britain had invaded the country under the pretext of re-establishing law and order and restoring financial stability. Egyptian finances were admittedly in a mess and needed sorting out. Huge debts had been incurred through the wild spending of the ruler – the khedive. The British determined to put things right and decided that a brief occupation was the answer. There was no question of a long stay or of annexing Egypt to the British empire. The solution was much more simple. The British presence was to be temporary and to be represented by an agent and consul-general who would advise the Egyptians on how to run their country. This slightly absurd situation worked – from a British point of view. Financial stability was restored and numerous Britons were brought in to help run the country.

Things did not change much until the Great War when Egypt

became a theatre of operations against the Turkish armies. Britain in
a way formalized the situation by declaring a protectorate over Egypt
and deposing one khedive and appointing another as sultan. The
Egyptians gained little; the British consul-general became high
commissioner. But things would never be the same. The war put an
end to one way of life – the Victorian confidence of empire, the
sureness of touch of a great proconsul and his minions. New ideas
were stirring in the world at large – ideas of independence and self
determination – and Egypt's nationalist leaders wanted to put an end
to foreign domination, foreign soldiers and foreign advisers. They
could not quite do that, but after a nationwide nationalist disturbance
in 1919, the British took fright, signed a treaty in 1922 which gave
Egypt limited independence and meant fewer Britons running the
country and on a different basis. The British had to take some note of
the king (once the sultan) and of Egyptian politicians. This basis did
not really change until 1952 and the Egyptian revolution – although
another world war (1939–45) once again skewed the relationship.

The imperial Anglo-Egyptian relations ended better than might
have been hoped, without prolonged wrangling and bitterness. That
was hardly in the Egyptian character. In July 1952 a group of young
officers led by Gamal Abd al Nasser staged an almost bloodless coup.
The King, Farouk, corpulent, unattractive and very corrupt was
deposed and allowed to sail away from Alexandria in the *Mahrousa*,
the royal yacht, to exile in Europe. His bloated figure was often seen
in casinos, night clubs and expensive restaurants, not a good
advertisement for royalty. British soldiers, officials and teachers left
Egypt and it took some time for Britain to come to terms with
Egypt's new independent rulers and her own position of weakness.
Once (during the Suez crisis in 1956) there was a foolish and
pointless attempt to turn the clock back.

How some men stayed and others left

What was it that attracted men to serve in the Middle East, leaving
the prospects of a safe and secure career at home? Of course, reasons
were varied – adventure, a sense of service, escape, sometimes
health. A career in the empire was natural enough and one of several
possibilities open to ambitious young men. If it meant a life of
hardship then that was accepted. The rewards of helping the less
fortunate and of serving the empire were sufficient. Service in India
was the plum career, while other areas had their own attractions and
difficulties. In the Middle East numerous possibilities were available.
From 1899 on, entry into the Sudan Service carried élite status.

During the time of these tales – 1882 to about 1952 – the British were 'running' Egypt, in order to protect the Suez Canal and to keep others out. In the period before the First World War they had to provide many administrators in government departments and a hierarchy of officials. Egypt was by the far the most important British 'possession' in the Middle East and Cairo was looked upon as the headquarters. Slowly, other areas were acquired and more administrators were needed – in Palestine, Iraq, Jordan, in parts of Arabia and in Sudan. In other countries imperial interests required the presence of a British consul whose task was to show the flag and to remind the locals that, although he might be a mere man, he had the might of the British empire behind him.

Those who decided to join the Foreign Office could do so in a number of ways, one of which was through the student interpretership entry. Young men sat a written and oral examination largely in languages and the best of those who passed were chosen to start their career in Constantinople. Harry Boyle was a young man from the Lake District, largely home educated and non-university, who passed the examination brilliantly in 1883. At the age of twenty he travelled to Turkey to study at the Interpreters' School on the Bosphorous to prepare for transfer to the Levant Consular Service. He soon mastered Turkish when in 1885 to his great disappointment he was transferred to Egypt to work in the British administration.

The Levant Consular Service was established in 1877 in order to staff consular posts in the Ottoman empire, Egypt, Persia, Morocco and elsewhere. It was very much a junior service to the Foreign Office and offered few prospects of promotion. The senior posts were consul-general in eight towns and cities, including Constantinople and Beirut, and nothing more. One disgruntled member wrote of the service that servants of the crown could expect 'prospects of personal distinction, of substantial emoluments, or comfortable conditions of life. The Levant Service offers none of them even to its most accomplished members.' It was said to be 'a good service for a boy without much brains, without much ambition, and with a moderate private income.' Or in the words of another commentator: 'The consuls belonged to the lower orders, with little pay and less esteem, clerking and issuing visas and repatriating drunken seamen.' Nevertheless, many men did serve therein, including a number whose names glitter in the story of the British in the Middle East.

Thomas Rapp had survived the trenches of the Somme, injured but intact, and he had to turn in 1918 from thoughts of war to those of a future career. He had studied at Cambridge before the war:

The armistice had found me still on light duty, in command of a squadron of cadets at No 6 RAF Cadet Wing at Bath. The demand for demobilisation now became irresistible and within weeks the unit was disintegrating in the general helter-skelter to return to civilian life. Like others I had to begin to think of finding a niche for the future.

It must have been the unconscious desire for a life of movement that led me to think of service abroad, but it was pure chance that gave direction to what was at best a vague idea. One evening I was desultorily scanning various service Year Books and came across the Foreign Office list. Of all the public departments this was the one of which I knew least, in fact nothing at all. Nor had I any conception of the roles played by diplomats and consuls. The Foreign Office List informed me that candidates for the Diplomatic Service should possess a minimum private income of £400 per year. Clearly it was not for me, and I put the book back without bothering to investigate the qualifications of consuls. But surprisingly, the very next morning, the *Times* carried a leading article on the importance of the Consular Service in the period of post-war reconstruction.

When I went for another look at the Foreign Office List, I found that there was no debarring income qualification for consuls and that an intending entrant should write to the Under-Secretary of State for the necessary application form. The application form was completed and sent off. The need for candidates was evidently greater than I knew, because only a few days later I was asked to present myself at the Civil Service Commission to submit to a summary form of examination. Without any time for preparation, or idea of the nature of the tests, I made a miserable showing and was prepared to regard the Consular Service as a write-off. My surprise was therefore the greater when I received a telegram inviting me to appear before a Selection Board composed of senior members of the Foreign Office and leading representatives of the City of London business and finance. Here fortune favoured me. I had still only the vaguest notion of a consul's functions, but I was tipped off by a candidate who had preceded me before the Board that I would be asked what was my conception of a consul's role. The question duly came and, on my murmuring something about the general protection of British interests and persons abroad, a City voice boomed out 'and the furtherance of British trade'. Again I survived and, having been accepted as a probationer vice-consul, was instructed to call on the head of the Consular Department to discuss future plans.

Rapp was immediately sent to Cambridge to study Arabic with other young students and after two short terms he was warned to be ready for posting abroad. There followed a long and colourful career in the Middle East and we shall come across him again.

Herbert Addison turned to the Middle East for a climate which might improve his health. Not many Englishmen followed that example; most looked upon Middle Eastern weather as one of the many burdens to be borne. Addison, a Yorkshireman with a degree in engineering from Leeds University, began to think that a post abroad might solve his problems:

When, early in 1921, the doctors said that they wondered whether it might not do me good if I went to live in a warm climate, I didn't imagine that they were merely trying to get me off their hands. They really had tried very hard. But they were not having much luck. Nor was I. My complaint still kept gaining on me. So this was not the time to refuse one more chance of recovery, especially as the thought of warmth and sunshine was acceptable enough for its own sake. Besides, there was brother Frank in Khartoum who ought to know quite a lot about warmth and sunshine. What did he think of the proposal? By this time my brother had spent long enough training the Sudanese boys in the instructional workshops of Gordon College to be mechanics and craftsmen. As for Khartoum as a health resort my brother's response to my enquiry was prompt and emphatic. What he said in effect was 'For heaven's sake don't come here.'

Then, some time in July, a message came to me in Colchester out of the blue. It was a letter from my Egyptian university acquaintance Abdel Meguid Omar. Writing from London, Omar said that as he wanted someone to talk to he had looked up my address in our professional register and now wondered whether we could meet. Without delay I fixed up a meeting-place with Omar. During the lunch he explained why he was in London. When I in my turn began to turn the conversation in the direction of health resorts in the sunshine, Omar at once became interested. It appeared that as a secondary commitment during his stay in London, he wanted to recruit staff for the Egyptian Government School of Engineering near Cairo. For some time he had been Vice-Principal of this school, and now he was Principal-designate. Specifically, he said, there was a vacancy for a lecturer in Hydraulics. So why should I not go out to join Omar in Cairo? Although convinced that I had the right qualifications, he could not then formally engage me, but on the spot he got me to write out an application for the post. This application, he promised, he would forward to Cairo with his own full recommendation, feeling pretty confident that if I cared to present myself at the School of Engineering he would be able to do the rest. It was in this buoyant spirit that Omar and I parted.

Addison did become a teacher and later a professor and he stayed on in Cairo until 1952. Being in Egypt had different effects on different men. Addison found his life there full of the 'pleasures of Anglo-Egyptian co-operation' (as he called his memoirs) and stayed as long as he could; some left soon, disillusioned with life abroad.

Thomas Russell was descended from the Dukes of Bedford of Woburn Abbey, born to privilege and position. He went to

Haileybury College where the traditions of serving the empire, usually in the army, were very strong. However, he rejected the army, the church and the Indian Civil Service as possible careers. Russell had a cousin in the Egyptian Ministry of the Interior who visited the family home in 1901. Entranced by his cousin's tales of life and work in Egypt Thomas Russell determined to follow him in his career there. After Cambridge he became a sub-inspector of the interior and threw himself wholeheartedly into what became his life's calling. He specialized in police work and was a unique character in his ability to get to know the seamier sides of Egyptian society. His introduction was dramatic enough:

It was decided that before taking up my appointment as Sub-Inspector of Interior in the provinces I should be put through a month's intensive instruction in the routine work of the Alexandria police. For this purpose and to save me the expense of living in a hotel I was given the rest-room of a small coastguard fort inside the dock area. The place swarmed with rats which every night scavenged the earth-closet, and it was no surprise to me to learn that the previous English occupants of the building had contracted typhoid fever. My days were spent in police instruction at the Manshiya police station near by and my nights till 2 a.m. at the Labban police station in Sisters Street, all the lowest quarters of this cosmopolitan seafaring city. The Labban area contained a registered prostitute quarter where the tariff was as high as a dollar, and the famous Kom Bakir slum, where the recognised price of two piastres (fivepence) was often violently disputed. For sheer squalor, filth and viciousness nothing can have equalled Labban on a wet January night in those years, and I could have strongly recommended it to anyone who wished to cure a nice young man, fresh from England of any preconceived idea as to the glamour of the houris of the East.

On the basis of this clear-eyed view of Egyptian realities Russell built up a wide experience during the next twenty years. He was incorruptible and deeply respected, except by those whose nefarious activities he stamped upon. His career seemed settled when the basis of the Anglo-Egyptian relationship was changed by the treaty in 1922 and Egypt was given a measure of independence.

Three years earlier the Egyptian population had risen up in revolt against the hardships of the war and against the continuing British occupation. Many lives were lost and discontent was so widespread that Britain's hand was forced. Negotiations led to the signing of the treaty and Britons working in Egypt were to be employed on a different footing from then on. Russell had to decide whether to stay on under new conditions. His devotion to his work and his desire to help were so strong that he did stay. As he wrote to his father in October 1920 before the new treaty was signed:

I personally think the Treaty will go through. What interests all of the English officials particularly and personally is our own future. The Treaty gives inferior independence to Egypt and the power to keep or dispense with any English official they like. They could give us all the sack: personally I don't think they'll be so foolish. They will certainly get rid of a good many they dislike or know to be inefficient but if they are wise they will keep a large number for some years. Everybody tells me that I am certainly one of the first they will wish to keep! Well, it will not depend only on what they want. One must wait and see what terms they offer.

Every English official will be given the option of going within the next two years and will be given good compensation. The other thing that remains to be seen will be whether it will be possible for an honest Englishman to work under Egyptian masters. Personally I think it will for certain Englishmen whose past record, personal character etc. will safeguard them against native superiors trying to get them to do 'jobs' or dirty tricks.

Anyhow the future does not worry me for the present. I expect to stay in Egypt and I think it is one's duty, if asked to stay, to do so and help the Egyptians through some difficult years, provided always that they make it worth one's while to do so.

Ever loving son, Tom

In 1922 Russell was offered the command of the Palestine police, in 1924 the chief constableship of the East Riding of Yorkshire. He refused both, finally deciding that his place was in Egypt. He retired as commandant of the Cairo police in 1946 and stayed on in Egypt until 1952. Others found it difficult or impossible to stay on. Young who, like Russell, had been an inspector in the Ministry of the Interior, had gone out in 1899 as a school teacher. In 1924 he came to the opposite conclusion from that of Russell:

I elected to go in 1924 and wisely for I saw that Zaghlul [the Egyptian leader] was anxious that the first Department to be cleared of British control should be the Inspectorate of the Interior. The position of British officials in all Ministries, but particularly in the Ministry of the Interior, had for many months been difficult. Before leaving the Egyptian Government service in April I obtained an interview with Zaghlul. It was short and his manner cold. He said he remembered me. That was all. But when I paid a farewell visit to the late Prime Minister my treatment was very different. Tewfik Nessim Pasha pressed my hand and expressed his deep regret at my departure and his wish that he could have prevented it. It was sad parting with so many of my Egyptian friends but perhaps I felt most of all taking leave of my Police orderly who told me so great was his grief at our separation that for the last three days he had ceased to eat.

Another great parting of the ways took place in 1952 when Anglo-Egyptian relations were at their lowest. Nationalists were rebelling against the continued British army presence and as a sign of Egyptian determination after one particularly tense clash at Suez, the Egyptian Council of Ministers issued a decree late in 1951 authorizing all government departments to dismiss British officials still in their service. Herbert Addison had then been teaching at Cairo University for thirty years. Had he to go?

1951/2. So we were out. Or were we? Could the decree be challenged? Could it be contested? Apparently not. Then what were we to do – where were we to go? So far as the Egyptian authorities were concerned, we could stay in Egypt or leave the country whenever we liked. But as most of the 160 odd officials had to find a new way of earning a living, the majority chose to travel to Great Britain as soon as they conveniently could. Not that it was convenient at all, for flats and furniture and belongings had to be disposed of in haste and on unfavourable terms. A whole way of life had collapsed.

When I got to Port Said in the middle of February, the place looked glum and deserted. In Simon Artz's, the shop assistants outnumbered the customers. Above the shipping offices and the consulates, the flags of many nations flew at half-mast. In London, crowds were watching the funeral of King George VI. It was not until late on Saturday night that the *Orontes*, faintly floodlit, emerged from the Canal. The Orient people had given me a good cabin. So after we were under way I could lie in my berth and watch the lights of Port Said as they faded away: by the time they were all very faint except for the flash of the light-house, I was ready for a long, long sleep.

Addison, more deeply than most, pondered on the profits and losses of a career in Egypt. Sailing home with the P and O his thoughts wandered over his life, the justice of his dismissal and prospects of career and pension:

With ten days at sea ahead of me, surely I could be allowed a little time for meditation – reflection – anticipation? There was plenty to think about. What did not trouble me were feelings of resentment about my treatment in Egypt. I could understand why my colleagues thought quite otherwise. They could not see any justice anywhere. They felt ill-used and humiliated – and with every possible justification. They intended to seek redress as soon as ever they could – redress, compensation, indemnity, restitution, reparation.

Some 160 British officials (mainly teachers) had been dismissed. With their organization – the Association of British Officials of the Egyptian Government – they began to press the British government for some form of compensation. A ten year struggle followed involving Britain, Egypt and the ABO. Remarkably, the Egyptians agreed to pay over £165,000 in settlement of all claims put forward by the '1951 officials', remarkably in terms of Anglo-Egyptian history. Addison concluded at the time:

We could now look at the whole company of British officials of the Egyptian Government, from the era of Scott-Moncrieff and Milner and Lord Edward Cecil and Willcocks to the era of Malcolm Muggeridge and Bonamy Dobree and my own colleagues at the Faculty of Engineering at Giza. Whatever they did for Egypt, many of them helped to make the country a very pleasant place for me to live in.

Amongst this great company, the '1951 officials' formed quite a small proportion. Of the others, some are still alive today, still benefiting from Anglo-Egyptian co-operation. Their share in the partnership is to receive the pension payments to which they are entitled – pensions for which very few of the '1951 officials' had qualified. Obligations that the Egyptian Government undertook in the time of Cromer, in the reign of the Khedive Abbas Hilmi, in the reign of Queen Victoria, are being honoured today. Egypt has been a Turkish province, a British Protectorate, a Kingdom, a Republic; King Farouk and President Nasser have come and gone: but the Egyptian government still keeps faith with its former British officials.

TWO

A PRISONER OF THE LORD

Boyle in Egypt 1885–1907

The second consul-general whom England sent to run Egypt was such a powerful personality that he quickly came to dominate both the khedive and the government – a *de facto* governor-general. No Egyptian questioned his word, for that matter no Briton either. In addition, the distance from London and Whitehall's willingness to follow his advice gave him tremendous power.

Sir Evelyn Baring (who later became Lord Cromer) ruled from 1883 to 1907. He came from a well known banking family – Baring Brothers – and his official reputation was that of a fierce, humourless dictator – nicknamed 'the Lord' or 'Over Baring'. To those who knew him more intimately he was a lovable boss, full of fun and wit. He was very loyal to his subordinates and they were devoted to him and prepared to work all hours. Harry Boyle was one such and he established a close working partnership with Cromer who came more and more to rely on him. Their most famous activity in Egypt was the long, almost daily walks they took together in all temperatures along the banks of the Nile, during which they endlessly discussed Egypt's problems. From this Boyle earned the nickname of Enoch for, as in the Bible, Enoch 'walked with the Lord'.

The deep affection between the two men must have allowed Cromer to overlook Boyle's eccentricities. He appeared untidy and unwashed all his life and never learned to button or tie anything. His collar was often fastened incorrectly and his tie askew. When he went to Cairo in 1885 he took with him his Montenegran servant Giuro who begged Boyle not to acknowledge him in the street as his master was such a walking reproach to his skills as a valet. Boyle was a large shaggy man, with a long, lugubrious face and a drooping moustache the ends of which appeared to tail off into areas of neglect. His incessant work for Cromer did not prevent him from leading a full

life outside his office, walking, riding or dining and talking
incessantly. As leisure before television or radio was largely these
pursuits, whether at home or abroad, life in Cairo was not noticeably
less pleasant than in England.

Boyle wrote daily letters to his mother which she carefully
preserved. He was a master pen and his letters are exuberant, full of
the joys of life and work, a vivid and detailed account of his time in
Cairo written with irreverence, wit and insight. In October 1899 he
wrote to his sister (?), 'dearest Tommie', a revealing letter which
detailed both a day's work and what he believed the English were
trying to do in Egypt:

We carry on our glorious existence here as usual, partly lazy and frivoling;
partly energetic and intelligent, always full of varied interests. One sees all
sorts and all nationalities of men, good and scoundrelly, hears tales and sees
instances of every human virtue and defect (mainly the latter). We are
grafting English ideas and habits of thought on a mixed Oriental and
Levantine mass of Heterogeneity, and of course it has to be done slowly and
with care or the result of the new wine and old bottles ensues.

I think you know the way this country is administered: it is undoubtedly
unique. From 9 a.m. till about 10 or so, the different Ministers and English
heads of State Departments pour in one after the other to consult Lord
Cromer as to the various pending questions of the moment – financial,
military, educational, public works, sanitary, in fact the whole management
of a country of 10,000,000 people with a vast Sudan dependency. In all this,
the most important part of the whole work, no writing passes, all is by word
of mouth. Meanwhile, I have got through the various cypher telegrams
come in the night, read the letters (countless, in all languages), and we are
ready for despatches (not many of them), telegrams to F.O., Sirdar,
Abyssinia, India etc. etc. All morning, besides these works Rodd and I are
constantly toddling in and out to different waiting-rooms to interview every
sort of applicant and visitor for the most miscellaneous matters. Foreign
diplomatists in Parisian get-up; ragged Bedouin sheikhs from the desert,
with the dromedaries tethered in the garden; slimy Greek contractors,
Frenchmen and Italians intriguing for contracts of Public Works; escaped
slaves from Harems (two here this morning); fellaheen screaming for
reduction of their taxes; officers getting instructions as to the management of
provinces in Central Africa – and so on, a perfect kaleidoscope of humanity.
Then the everlasting rain of letters, petitions, and references to the Lord by
every man or woman in the country who thinks his rights, legal or personal,
are infringed, and comes here for impartial justice. Amid all this fussing, all
working together, but without any strain or differences, we get through an
enormous amount in the day, and have generally succeeded in righting some
wrongs and making somebody happy.

This work continued even on Sundays. Writing to his mother at her home, Eller How, in the Lake District, Boyle described one such Sabbath:

Cairo, 13 January 1907

Dearest Mother,

I wonder what you are up to at this moment as is – 11.30 a.m. here, so 9.30 chez vous. On my side, I am in the Chancery, three typewriters going at once, Holher and Lyons pegging away for dear life (the virtuous Craig does not come on Sundays), the Lord bounding in every five minutes with fresh materials of sorts and saying 'I think with an effort we might just manage to get this little trifle off our hands today' or something of that kind. Every five minutes too a kavass comes in and says to me: 'Mr—or Sheikh—or—Pasha want to see um' and I roar 'Tell him I'm not at home, tell him it's the mail-day, tell him to go to the Devil', with extreme fury, and all the while I go on scribbling to a small person at E.H. All this under a glorious sun, windows wide open, looking out on a bright garden blazing with flowers. I need not say that I am most fit.

And even during the night:

19th December 1899

On Sat. night I had gone to bed; rather tired after a long day of miscellaneous things, and at midnight came a furious hammering at my door. I looked gingerly out of window (as I always do on such occasions; isn't that being a good prudent youth, eh?) and saw our excellent coachman Cole, who gave me a note adding 'is Lordship said as ow I was to find you somewheres and and you that. Is Lordship did seem in a hawfal urry.' I did not know what had happened, as the note only said: 'Most important work; come at once', so I bundled into my dress things again and scampered down on Cheese (who lives next door) with no saddle and in a horrid temper at being dragged out of his warm bed. There I found the dear old gent, quite radiant with a tel from Lord S. (Salisbury) 'most pressing and personal'.

Boyle was needed at 2 a.m. to send off a telegram to Khartoum. Frequently the demands of other people caused Boyle great bother, particularly as he was considered to be Cromer's *éminence grise*. He therefore had to deal with endless queues of petitioners hoping for favour or advancement, and was often the filter which kept the importunate away from his chief:

Cairo, 27 August 1900

I have a fair amount to do, enough to keep me going all morning. Petitioners keep on flowing in as usual. This morning I have had already:

One Greek woman who has lost her six grandchildren and wants us to find them; one Syrian who wants to join H.M.'s army; 17 dismissed black soldiers from Zanzibar who want anything they can get; one Frenchman and his wife who says if we do not give him a post in the Sudan he will shoot himself and the lady at our gate. I have not heard the report. One beautiful lady with a seductive smile who wanted a letter from me to the Director of the opera to get an engagement; two Jew-bankers accused of having perpetrated a gigantic fraud, and who wished to tell me the 'simple facts' so that we might interfere with the courts on their behalf. Not much we don't! You will agree that this is not a bad list for from 9 to 11 a.m. Now I must prepare for some more, so good-morning.

Tourists descended on the British officials during the season and with their absurd questions and notions based on half knowledge and prejudice drove them to the edge of despair:

Cairo, 30th March 1900

Dear Mother,

Nothing to tell you except that it has been uncommon warm all day – up to 93 – and that all our remaining visitors are scuttling. What a comfort it is when they have all gone and the place gets a little quiet and respectable again.

We old Cairenes cannot abide these floods of globe-trotters swarming all over the place with their insane costumes and ridiculous questions (pray don't think I'm in a bad temper, on the contrary I am most affable and grinning). Did I ever tell you any of the sort of things they say? We must have been asked scores of time if we 'spoke Egyptian'. Lady Carlisle told me she could have no opinion of the boasted industry of the fellaheen as long as they had no hayricks! One young woman asked whether the Mohamedans in Egypt *still* worshipped cows as they did in Pharoah's time; and another anxiously enquired of the Lord if he often had to 'hang people' himself. He said no, he only *blew them up*, like the mutinous sepoys. One delightful old gentleman told me that he had never realised what a great man Mehemet Ali Pasha [ruler of Egypt who died in 1849] was until he saw his Pyramid!!! The Bishop of Salisbury told me that he saw 'the eyes of the Egyptian girls full of unsatisfied longing for the benefits of a higher culture and knowledge of better things.'

Summers at rest

In the summer Cromer returned to England and Boyle was his own master. Things were more relaxed and the frantic tempo of life slowed down. A great peace reigned:

Cairo 12th July 1904

Dearest Mother,

Here I am in the plenitude of repose, but I have no news for you except that it suits me admirably and that I am most fit. This is my present programme:

8 a.m. Got up – not quite with the lark, but near enough – went down to the river and swam Pajags [his dog].

9. Breakfast at Agency on terrace; 4 poached eggs with buttered toast, bread and marmalade. At breakfast when Murison came in and stayed chittering till 10.

10–11. Wrote a long letter to a young woman in England who has written to consult me as to whether she should marry an Egyptian Bey who has proposed to her. Drew an appalling picture of her future life here if she does so, giving her an idea of Moslem views and habits in those matters.

11 to 12.15. Read Arabic press on verandah. Mustapha Beyram called for a moment, also an Abyssinian boy to ask us to get his father out of prison, said father being in Abyssinia!

12.15. Went to town to call on lady who wanted to show me her boy, a prize child of 2. Was complimentary.

1. Declined lunch and went home, where bread and cheese with a half bottle of stout. Read Walpole's *Letters* till 2.30 with tobaccoes.

2.30 to 3.30. 40ww (oh lazy!)

3.45. Self and Padge down to Agency, hot afternoon, but not excessive.

4 to 6.30. Sat in the garden and read Buckel's *History of Civilization*. Pajags chivied ball and swam alternately. Tea and toast at 5.

6.30. Chief police officer of Traffic Department called in reference to some criticisms I had made to Governor of Cairo. Discussed traffic and kindred police matters till 7.45 when went home.

8.15. Dined Dr Nimr (the editor of the celebrated *Mokattam* paper) at the Khedivial Club, and discussed Turkish affairs till 11. Walked home with him and agreed to dine with him and his wife on Saturday.

11.30 to 12.30. Final cigar and read Life of Voltaire.

12.35. Tub.

12.45. Ruggins.

There is no record beyond that moment.

When the end of summer was approaching activity in the residency once again hotted up in preparation for Lord Cromer, whose return was viewed with pleasurable anticipation. Late one August a 'spring' cleaning was completed:

I find quite enough occupation and interest to keep me going. Among other things I have lately been destroying useless books and papers in the Chancery, and have got rid of two cart-loads. Talk of a spring-cleaning! I never saw one equal to this, either for masses of paper or for dust. I have carried on the operations in the splendid costume of a nightshirt and flannel trousers, both quite black with grime, and have presented a rather startling appearance to my visitors – among others being the Russian Agent who thought I must have gone cracky! However, that is now finished and things are in lovely order.

By October the return was imminent:

Cairo, 2 Oct. 1899

Dear Mother,
Behold the last day of the holidays! Everything is in order; the Agency is in unique condition. The four new English horses the extravagant Lord is bringing out will be here a few days after him, the Indian servants have returned from Madras where they take their holidays, and the last cartload of 100 tons of coal is just coming in. On my side, great things have also occurred; a benevolent landlord has repainted my house, walls, shutters and everything, so that it is a vision of splendour; Giuro has had tremendous doings inside, and such renovations have taken place that the dogs simply don't know their own diggings. I am going to sleep there tonight, and not sorry to do so. My gee-gees have also today resumed their winter quarters in their own stable next to my house, where I can hear if Cheese burrows out of his box and tries to get a bit of the other one's haunches to show there's no ill feeling. So altogether you see things are in good trim for the winter campaign.

The season

So the Lord returned and during the winter life was a series of receptions, teas, dinners and balls. Most of these would involve other Britons although occasionally other socially acceptable Europeans would be invited – French, Italian, others perhaps. A strict taboo was kept on the lower class European residents – mostly Greek or Maltese. As Cairo was both on the tourist map and on the way to India numerous visitors had to be entertained – from royalty downwards – life was quite a social whirl:

8 Jan. 96

Here all is in a state of hurry and confusion and work (of a social kind) which nearly overwhelms us. We have just written and are now sending out some 500 invitations for the Ball on the 15th – an appalling work. Then dinners, people to lunch, cards, rides, walks with the Lord in spare moments, take up all one's time. I am WAP [well as possible] to an extent which rejoices the hearts of spectators. Such lunches! Such dinners! Such breakfasts! enough to ruin a quiet family in food alone. I dine out nearly every night. Tonight there is a big dinner at Shepheards, and afterwards the marriage of the Khedive's sister. A tiresome midnight function.

18 March 1899

I have pottered all day in one way or another to my exceeding great contentment. Now I am going to a swell native dinner, at which there will be various Pashas, and a feed of about 30 courses, and a lot of dancing-ladies (which I hate), and I shall not get home till about three a.m. I have got rather out of the trick of these functions lately, though I used to be always doing them, but it has to be done sometimes for the good of the State. You may think it ought to console me for some boredom to know that we shall feed off gold plate (the nastiest thing in the world, by the way), and the Sèvres china – relics of the Ismail period – is the only kind of pottery allowed. My host is betrothing his daughter, hence the function. Luckily, the custom of wedding-presents does not hold in these parts! Now for it!

30 November 1897

Dearest Mother,
We are going to have a beast of a week, fussing with Royal Highnesses and Chamberlains, combined with a great deal of current work. The Great Joe and Mrs Joe [Chamberlain] arrive on the 3rd and will stay till the 6th, on which day the Lord goes to Port Said to meet the Duke. It will be interesting to hear what J.C. has to say, more especially coming just after Kitchener. Last time they were here I trotted them round Mosques etc; I hope they won't want anything of that kind again.

The galloping gourmet

Early in the mornings and on holidays Boyle seized every available chance to go out riding. The peace of the pyramids before the tourists arrived was a welcome contrast with Cairo bustle and he revelled in the hard exercise and the company of the animals. Despite his unprepossessing physical bulk he was obviously a very accomplished horseman (or occasionally camelman):

6 April 1899

In spite of everything, I get my long morning rides regularly each day from 7 to 9. How often I wish you and the A.P. [aged parent – his father] could see the views! Perfect cloudless mornings, the sky a most profound blue, the whole country a mat of brilliant green vegetation, dotted with brown villages and clumps of palm trees here and there, and at the back the bare Mokattam hills and the long stretch of desert, glowing with a sort of rosy tint in the early part of the morning. When one gets onto an eminence and sees all this, with the blue Nile (though muddy enough close to) flowing through it, the view is absolutely perfect. If I am riding alone, I make all sorts of enquiries among the people, who know me very well now, hear diverse complaints, redress wrongs like another Quixote, and often come back with some story which I send on to the competent authorities of the Government for enquiry further – which is not only very interesting but useful to the cause.

4 May 1896

On Wednesday we had a great day. The Count (Jean de Salis, Councillor at the Agency), Hohler (the boy from Constantinople) and I extracted a *whole holiday!* from the Lord. Started at 10 and rode to the Pyramids of Sakkareh, a ride of about 20 miles across cultivated land and desert. We sent on our grooms by train and donkey with a gorgeous lunch and drinks; we had a noble time, then visited the amazing monuments which I know well but the others had not seen – and got back at 8. Cheese [his horse] fresh as a daisy, we rather smelly as it was a snorting hot day, about 96 degrees in the shade – of which we had none.

13 April 1899

I am glorious W.A.P. and the weather is divine – just my sort, very warm and dry. Nearly all the tourist-demons have scooted.

On Monday I had a noble day. The Lord was away all day inspecting railways in the Delta, so I had a whole holiday. A young Sheikh of one of the desert Bedouin tribes happened to be here with some of his prize dromedaries, so he proposed to me to do a real first-class camel ride. Accordingly, we two started early, on a most superb morning (temp. in shade in Cairo 86), and did a 46 mile run like birds. It was quite magnificent and I enjoyed myself enormously. The dromedaries were most splendid beasts and simply flew. On the way home we sang to each other (!) and produced most sweet sounds in the desert. My Bedouin chanted love songs and heroic melodies of his ancestors, and I gave him select pieces of your repertory. He much appreciated 'The Brook' and also 'The Fishers of St. Ives', but he liked 'The place where the old Horse died' best, as the meaning of it was more in his line. You would both have howled with mirth if you had seen us tearing along, his burnouse flying in the wind, in the blazing sun over the illimitable sand and rocks, and pouring forth 'Maud' etc. in the most tearing spirits. Altogether, it was a most delightful excursion, and I felt quite up to the old fox-hunt days.

In addition to his riding Boyle enjoyed the other good things of life that Cairo had to offer – food and drink. He ate well, at official and private dinners or by himself on his verandah. His breakfast set him up for the day, or at least until it was time for lunch:

6 August 1906

I have just had a tremendous breakfast so am up to it all. I often wish you could see my breakfasts! Three fried eggs with lots of ham or bacon; toast and marmalade; three cups of tea; ending up with a brace of mangoes or a whacking bunch of grapes. Not bad, what do YOU think?

4 October 1902

Dearest Mother,

No news for you again this time. Here we are in the middle of the usual phase at this moment, gradually getting accustomed to the heavy – and excellent – lunches at the Agency, at which we keep up a continual stream of chaff and jokes the whole time, while we put away large stores of the most admirable foods and drinks.

The temptations of excessive drinking in the hotter climes of the Empire were notorious – there was too the necessity of fighting off the effects of strenuous exertion in the often appalling heat:

Cairo, 23 November 1901

Dearest Mother,

Here we are again, as the mail is early this week. Nothing to tell you except general festivities still going on. Last night I dined with my friends the Alstons. He was in bed with a 'sun-head', but Mrs A and I had a festive dinner and sat smoking cigars at table till 11, when he appeared, cured, and we drank milk-punch till 1.15 a.m. There's Tom and Jerry, or Life in London for you! I chuckle over your terrors as to my becoming an habitual inebriate. Know, unbelieving one, that I drink SODA-WATER only at dinner, taking my little whack of Port etc. after.

Cairo, 24 August 1899

I have got no news to give you except that I am W.A.P. and have got rid of my prickly-heat. Tell the A.P. that, after many years of experiments, I have at last discovered that the best drink for these countries where one wants to allay thirst and at the same time not lower the system, as is done by great quantities of spirit and soda, is certainly a mixture of porter and soda-water, in proportion of one to two. I find it admirable for a lunch drink; it does not make one sleepy, but on the contrary seems to act as a mild and invigorating tonic. Of course, *he* will say 'water' but I should (or rather should not) like him to try that of old Father Nile in his green or red periods.

Out and about

Occasionally Boyle accompanied Cromer on trips of inspection outside Cairo, one most memorably in 1898 by boat up the Nile:

23rd February 1898

Dear Mother

We have just returned from our great expedition, which has been a great success in all respects and has done us all an immensity of good. I was quite WAP before, but 950 miles of river air seems to blow off some cobwebs and freshen one up nevertheless. The Lord and Lady are very fit, he especially being in tremendous form.

When I sent off my last scrawl – I think on Thursday – we were on a stiff clay reef, stuck fast with a huge bare mountain range above us and illimitable desert in front. All efforts that night and next morning proved quite useless, and only seemed to make us settle firmer in the mud. So after lunch on Friday, we thought it was a bad job altogether, and the Lord and I set off in one of the steam-tugs to go to Nagd Hamadi, the railway terminus at present, and arrange for taking ourselves and all our servants and belongings down to Cairo in the express next day, a run of 13 hours and a sad fiasco to our happy river trip. After making all our arrangements, we went up to the enormous French factory for crushing and refining sugar which is there, to thank them for sending us tugs and men to try to get us off. These noble fellows, however, would not hear of our going without another more serious attempt, and at once proceeded to prepare and send off to the scene of action (an hour and a half's steaming South) three more tugs, making five in all, a first-class French engineer, and every description of winch and chain cable. We then steamed back to our desolate wreck and ladies, and by 5 all the allies arrived. That night our Captain – a most excellent fellow – with the engineer and our crew, sounded, measured, and did everything in the most scientific way possible, and we determined to make the great effort next morning. On coming on deck next day, we found a most amazing spectacle. By this time the local authorities had heard that the great man was a prisoner, and had sent out orders for a levy 'en masse' of the population to help. The result was that there were about six hundred men already there, and the whole country was alive with more pouring in on all sides, on foot, camels, horses and donkeys, with mounted police, and armed bedouins with rifles. We were rather appalled at this, but it could not now be stopped. When everything was ready we commenced operations. It was a most tremendous business. The five tugs pulled and hauled; several hundred dusky natives – very airily clad! – surrounded the steamer and pushed; six three-inch cables and two chains snapped like threads; but our engineers were indomitable, and at last she stirred and inch by inch swung towards the deep water. When she went off with a plunge into the channel, all our wading Egyptians were dragged after her, and as about 20 of them could not swim a stroke we very nearly had a nasty catastrophe. However, we dragged them all through the windows of the saloon and cabins, and fortunately had no losses. We had been aground there exactly 48 hours. After that, we came merrily on, sticking four times more, but only slightly, and had no more adventures.

We got back today at 2 p.m. having been away just over a fortnight, and had a most enjoyable trip. Though we took a lot of books, neither the Lord nor I read a word, nor wrote anything except some telegrams – of which luxury, by the way, we received 19 at one stopping-place. We had huge appetites, went to bed at 9.30, got up at 7, and prattled most merrily all day. So you see altogether we had a very fine time. Now for a state dinner offered to the traveller by the Staff.

The attractive side of his chief being so much in evidence to Boyle he reports with delight the stories he hears of Cromer's fearsome reputation outside. It is not clear whether he reported them to the subject himself:

20 March 1901

I am extremely well and had a pleasant run to Alexandria where I just saw the sea, stayed two hours and then back. I hate that flourishing 'commercial centre'. I came back in the train with two American ladies who asked me if I knew Lord C. On my saying I did, they told me what a brute he was, always abused and d..ned his staff (there is some truth in that) and that no one could stand being with him for more than a year. I said it was too awful to think of, and he ought to be ashamed of himself. I only hope I shall not meet them here anywhere, or they will tomahawk me.

Obviously the change of name of the British agent from Baring to Cromer confused some onlookers. According to Boyle:

A splendid old French nobleman asked Lady Cromer at dinner if the Egyptian people 'did not feel it an immense relief to be under the gentle sway of her admirable husband after so many years of suffering under the brutal and unutterable tyranny of that inhuman monster Baring, who had so long disgraced the British name in Egypt'. That will settle you for this time. Now for dinner as I am almost too thirsty to write, after a long hot dyke walk with the monster.

In many letters to his mother Boyle reports on his long walks with Cromer. These almost daily occurrences were not stopped by excessive temperatures when every sensible Egyptian took to the shade or his bed:

3 May 1900

I have no news about myself except that I am WAP. The heat always seems
to be my element, and I can always sleep at night when other sufferers are
seeking rest (and not finding it) by putting their beds on roofs, in gardens
and so on. The Lord is also very fit and a source of constant amazement to
the Egyptian aristocracy and the foreign Colleagues when, as they go for
their usual 'carriage exercise' they see him playing tennis with nimble
soldier boys, larding the lean court copiously, or else starting with me along
a sun-parched Nile dyke, not an atom of shade from start to finish, the
only human creatures to see being the shepherding bedouins or the sturdy
but smelly cultivators. Many of them think he is quite crazed, as
such proceedings are incomprehensible to the foreign mind, but we know
better.

A great sadness came to Cromer during his time in Egypt with the
death of his first wife. The staff in the agency had a great affection for
her and deeply shared his sorrow. Boyle's letter to his mother at this
time was touchingly full of typing errors:

20 October 1898

Dear Mother

I can absolutely give you no idea of the appalling time we have been having
since Sunday evening. I have no doubt, nor has any one else, that except in
the case of Royalties no such amazing demonstration of feeling has often
occurred. Telegrams have rained on the Lord without cessation from all
parts of the world; Kings, Princes, foreign Governments, Ministers,
ecclesiastical Dignitaries and personal friends of all kinds, have been wiring
sympathy and condolence. We have had to reply to all these, and the labour
and the cost have been gigantic. In Egypt itself, all the foreign communities,
the various religious bodies, the British subjects without exception, the
native notables, and a large number of humble people quite unknown to us,
have come forward and expressed their sorrow at the loss of a kind and
generous friend in a manner which astonishes us all.

   As for the Lord, I can only say that he has, besides the deep sympathy,
the sincere admiration of every one who has come near him. He is well,
does his work like a man, and goes out with me for a two hours walk every
day, since, and including Monday. He is really a great man. He has given
me some familiar relics of the dear Lady. One, a book, I shall send home for
safe keeping. You will like the inscription in it. The poor Lady's coffin
leaves for England this evening. It seems hard to realise even now.

Three years later the agency was bubbling with the news that the
Lord was taking a second lady to wife, Lady Katherine Thynne:

29th September 1901 Cairo

Dearest Mother

I suppose you will have seen in the papers by now the remarkable piece of news which we received by a cypher telegram yesterday morning, to our great amusement, a little surprise, and much satisfaction. It has created the devil of a sensation here, but is universally approved. The lady is quite suitable in all respects (I take it that you do know, but in case you don't – the Lord is going to take a Countess). Her age – 36 – is as it should be; she is a Marquis's daughter and sister; very good-looking; and by the testimony of all who know her extremely nice in all ways. So the old man could not have done better all round. It is undoubtedly a very good thing for everybody. He *must* keep more open house, give balls, and so on, in his position here. This he could not possibly do without a lady to take the lead. Again, it is essential for Cairo society to have a woman of that sort of rank and position to keep things as they should be. It was a dog's life he led here; solitary dinners every evening and playing patience till after midnight is not an existence for a man of his sort. Of course, we all regret the dear lady – no one, you may be sure, more than he – but one must look facts in the face. We shall know more about things on Wednesday: meanwhile he is not coming back till the end of October, so my cow will only have my breakfast to provide for.

By 1907 Cromer had been running Egypt for more than twenty-five years. He was sixty-six – but he was ill and tired and unable to face the ceaseless demands of government. Boyle was torn between sadness at his going and a relief that the Lord would now be able to rest at the end:

SECRET Cairo 27 March 1907

Dearest Mother

I have something to tell you which – though it does not concern myself directly – will I know give you a good deal of distress, though it was one of those things which must inevitably come sooner or later. I must say, first of all, that NO ONE AT ALL is acquainted so far with what follows except Lady C., Findlay and myself, neither here nor in England, so I need not ask you to keep this absolutely to yourself alone.

The time has come when the Lord must go. His health has entirely given way, and if he is to have the few years yet remaining to him in anything like decent comfort he must leave this place at once, i.e. in a couple of months or so. His mind is as sound as ever, but what is amiss with him is that his digestion is entirely gone; he can take nothing, suffers torments of dyspepsia, and generally is in so weak a state, owing to want of nourishment and to constant pain, that he is totally unfitted to grapple with the terrific work of this place. The doctors have now expressed their decided opinion that it is a hopeless fight and that in ordinary justice to himself and his family he must make up his mind to take the plunge and retire. This place requires a man in robust health and strength to cope with its immense difficulty and complexity.

I know you will be sorry for this, but personally I have been seeing it coming for so long that I am familiarised with the idea and shall not regret seeing the fine old man get a little repose which no man has ever better deserved, and I devoutly trust that the climate of England may to some extent restore his health for a bit. You will understand the Lord's state when I say that, for weeks and months past, he has taken NOTHING but Benger's food for Infants and is unable to digest even that.

Less than two months later Cromer left Cairo. The parting of the two friends of twenty-five years was stiff upper lip, surname and formality and a shaking of hands:

Very Private 8 May 1907

Dearest Mother

My parting with T'Owd Mon was short but rather painful. I did not go to the station (where he had a royal send-off with military escorts, salutes of cannon, huge crowds and so on. It was an official ceremony and a fine sight) – but on Monday morning, just before he started, when all was quite finished, I went into his room and he said 'You know Boyle, I'm not much of a hand at saying what I feel, but whatever I said I could not express what you have been to me all these years. We have been through – many things together,' then he broke down and could say no more. I could not answer him at the moment, and there was no need, so we shook hands and I went away. After all, that is the best display of eloquence with which old friends can part. He is a fine man; in all these years I have never heard him say a word, do an act, or – I know – think a thought which was in the least degree small, personal, or unworthy of a great mind.

Of cats and dogs and other animals

Following the mores of his class and time Boyle thought more of animals than of the lower classes of Alexandria and Cairo. They were a relief from human company. He was ready to take on all sorts of animal causes and was besotted with his dogs to an extent which amazes even in these days of a corgi owning monarchy and the hysteria engendered by Crufts Dog Show. Dogs ate with him, slept by him, walked and played with him. In the beginning there were two favourite dogs, Toti and Molo who grew old in Cairo and eventually died there. We first hear of Toti, a sort of terrier, in 1897 in a letter home and we can follow his adventures in detail. Molo appears a little later:

10 January 1897

Toti is extraordinarily well and quite lovely. I have also got at my house an angelic cat named Violet; she has lost one leg, poor beast, and is most amiable and a great addition to my establishment – tho' the Philistines jeer at us.

20 June 1899

There has been a great heat in the last few days, the temp. having been between 103 and 106 each day. The nights have been very trying for people who are affected by heat; poor old Toti has had a dreadful time, sometimes he can hardly breathe, and the night before last I had to get up at 3 am and put him in the ice-box for a time!

10 September 1899

My pup-dogs are all very fit. Totangie is lovely though quite gray, and Molo is the joy of all beholders. Cheese is also magnificent, though he has not got one sound leg in his dear old body. The other gee is all right; it was only that his hoofs had grown too long.

27 August 1900

My precious Toti has been very ill, so much so that I thought I was going to lose him. However, stiff castor-oiling and a diet now of raw meat minced small seems to be pulling him round. He chased a cat this morning, which is a good sign.

Cairo 28 October 1900

I am in such a desperate state of heat and breathlessness from a romp with Molo on the terrace, that I am quite unfit for duty. It is a blessing that there are no overlookers of our garden or the spectacle of a stout elderly gentleman playing riotous hide and seek with one frisky dog while another solemn dog looks on with appreciation and occasionally joins for a moment, would be too much for their respect for H M's Agency.

17 November 1901

Toti is sitting here smiling from ear to ear with a blue ribbon round his old neck, looking a perfect angel on his Sunday out. Molo is rather low as he has been kicked by a camel and is stiff and sore. (The weather is divine. By the way, what appalling storms you seem to have been having. I hope none of our trees went.)

12 September 1902

My ancient Toti keeps in marvellous form. He even jumps!! But he does not like going up and down stairs so has to be carried. The odd thing about him is that at night, when he sleeps, he quite loses all consciousness and can be pulled about and thrown up and caught etc. without ever waking or knowing anything about it! Never was such a precious.

25 June 1903

My old Totie is getting dismally old. He crawls along and cannot climb upstairs except one leg at a time. He can only just see, but I am sure he enjoys his life so I can't bear the idea of removing him. He is now nearly quite white all over, all those bright marks you have in the old photos having disappeared.

20 December 1903

It is the most glorious and divine day you can imagine, temp. about 80 in the shade, and I am going to take my pup-dogs out on the terrace (which they now share with the Hon. Evelyn Baring [Cromer's son] with whom they are on the best of terms). He and his Ma are exceedingly fit and quite beautiful – both of them. Toti is now pining for his Sunday sun-bath, and I know you won't grudge it to him so off we go.

18 July 1904

I really can't write any more as I am distracted by the screams of Toti who is being washed by Giuro in the pantry. I must go and comfort him. He does not take his baths nicely, not that they hurt him, but he is so feeble that he hates anything out of the usual course. I will go and give him an extra kiss from you to encourage him.

18 March 1906

This will not be a long letter as, though very well, I am rather sad. My poor Molo is dead. On Friday morning he was with me in the Chancery, having breakfast with me as usual, when suddenly he gave a jump forward, fell on his side, and in five minutes was dead with apoplexy. Luckily he did not suffer, but it was a horrid blow. He was such a dear. Toti still remains, a monument of old age; he knows nothing of his loss. I must now devote myself to training up Puzzooz in his father's steps, but he will never be equal to him.

21 June 1906

Puzzooz is a wonderful companion; even if one were apt to feel solitary – which I never am – it would be impossible with such a cheery little beast about. My poor Pollywog-dog (Toti) now never leaves his room.

Toti eventually went blind and died at the age of twenty-three. He was replaced in Boyle's affection by Pajags who was as lively as his father once had been:

17 May 1908

Crikey! it has been steaming hot these last few days. I am having a poke-bonnet made for the Padge as he suffers so much from the heat I am afraid of his going off in an 'appleplexy'; he will look a perfect saint in it but I fear vulgar people will jeer at him when he takes his walks abroad. But in our family you know we do not care 'a little D' about that.

With his love for animals Boyle expended his energy in saving horses from maltreatment:

10 July 1902

How are you? I and all mine are very fit. What do you think I have just done? I am uncommon proud of myself! I have just run a good half mile!!! And run too like a certain youth used to cut over the fells. I have not done such a thing for years. As I was going out to lunch I saw a man with a cart cruelly ill-treating his horse; I thundered to him to come and be arrested, when he bolted, cart and all, and went off. I swore I would get him and I did. After a tremendous run, he gave it up and rushed down a side street and vanished. I stopped the cart, got a policeman; the man was spotted and is now in chokey to be tried on three charges; 1. Ill-treating his horse; 2. furious driving; 3. leaving his horse and cart unattended. But the main thing is my athletic feat! If you could have seen that stout middle-aged gentleman cutting along with his hat in one hand and a cigar in the other, you would have been astonished. Two Highland soldiers joined in for a time, but they soon had enough of it, and I had the glory to myself. As you may imagine, such games with the thermometer at 97 in the shade are pretty warming, so I have had to change all my garments and have a good tub. But it was worth it for the fine old exercise again.

22 June 1903

This morning I rode out to the stone quarries, about 8 miles out in the desert, and arrested 14 horses in a most deplorable condition, after a most fiendish row with the quarrymen. I believe 12 of them will be shot by our SPCA this afternoon. I thought once the men were going to show fight, but rightful authority and the free vernacular language carried the day at last. I do enjoy these little episodes!

Boyle's boil and other plagues

Although life in the Middle East was very pleasant it had a not so attractive side. Climate, disease and lack of hygiene all caused various kinds of afflictions – cholera, plague and typhoid. Cholera was the most feared and occurred several times during Boyle's period in Cairo. Europeans on the whole did not succumb as they took stringent precautions. Others, not so careful or not so lucky, fell prey to the epidemics. In 1883 a severe outbreak had caused more than 25,000 deaths in Egypt. In 1896 it broke out again in much milder form and was back in 1902:

Cairo 25 July 1902

Dearest Mother

So you see we have got the jolly old complaint again after all our efforts. Once it gets into the country, it is pretty well bound to go through. I am extremely fit and a perfect Solomon about 'precautionary measures'. I suppose you would like to hear something about them, as you are one of those happy millions of Britons who have never seen a good Eastern epidemic. First, I am living at the Agency. Oh the noble coolness of the nights and the splendid North wind up the river and the glorious dawns over ditto! What a difference after the sweltering nights in town! Of course, one has to be careful about sitting out before going to bed, so as to avoid chills. Secondly, water. I never touch it except in a bath and for teeth purposes, when it is boiled. Milk, thoroughly boiled. Butter, abandoned. Fruit of all kinds, ditto. But oh these native friends of ours! They beat anything. For conscience sake I collected the whole lot (now 42) yesterday morning and made them a speech; told them that all depended on water and fruit, and that I would have as much water boiled every day as would suffice for them all – and even their families – if they would promise to take it away and use it only. Of course, they all said 'Hadir, ya Bey' (certainly) and so I gave orders. On coming in at 3 o'clock pm I find three of them drinking freely from the trough in the stable-yard! So I give it up and only look after the European servants – three in number – who are sensible enough, being English and German. It is hopeless to try to change their notions, so down they go. It still remains to be seen how far the thing will go; it died out with extraordinary rapidity in the Hedjaz (one of the dirtiest places in the world); has done the same in the town in Upper Egypt where it first appeared, and may very probably do the same here. But the boredom of it!! the quarantine in foreign parts, the disinfections, the expense. Fortunately there is no panic among the European (Levantine) population here.

8th August 1902

The cholera is diminishing here, but has broken out at Alexandria; it will probably be worse there as that happy town has a most filthy population of low-class Europeans, all in a panic-stricken state. It will probably disappear from Cairo before long. A propos of cholera, I must tell you a characteristic anecdote: an acquaintance of mine, a Copt functionary in the Ministry of

Finance, was terrified of the complaint. His habit was to drink a bottle of brandy a day; last Friday he felt rather cheap so took a dose of caster-oil; as he felt feeble after this, he took all his bottle in the morning. This made him feel better, so in the afternoon he drank another! This so encouraged him that he said he did not care a D for cholera and ate a whole enormous water-melon for dinner. The sanitary authorities heard that he was ill, so carried him off to the cholera hospital, where he passed the night, protesting. Next day the doctor said he had no cholera, so he returned home, and in his general feeling of joviality, drank another bottle (making 3 bottles of brandy in 24 hours). He shortly after had a fit of apoplexy and expired; aren't they genial dogs? One of Borg's cavasses died last week, as I think I told you. He also was in a state of blue funk, so to make sure of being safe, he lived on melons and pickles, with the natural result.

Boyle dismissed the epidemic as negligible in a letter to Rennell Rodd in October 1902:

We have had an eccentric sort of summer; I have revelled in the dolce etc. here, and from my terraced rock have watched the others tumbling in the Alexandrian waves. I could not work up any enthusiasm about the cholera demon; he seemed to me a very one-ass sort of epidemic when one compared him with the great efforts of 65 and 83. One felt no sort of heroism in being here, but only boredom at being denied fresh fruit and having to put boiled milk in the tea. You remember the old rules from 96. Findlay (whom we all loved greatly) grappled the microbe in person and threw it heavily, doing really admirable work in getting an effete municipality to adopt some elementary measures of cleanliness in the streets of Alex. and also to prevent the population from drinking essence of dead dog and rotten cabbage stump from the Mahmoudieh.

The epidemic of 1902 was still remembered in Egypt when there was another outbreak as late as 1947 – long after Boyle had left. Thomas Russell was writing home in October:

The main conversation here these days is the cholera. So far there have only been half a dozen deaths in Cairo. Of course it is a very different thing now from the last epidemic in 1902 when there was no inoculation known and none of the modern methods of nursing.

25th October 1947

My Dear Father
Our little cholera epidemic goes on gaily and gives us a great deal to talk about! We have all been inoculated including the servants' families, with some difficulty as there was a great shortage of vaccine at first and it is

popularly believed that most people are getting a dose of sterilized water! We have a large basin of disinfectant outside the back door and every one is supposed to wash their hands in it before coming into the house. The water supply is considered safe and it is heavily chlorinated and the bath stinks of it and the tea tastes of it. But we boil it all the same. All fruit is plunged into boiling water and so on. Then you tell the upstairs servant you want some drinking water and you find he went and took a jug from the bathroom and filled it from an open saucepan on the fire! Of course it must be boiled in a covered kettle and poured direct into a sterilized bottle, stopper and all. The only thing is to thoroughly put the wind up the servants and then they do take some trouble. If the river got infected of course we should have to take much more trouble over it all.

There were over 500 deaths a few days ago but they dropped again the last two days but there is no question that it is increasing and they are very worried about it. It is an enormous expense to the government and a great loss financially as well, for all trains (nearly) are stopped, and no one can move without permits, and the country is at a standstill over it. There are lots of good stories, one of which is the following denied in the press two days later. A vegetable cart coming in to Cairo, stopped at the control post, where they make them wash the vegetables, was found to have under the cabbages, two corpses, who had died of cholera!

Apart from the major diseases such as typhoid, living in the Middle East had numerous less serious irritations. Boyle ran the gamut of them but remained very cheerful; some he rather inflicted on himself, others were unavoidable. The proximity of so many animals did not seem to affect him:

4 May 1896

All goes well here and I am WAP as you could wish except for small Nile boil on my right thigh which has bored me for a few days. Murison has bored it in return and it is now vanishing. Nobody escapes one or two at this season.

Two days later

Dear Mother
No news, WAP to the highest extent; *both boils* all right.

Greed, however, exacted its revenge.

20 September 1899

I am amazingly WAP but yesterday I had a stormy day. It was rather a case for Tennyson's line: 'I thowt t'were the will of God, but Miss Annie she said it were drains', in this way. On Monday morning I had a superb breakfast

of oysters; (there is an R in September); appalling results. I was engaged to
dine with Murison on Tuesday night, but wrote round to say 'No go *chill*'.
The devoted man came scampering round at once and laughed indecently.
He said 'Beastly *greed*, having oysters for breakfast, serve you right'.
However, I am right as a trivet again and am going to dine with the Lancers
tonight and make old Cheese sweat in the morning.

Plagues of the non-medical variety came in the form of various
insects – in addition to the ever present *moustica domestica*.

                                                          9 May 1909
The weather continues very hot, and the flies are really a record. No one has
any recollection of such a plague; there can be no doubt that it is worse than
the original one instituted by Moses, as Pharaoh would certainly have let the
Jews go at once under these circumstances. But beyond being annoying they
don't do any harm, and I grin at them myself, but lots of people are driven
quite frantic. The evenings are divinely cool and enjoyable; last night we
dined here outside, on the Nile terrace, which was noble.

                                                          18 July 1904
On Friday night we had an outbreak of mayflies, fat white harmless things
that die at the least touch. The whole town was a mass of them, and the
streets round the electric lights looked as if it had been snowing. At the
Club at dinner it was a quaint sight; all the foods and drinks were covered,
the verandah a slippery mass, on which the waiters went tumbling about
like clowns. I have not seen such a visitation since the ant flight at
Khartoum in 1898. However, they have all disappeared again. In spite
of this trout-like diet, you will be pleased to hear that I am extremely
fit.

                                                          15 May 1902
Now I think I had better go, as I am ruining the type-writer by the
perspiration which is streaming off my manly brow as I write. Moreover
there are four enormous locusts, each about five inches long, banging about
the room, and I hate getting a locust in my hair. What joy you would find in
a good broiling hot day in Egypt with all its attendant delights!!

Leave taking

Once Cromer had left Egypt much of the delight Boyle had felt in his
work disappeared. Although he liked and admired his successor, Sir
Eldon Gorst, a mild, amiable man, he began to think about moving
on:

5 December

Last night, I had another tête-à-tête dinner with JLG [Gorst]; he is most extraordinarily clever and amusing; his intellect is really something quite uncanny and simply paralyses people who don't know him well. I have advanced further in my plans for future proceedings. The FO are quite ready to give me the first vacant post, to my liking, which presents itself to disposal; but naturally one never can tell at what time the opportunity may occur.

I shall be in many ways most sorry to leave here. Not for the country, of which I have had a great deal more than enough; but the Gorsts are so intensely kind and nice that I leave them with boundless regret. But they see it quite plainly as a necessity. I am consequently taking steps to wind up my affairs slowly; I have not renewed the lease of my house, taking it on – by the great courtesy of my Armenian landlord – by the month only. At the end of the year I cease to be a member of the old Turf Club – as I think I said before. The only thing which worries me is Giuro, how to dispose of him. But I hope that Murison will manage to solve the problem. Now I must paddle.

Eventually Boyle received notice that he was to be posted as consul to Berlin. What worried him most was not leaving Cairo, his work, or the fate of Egypt but his dog Pajags. What would happen to him?

20 August 1909

I am very fit, but if you don't find my letters very cheerful these days you will know that it is this dog question. It hangs over me like a black cloud day and night. Of course, I am not such an ape as to be affected in this way merely by the dog's death; if he died a natural death or was killed by an accident, I should be quite undisturbed; that is the way of the world. But the point is that I am murdering him myself. However. I shall be thankful to be gone and finished. This state of affairs is very tiresome. Yesterday all the kavasses of the Agency came to me and said that now I was going they wished to leave the Agency and take service elsewhere. I turned them out of the room and told them not to be idiots. They went in tears, but all this sort of thing is trying when you are contemplating the cowardly murder of your best friend. All kinds of weird creatures, of whom I have no knowledge whatever, keep coming up to me in the street and drivelling in the same way. It is as much as I can do not to fly at them! Good-bye for the time. I wish Pajags were dead and I was off this afternoon.
Your Harry

So Boyle did depart from Cairo, without killing Pajags but leaving it behind. He spent some time with his mother in Eller How before going on to Berlin. A leaf from her diary rings down the curtain on his Egyptian days:

Tuesday 28 December 1909

Another nasty wet day. So disheartening! At breakfast all brightened by a letter from Lord Errington to my dear Harry, saying he need not go to B. for some time yet, and is to have another £100 a year! Oh to be more thankful! Busy about nothing all morning. Bright lunch with my treasure (potato-hash, H. does so enjoy it!). In the afternoon *rather tired*, but cheered by nice tea with my precious son. He presented me with an empty 'pioneer' tobacco tin of his!!! Oh how good and dear he is to me! Quiet cosy eve, H. reading 'Consular Instructions' (quite unnecessary in this case I should say!) and then Diary to me; he has only alluded to 'Pajags' 1087 times today! I trust the dear boy is not unwell, but it is not a good sign. Finished brown-wool socks for dear Mary's bazaar and went to bed at 12.30. Still sheets. Oh for a little finer weather!

That is not quite the end. Boyle revisited Egypt in 1921 to report on the situation. Earlier Pajags had been brought back to end its days romping and walking in the rain of the Lake District. In 1921 it was nineteen and dying of old age and exhaustion. Boyle was then in Egypt. The terrier died a soldier's death, shot by a gamekeeper who had taken it for a poacher's dog.

THREE

A GALLERY OF EGYPTIAN CHARACTERS

Travelling with the khedive 1908

Through the pages of our writers strides a whole gallery of characters, British and Egyptian, who meet and interact with each other on occasions ranging from the most official to the most informal or even improper; ranging in rank from the khedive himself to the lowliest prostitute. These meetings, however brief, between Briton and Briton, Englishman and Egyptian, span the whole gamut of imperial intercourse.

Starting at the top was the despised khedive, the 22-year-old Abbas who had ascended the throne in 1892. Although so young he had had the nerve to stand up to Cromer and a coldness developed between the two men. The Lord could not tolerate any opposition; Boyle loyally followed his master in this attitude:

This morning we all toddled off to the Palace to congratulate H.H. on the anniversary of his accession (?!). He was shifty as usual – and is even *fatter than I am*!! He is behaving quite vilely and we anticipate having to sit on his head before long. He is a quite amazing product for folly and falseness and all the loathesome political vices – ugh!

The British thought him totally corrupted by a Parisian education. By 1904, however, a sort of accommodation had been reached between the two sides. Boyle again:

Cairo, 10 November 1904

Dearest Mother,

I wish I had some news for you but, except that I am extremely fit, I have none at all. The weather is perfectly noble, not a fault to be found with it in any way. We have not had a drop of rain for ten months! What do you think of that? Yesterday was the usual Birthday functions – viz. a review in the morning, a lot of visits all day, and the swell feed here in the evening. All went off very well. For the first time, the Khedive appeared at the parade and took the salute. We are like brothers now-a-days, and he and Dominus swear by (not at) each other. Long may it last, but I have doubts. His Highness is always sending me complimentary messages as if I was his dearest pal, whereas he cannot abide my very name. We did not go to his reception last night, as we had our own dinner on here. Polums (dog) is very well and begs to send his love to that little puppy in England. He celebrates his 19th birthday next week, but the Khedive will not be present. He only asks his old friends.

The khedive appears in the following extract in a more curious light with his entourage of attendants, particularly his exotically named English yet aitchless butler Frederic. John Young had in 1908 been asked by the ruler to survey and map a large property he had recently bought in the Dalaman valley in Anatolia. Two years later the khedive invited Young to accompany him on a visit to his property to continue his survey. Young readily agreed:

We sailed from Alexandria in one of the Rumanian Company's steamers bound for Rhodes and Constanza. The ship was very full but a number of cabins and berths had been reserved for the Khedive's suite which included a Swiss agricultural expert, an official from the Ports and Lights Administration and a civil engineer, all of whom were to give advice on the management of the Dalaman estate. I found myself by good fortune sharing a cabin with a British Officer in the Egyptian Army who was going on leave, and my servant, who had never been in a steamer except the Government launch *Togo*, when he was unpacking my things in the cabin saw the British Officer's toothbrush on the wash-stand and said: 'I see the ship provides you with a general tooth brush so perhaps you will not want yours.' A few minutes after we had left the quay we slowed down opposite the Khedive's yacht the *Mahrousa* and the Khedive came alongside in a launch accompanied by all his Ministers who salaamed with great ceremony as he mounted the gangway.

The Khedive dined in his private cabin but came on deck after dinner and spoke to me. He said he was glad to be off for a holiday and that Dalaman was always in his thoughts. He would have it drained and irrigated; 'I will make the estate pay. Already I have discovered a kind of grass which grows naturally in a part of the valley and I have had a quantity of it shipped to Alexandria. I find that when it is dried and cut up it makes excellent fodder for cattle. And now on board we are a party of experts. We have with us a Swiss Agriculturalist and a specialist on harbour making. We have an engineer and we have a doctor who will give us all quinine three times a day to keep off malaria. And we have Mr Yong. We are a party of experts.'

We reached Rhodes the following afternoon where we transhipped into Prince Muhammad Ali's yacht which was awaiting us there. The steamer had not ceased moving before we were hemmed in on all sides by so many small rowing boats that the dinghy sent from Prince Muhammad Ali's yacht could not be discovered. The deck became crowded with arriving and departing passengers whom the united efforts of the Khedivial suite and the bodyguard of ten soldiers failed dismally to control. No one knew the whereabouts of anybody's luggage including that of the Khedive and the Khedive himself, who could not find his dinghy, was swept off his feet into a small boat and conveyed by gesticulating boatmen to the yacht. 'His Highness' yacht is just starting for Asia Minor,' shouted the Court doctor running rapidly past me and jumping into a boat already overloaded with luggage. 'Be quick!' 'Quick!' we each cried to the boatmen. 'Extra pay if you reach the yacht in time,' and we swayed our bodies in rhythm with the rowers.

As we approached the yacht we saw signs of great activity. The Khedive and the Court *Imam* were running up and down the deck trying to sort out their luggage and asking questions which no one could answer. I heard His Highness exclaim: 'Where is my bag? I cannot see my bag anywhere. This is not my bag. It is Mr Yong's bag. Do you see mine?' To which the Court *Imam* replied: '*Mafeesh* (It is not here).' We arrived on board. Had we delayed the departure? By no means. It was not till after midnight that the yacht weighed anchor. At sunset when the luggage difficulties had been safely settled and the Khedive had found his bag the Court *Imam* mounted to the hurricane deck and walking round the mast as though it were a minaret called out to sea with a ringing voice the summons of the evening prayer. The English butler Frederic showed me my cabin and the arrangements of the yacht.

At the head of the companion leading down to the dining saloon were two small cabins set apart for the Khedive. Opposite, on the other side of the corridor, was a saloon for general use and below the companion was the dining saloon furnished with two tables. I took the precaution to learn from Frederic that dinner was at 7.30, but the other experts seemed unaware of this and they wandered aimlessly about the deck apparently without expectation of food. Just before 7.30 as I was sitting below in my cabin I heard the Khedive remark on deck to the harbour expert, 'Avez vous faim Monsieur?' 'Non monseigneur' replied the expert undecidedly. 'Jamais' . . . but at that moment he was interrupted by the ringing of the dinner bell and we all assembled in the saloon.

'What wine will you drink?' enquired His Highness genially as he removed his tarbush. 'White wine, thank you Sir' we all answered quickly as Frederic uncorked a small bottle and sparingly handed it round. 'White wine and water' Frederic seemed to say for after pouring a thimbleful of wine into my tumbler he filled it to the brim from the water jug and then shutting the bottle in the cupboard turned the key. Hardly however had we begun to feel the first glow from our cups when the electric light went out and the Khedive remarking 'I must look after this at once' left the saloon. That was the last we saw of His Highness for the evening and we were left to finish our dinner with our wine and water by the light of two candles. 'Is there any more wine?' the engineer ventured to ask, but he did not ask again. Frederic seized the water jug and filled his empty tumbler. He also filled the doctor's tumbler and my own and after calling for a fresh jug of water walked across to the other table and supplied the harbour expert and the agriculturalist. 'Non, non' expostulated the agriculturalist, but Frederic filled the tumbler to the brim. After that no one asked for any more wine.

'Good morning!' I called to the harbour expert early the next day stumbling over the top step of the companion into the little saloon. 'Not a word' he answered in alarm. 'His Highness is asleep.' 'Hush!' said the Court *Imam* putting his finger to his lips. *'Effendina* is asleep. Not a word. Move as though you walked on air. He has been mending the electric light and then he would not got to bed until we had completed the voyage and had come to anchor and now we are indeed safe. Thanks be to Allah! Safe from the dangers of the sea!' I looked up and saw the well remembered Bay of Kille. ''Is 'Ighness is gone to lay down' whispered Frederic coming up on tip toe. 'There must be no talking.' 'No talking' echoed the Court *Imam*.

It was impossible to remain with the rest of the party without being reprimanded by the *Imam* or Frederic so I strolled towards the bow and began to examine the shore. A boat put out and came alongside. Two of the occupants hailed the yacht. 'Why there is Mr Yong' cried one of them and I recognised Amin effendi, the *Mamur* (official) of the Dalaman estate. 'How are you, Mr Yong? Here is my colleague Herr Wilhelm Schwartz.' 'My life is quite wretched' said Herr Wilhelm Schwartz. 'I have lived for six years in Vienna and my wife has come straight from there to Dalaman. Now we live in a marsh. It is no pleasure for my wife to put on her best clothes. There is no one to see her. She cannot go to concerts. She can see no shops. She cannot dine out. She cannot visit my mother. She has no happiness in Dalaman except the gramophone.' 'Hush!' said the Court *Imam* running up to the taffrail. 'Hush! His Highness is asleep. No more until the afternoon.'

It was not until after lunch that His Highness arose refreshed with sleep, when all our party set out in a small steam launch to visit the points of interest in the neighbourhood. We landed at several places, and as we were about to embark for the last time a little dog jumped out from behind a shepherd's hut and bit one of the experts in the calf of the leg. If anyone had to be bitten I would have preferred the Court *Imam*. At sunset we were all dosed with quinine. 'How much must I take?' asked His Highness. 'Three Monseigneur'. 'I cannot take it. It is impossible.' 'It is necessary Monseigneur. Ah! There is one gone. Now for another! Good!' 'That will do *Monsieur le docteur*. Two are sufficient. I have no fever.' 'Take a third,

Monseigneur.' 'It is impossible.' 'Courage, *Monseigneur*. Ah! Bravo, *Monseigneur*!'

The next morning Frederic called me at 5.30. I could hardly believe my ears when he told me the time. Frederic explained that the Khedive was starting in half-an-hour for Dalaman. No one the night before had any idea that he was leaving the yacht. All was arranged. 'Frederic! Frederic!' I heard from above. 'Frederic! Where is Mr Yong?' 'It is 'Is 'Ighness' said Frederic disappearing up the companion, and I was left alone. I dressed and came on deck to find all in confusion. The Khedive was rapidly pacing up and down dressed in helmet, white Sudanese cotton coat and yellow riding breeches. He was surrounded by a crowd of attendant° amongst whom I could see an effendi, Herr Wilhelm Schwartz, an Egyptian Officer, the Captain of the yacht, the experts, the Court *Imam*, the Court doctor and all the crew, Every now and then he asked a question. 'Where is Amin effendi?' 'Here, Sir!' 'Send me *Monsieur le docteur* at once.' 'I am here, *Monseigneur*,' replied the Court doctor from his side. 'Is Frederic here?' 'I am 'ere, Sir!'

Suddenly he paused and exclaimed, 'Where is Mr Yong? Ah! Mr Yong! Bad news has arrived. I hear there is a wicked brigand called Chokajik living in the very country through which you will pass and if he captures you he will most certainly demand a heavy ransom from me. The son of an English lord was captured by him last year and his father was forced to pay as much as £1000 before he was liberated. I wonder, Mr Yong, how much he would ask for you?' 'I don't think' interrupted Amin effendi, 'that Chokajik could ask as much as that for Mr Yong. I don't think he would ask more than £100 or possibly £150.' 'Ah! that is better' said His Highness with a sigh of relief. 'Then it is not such a serious matter.' 'But is it safe for Your Highness to ride to Dalaman with this brigand in the district?' queried some flatterer in the crowd. 'I have no fear', bravely answered His Highness as he stepped into the launch. 'And as for Mr Yong he is a man of gallantry.' An hour later the Khedive disembarked at Kille and I watched the calvalcade climb slowly through the pine woods and up the hill: His Highness first, like a general with an uneasy seat; next the bodyguard; then a long line of attendants and baggage animals; last poor Frederic mounted on the worst horse of all.

Young was fortunately not kidnapped, and spent the next days surveying and mapping the beautiful local countryside – orchards of apple and cherry, fields of ripe barley and even wooded meadows in which a cuckoo was calling. When his work was over he travelled to Constantinople to report to the khedive in his palace:

I had a very interesting interview with His Highness, who seemed much pleased when I presented him with the map. When the interview was concluded an official of the Palace showed me round the principal rooms, took me to look at the view over the Bosphorous from the top of the tower and drove me in a small pony carriage round the dairy farm and finally brought me back to lunch with the Khedivial suite. After lunch there was a sudden and violent thunderstorm. Heavy rain fell followed by a shower of exceptionally large hail-stones, which seemed to delight the suite for they all, including my friend the Court *Imam*, ran out into the garden, picked them up and ate them. Even the wet grass did not deter them and it was an absurd sight to see the Court officials, most of them clad in tight fitting frock coats, eating and relishing hail-stones. The storm soon cleared and I returned to Constantinople in time to catch my steamer for Constanza and from there to travel across Europe on leave for England.

Anglo-Egyptian friendship?

Contacts between the British and the Egyptians were usually limited to formal meetings between officials at various levels or between the British and Egyptian petitioners of all kinds. Rarely were friendships formed beyond the call of duty. The British claimed they saw enough Egyptians during office hours not to want to meet them at home or club and there were feelings that friendships with 'inferiors' were not quite right. There were interesting exceptions. John de Vere Loder was a bright young lieutenant who at least made an effort. A scion of the upper classes, he went to Eton and was only nineteen when the First World War begun. He served in Gallipoli and Egypt. He brought all the prejudices of his class to the attempt to get to know and understand an Egyptian family. These he described in letters home to his father at Wakehurst Place, Ardingley, Sussex:

Sidi Bishr 25 June 1916

Dear Father

I am trying to make the acquaintance of an Egyptian family whose garden overlooks my tent but it is the most difficult thing imaginable. They are the most exclusive and retired people possible although they are Christian Copts and take a pride in being very English. They asked me to play tennis the other day. I arrived and found 3 youths there to play with and although the whole of the rest of the family sat and looked on from the verandah close by I wasn't introduced to one of them. I daresay we shall get on better after a time. Much love from your loving John

1 July 1916

My acquaintance with the Egyptian family next door is progressing slowly, but it is hard work as although they want to be as English as possible I think they are rather frightened of public opinion if they allow their women folk to make the acquaintance of strangers. However, I am very friendly with all the boys and little children. Only a suitable opportunity is required for me to be introduced to the parents, after which there ought not to be much trouble in overcoming their prejudices. Where there is a will on both sides there should easily be a way. At all events the eldest boy has asked me to come down the Nile from Cairo to Assiut (a 3 days' trip) in their motor boat if I can get a week's leave in August. They are really quite nice people and most interesting as to their ways and behaviour.

6 July 1916

I am getting on well now with the Egyptian family next door and have been introduced to the whole lot at last. It is rather nice to have civilian friends about. I forget if I told you that the eldest boy goes up to Trinity, Cambridge, in September.

24 July 1916

Dear Mother

Herewith more about my Egyptian friends which may interest you. The entire family lives together as much as possible. There appear to be 3 principal branches by name Wisa, Alexen, and Khayat. They have 3 houses side by side here and 3 houses side by side at Assiout where they spend the winter. They are Copts by nation, American Protestants by religion and wealthy cotton-growers by trade. I do not know the parents very well, I have met Alexen Bey several times and he appears to be a typical 'notable' quite willing to lick English boots if it paid him. The girls have been well brought up by English governesses. Their manners and customs are naturally a bit odd to our ideas, but are a very tolerable English imitation considering the fact that most of them have never been to England. Partly owing to ancient prejudice and partly to Mahommetan environment their womenkind hold a rather indefinite position. Although they are fairly decently educated and allowed reasonable freedom it is not easy to get to know them. One is not introduced to them until one has known the menfolk some time and they know what sort of person you are. This is partly due to the fact that they lead a very narrow existence. They see very few people outside their own family. As Copts they are members of a small clique looked down on by most other Egyptians and as Protestants they are separated from many Copts. Their outlook on life wants broadening by contact with outsiders, from lack of this they are very shy and reticent at first with strangers.

As usual in hot countries they don't spend too strenuous a day. They stay indoors most of the morning, lunch at 2 p.m., sleep till 4.30 and then begin the strenuous portion of the day. They usually play tennis in the evening, dine at 9 p.m. and go to bed at 11 p.m. Altogether they are quite nice people making very praiseworthy if only partially successful efforts to be English without anyone to show them how. If the whole lot came to England for a year or two it would make all the difference. The basis of their nature is however Eastern and will always remain so. I don't think they would ever absolutely grasp the English point of view as to politics and diplomacy, though they would be very offended if you told them so.

Loder also described various citizens of Alexandria as seen by an English soldier:

21 February 1916

Dear Father,

I have never seen such funny people as the natives here. They are a low, thieving, lying set of ragamuffins, but most amusing.

The *Omdeh* of Siuf is the headman about here to whom most of the people owe allegiance. He is a little wizened man in a black gown with a white turban round his tarboosh and rides about on a frightful skewballed tub of a pony, carrying a little sjambok which is seldom idle. By his own account he is an ardent Anglophile. To emphasise this he invited the Camp Commandant and his Staff one day to a lunch lasting 4 hours provided by his Italian son-in-law who runs a fried fish shop in some back street of Alexandria.

Near the tram station and at various points of vantage about the camp there are donkey enclosures, each under a native policeman. As the unfortunate soldier passes, an avalanche of donkey boys dragging their wretched animals along with them sweeps down upon him. If he is wise he will select an animal quickly and cut a way through the throng with stick and spur, else a conversation something after this kind ensues:–

1st donkey boy (pushing his animal in front of prospective fare so that he stumbles over it): 'Take me donkey, Mr Officer; vary goo–ood, vary ni–ice donkey.'

2nd donkey boy (charging through the scrum and ousting 1st donkey boy): 'No, no, Mr. Officer, he donkey no damn goo–ood; me vary clean donkey, 'gyptian donkey.'

3rd donkey boy (a powerful giant almost carrying a diminutive, underfed animal before him thrusts 2nd donkey boy aside with rough gestures and much voluble abuse): 'A–ah, Mr. Captain, he donkey bally limit, me donkey Lord Kitchener, take Lord Kitchener donkey.' (Meanwhile prospective fare hopelessly bewildered in the turmoil hastily bestrides the nearest moke. If he is not careful in mounting he pulls the saddle over and collapses on the sand. Renewed clamour mingled with cries for backsheesh from various claimants to the honour of having helped him up. Exit finally at a slow jog, donkey boy pattering behind in the sand uttering the usual gutteral long-drawn cry 'A–a–ah'.)

There is another strange class of being who only emerges at dusk; the lamp-lighter. The particular fifteen-year-old specimen who attends to the lamp near my tent rejoices in the name of Cicero. There is little he doesn't know about arc, oil or incandescent lights. He is invariably filthy dirty and has to all appearances worn the same pink print nightgown of a dress ever since I came here. Despite his tender years he has a 'plenty fine wi–ife'.

There is one more institution without which the camp could scarcely exist. It consists of a small compound enclosed by a high barbed wire fence into which all malefactors and vagrants are mercilessly cast. Among the inhabitants it is known as the 'cleenk'. Every morning two representatives of the civil police arrive and administer due chastisement to minor offenders with a stout bamboo cane before a highly appreciative audience. On special occasions the *Omdeh* himself is present to give a few extra cuts on his own account. You must not imagine however that the sufferers bear any ill will. They are at it as hard as ever next day and merely grin rather more broadly than usual when you kick them back into the 'cleenk'.

If time and the cost of postage permitted I could discourse at length on a number of other types who unconsciously make life rather more amusing than it otherwise would be. I refrain, however, from mentioning any others than the newspaper boy and the ordinary workman. The former is chiefly noticeable because of the desperately early hour at which he starts operations and the everlasting optimism which always inspires him to shout 'Vary goo–ood niooz papar this muarning; vary goo–ood niooz'. The latter does more work single-handed than a fatigue party of half a dozen Tommies and seems to enjoy it. At intervals he makes the noise he calls singing, but which reminds the white man of a cat fight and provokes him to throw bricks.

Master and servant

The relationship of the British to their servants was often equally fraught and the subject of numerous stories and jokes. It was the one unavoidable contact, often a relationship of amused tolerance and sincere affection on both sides. There is the story of a dinner party given by an Englishman in Cairo at which there was an inordinately long gap between the soup and meat courses. When all the guests had left the host asked one of his servants the reason for the delay. The answer was that the cook had suddenly died after preparing the soup and the servants, sure that their employer would not want the dinner to be broken up, had gone off searching for a replacement cook to prepare the meat.

The following account by Cecil Hope-Gill of the Levant Consular Service seems to be a variation on the above, although ostensibly from Morocco. He had a servant whose devotion to duty was such that:

One day after luncheon at which we had had guests, when my wife asked him why there had been such a long wait between the meat course and the desert, he had profusely apologised, saying, 'But I had to deliver my wife's third child, for we did not want to disturb the *Bashador* (local lingo for Ambassador and a common enough address) by asking him to drive her to the hospital', which I had of course promised to do.

John Young recounted his experiences with his stableman in the form of a scene which epitomized all his meetings with this particularly lovable and infuriating employee:

'El Usta Mohammed wishes to see you, Efendim.' El Usta Mohammed is my syce (stableman). 'Tell him to come in ten minutes – I am busy – and oh, bring me a whisky and soda.' 'Hadir,' says the servant and retires noiselessly. I am not really busy, but it is the first of the month, and I know that Mohammed intends to present his monthly accounts. I know what is in store for me and shrink from facing him – always. Sometimes it is three days before he can obtain an audience. Today I shall see him in ten minutes – probably. If only he wanted to talk about the ponies I should welcome him, for he knows them and loves them, but I cannot bear to discuss money questions with him. I sip my whisky and soda, light a pipe, and endeavour to steel myself to face him. I glance at my watch, remember an important engagement which must be kept before dinner, and am just about to ring and postpone the interview till tomorrow, when Mohammed settles the question by stumping into the room and out onto the verandah.

He is a venerable figure, gnarled and rugged, with the unmistakeable look of the man who lives among horses. In addition to his boots, he wears a white turban, an old officer's winter khaki jacket from which the badges of rank have been stripped, leaving their shadows in the shape of unfaded patches, and the usual voluminous white drawers. His face and hands, and the legs which emerge from the drawers and disappear into his boots, are jet black. He proceeds to fumble in his pockets, finally handing me a dirty little square of folded paper, which I take and open. The square of paper is a page torn from some book. At the top is printed in English the word 'Answers', and underneath are eight spaces separated by printed dotted lines. Upon this has been scrawled in pencil in almost illegible Arabic the monthly account. It is not Mohammed's handiwork, for he cannot write. Once a month he meets a literary friend of his own tribe in the open air cafe amongst the fig trees near the Sidi Gaber Mosque, and between the two the statement is drafted.

I sit looking at the paper, wondering dreamily where he got it and what is the meaning of the word 'Answers,' until, in turning it over, I find printed in English at the back the following:

Questions.

1. The Prose and Poetical authors you admire most?
2. The scenery you admire most?
3. A brief definition of Love?

and five other questions of an equally probing nature. So the paper is a page from one of those books which in my youth every English flapper used to keep for the persecution of her male friends. I have not seen one for twenty years, and the incongruity of its associations with those of the business in hand sets me laughing, and looking up at Mohammed's black, puzzled face, I laugh the more. He smiles at first, but the smile soon gives place to a puzzled frown. He is not of the type that likes being laughed at. Well, it is not my business to enquire where his clerical staff obtain their stationery, so I settle down to examine the account.

Occasionally an item is to me illegible, and I ask Mohammed to come to my assistance, but he cannot read. So we proceed as follows:

'What does it look like?' he says.

'It looks like one horse, five piastres.'

'No, it cannot be a horse. I have not bought one, and five piastres is too cheap.' Mohammed begs me to try again. 'Perhaps,' says Mohammed, 'Mohammed could read it.' Mohammed is the *sofragi* (servant). The worst of my household is that they are all called Mohammed. Mohammed the sofragi is rung for, and the document is presented to him. After studying it for some time he suggests that Mahmoud be brought into consultation. Mahmoud is the cook. He is also Mohammed, but one must draw the line somewhere, so we call him Mahmoud as the nearest thing. Mahmoud is duly fetched, and the document presented to him. He enjoys a great reputation for scholarship in the household, and we watch him with confidence. Being terribly short-sighted, as befits an oriental scholar, he raises the paper to within exactly one inch of his left eye, holding his head to one side, and fixing his right eye on the carpet, throwing it as it were out of gear. He then proceeds to move his head forwards and backwards along the paper.

'It looks like two camels,' says Mahmoud at last, not with much conviction, and amid general laughter.

I thereupon decide to dismiss the two experts, and to pass the item without further investigation. Mahmoud, who likes things to be shipshape, is not contented, and suggests going to fetch the man who wrote the account, but this I refuse and pass on to the total.

Dear old Mohammed! How did we solve our problem that damp summer evening in Alexandria ten years back, as I sat on the verandah and discussed finance with you to the sound of the breakers? Frankly, I cannot remember. Probably you carried the account away and, after a conference with all the syces in the neighbourhood, brought it back in a new form which triumphantly vindicated you, or perhaps in sheer weariness I accepted your conclusion in defiance of every law of arithmetic. Who knows? I still have your bill; I kept that particular one as a curiosity, because of the sheet of paper it was written on, and, as I look at it, your honest old, black face comes up before me, and I hear your high-pitched voice, and look at the phantom Captain's stars on your coat. All those things your scrap of paper has brought back to me; all those, and many more besides. Here on a dark winter afternoon, amid the greys and half greens of the Cotswolds, it has carried me back to the buffs and blues of the East, and filled my memories with happy sunlight.

Young had no affection for two of his other servants who proved to be neither efficient nor trustworthy. He wrote of one of his journeys:

Before leaving Cairo I secured the services of a young servant named Taher. This boy had been with a friend as second servant when he was on inspection in Upper Egypt and handed him on to me with the highest testimonials. I may say that Taher not only proved to be a lazy inefficient servant but he irritated me to such an extent that I dismissed him immediately on my return. My friend, surprised at finding that my opinion differed so widely from his own, asked Salah his head servant if he could give an explanation. 'The reason is clear', said Salah. 'When I was with your excellency in Upper Egypt I used to take Taher every morning behind a palm tree and beat him. Taher is one of those people who cannot work until he is beaten. As Mr Young did not beat him he has become completely useless.'

Another untoward incident happened at much the same time. My Government servant named Said had been proving unsatisfactory for some months past and he had to be dismissed. I accordingly paid him by cheque a small sum due to him for private services and he left my employment. To my surprise a few days afterwards I received a telephone message from the National Bank of Egypt asking me if I had paid my servant a cheque for LE50. I replied that I had done no such thing and was at once invited to visit the Bank where I would find my late servant together with the cheque in question. It appeared that Said had taken a blank cheque out of my cheque book and with this and his own cheque he had gone to a public letter writer whom he had requested to write out a cheque for LE50 to himself and at the same time to copy my signature. The public letter writer demurred. He said that as a public letter writer it was of course part of his business to forge signatures but that to do so he must demand a fee of P.T.50. This Said promised to pay. But when the cheque had been duly written and signed he seized it and handing over only P.T.5 ran off and disappeared into the crowded street.

The public letter writer was for the moment dazed at the smallness of the reward, but he soon recovered and went to the Police Station where he called out 'I am oppressed. An *effendi* promised me P.T.50 for writing a cheque with an Englishman's signature and when it was written he only gave me 5 and ran away with the cheque. There is no justice in Egypt.' The public letter writer was immediately detained, but as it was Saturday afternoon the Bank was closed and nothing could be done until Monday; when as soon as the doors were opened Said and a policeman walked from different directions simultaneously up the steps of the Bank and Said was arrested on presenting the cheque.

The trial some weeks later at which I gave evidence was most entertaining. Said in his defence stated that he was beloved by me, that I often wrote him cheques for five, ten or fifty pounds as a token of my good wishes, and he frequently interrupted the Egyptian Judge, who sternly called out 'Silence'. On being questioned I stated that I certainly had never written or signed the cheque, and I further pointed out that no Englishman would word a cheque in such a manner for the LE50 was written as 'Fifty hundred piastres', whereas I would have written either 'Five hundred piastres', or 'Fifty Egyptian pounds'. 'But', interrupted Council for the defence, rising and leaning over a pile of books and papers, 'in this year 1922 English people do not speak of one thousand nine hundred and twenty two. They say nineteen hundred and twenty two, just the way this cheque was written.' At that the Judge cried 'Nonsense'. Council collapsed. All his papers fell on to the floor and the Judge gave sentence: 'Two months', and Said passed out of the Court and for ever out of history.

A heart of gold: Hanem Aaref

In 1919 Egypt had risen up against the British in protest against the continuing occupation. Several bloody massacres took place including one at the railway station of Mellawi in Upper Egypt where a British soldier was hacked to death. What happened then is related by Judge McBarrett, working at the time in the Egyptian Mixed Courts in the region:

Conspicuous among the frenzied wretches who screamed and shouted about the mangled corpse were the women of the town ululating and clapping their hands in their joy over the heroism of their townsmen and clients. With them came Hanem Aaref – she too was of the sisterhood – but the only soul mindful of her womanhood. She wept and, pressing forward, sought to intercede and wipe the blood from the dead man's face with her gown and was beaten and driven off with curses by the mob. So rare a flash of humanity seemed worthy of investigation, so Hanem Aaref was sent for by the inquisitors. She was found to be in prison for some petty offence – an alleged theft from a client – a charge not without suspicion of being prompted by revenge for her action on the fatal day.

Before the examiners she told her story quite naturally and without the least embroidery. 'I went with the others', she said, 'to see – but when I saw the poor boy all bloody and beaten I could not help weeping – I thought of his mother so far away and what she would suffer when she knew how her son had been treated in a distant land. I tried to wipe the blood from his face, but they drove me off and beat me.' As she left the Court the members of the Commission rose and saluted this woman of the town. An immediate effort was made to get her released from the prison. The story was told in full to the authorities at the Ministry of the Interior with a request for clemency. The reply was remarkable – all the more so as it was signed by an Englishman. It was to the effect that the offence for which she was incarcerated appeared to be proved and that as it appeared that she was a woman of low character the Department declined to interfere.

Those, however, who knew the facts and had seen the woman were determined that her behaviour should not go without some recognition. A subscription was started privately and eventually some months after the rising a notice was put up in the Turf Club of Cairo. The response was immediate and finally the list was closed at the respectable figure of L.E.92.50, and I was entrusted with the delicate task of deciding on the form the presentation should take. It being no task for a mere man I at once called in the aid of Sister Margaret: this is the natural thing to do for Sister Margaret is the pivot of all English charitable actions in Egypt; moreover, she gets things done. She is small and frail, but one who doesn't suffer fools gladly and is an ever-ready helper in trouble.

Needless to say my call met with a ready response. We decided that Hanem Aaref must come to Cairo and give her own views of what she would like done with the money. Friends at Mellawi were appealed to – the lady it was found was nervous and a little uncertain of the reasons for which she was being sent. Her departure was announced once but on that occasion it appears that her courage failed her and she left the train at an intermediate station. The second effort was more successful and she arrived at Cairo Station – slightly fortified by strong waters – in company of an elderly Copt, apparently a personal friend, and an idiot brother of whom she takes charge and who never leaves her. She was met by an agent of the Cairo branch of the White Slave Traffic Society and taken to their Home and put to bed comfortably for the night. Next morning Sister Margaret brought her along to see me. I found myself in the presence of a lady handsomely but soberly dressed whose perfect manners – not even the perturbation caused by my lift – a novel experience – could disturb. Though much more prosperous in appearance than on the first occasion I had seen her, she was not otherwise changed – a gentle-mannered creature with a plain kindly face who conducted herself with perfect propriety and dignity and never once suggested by word or deed the sad profession to which she prolonged.

The rest of the narrative I give in Sister's own words: 'You will be glad to hear that Hanem Aaref has left Cairo safely. Her escort and the idiot brother went with her. We had an extremely amusing time; she is a woman of real character. She quite thought she was coming to Cairo to be hung, and she fortified herself for the ordeal by a fair amount of strong drink, but we put her to bed safely at the Refuge, and she was quite contented and happy the next morning. It was very difficult to find out what really would please her most. We suggested a comfortable little home with her mother in Minia – a little shop – some land, a husband, a monthly sum to be paid her regularly as long as our funds permitted; all these things she agreed to, but clearly they did not hit the mark. At last she produced some heavy gold bracelets. 'Why not give me some bracelets?' It seemed really the most sensible thing to do. She couldn't drink away bracelets, she would always be proud of possessing them, and they would constantly recall to her her really heroic behaviour.

So we took Hanem Aaref off in an *arabieh*, and settled ourselves in a tiny shop in the Gold Bazaar in the Mouski for a strenuous morning's work. For about two hours we tried on bracelets. Four men were employed (two at each arm) to press them into exactly the right shape and size. We had to call for soap and water to aid us in passing the bracelets over her hand. When they were finally fitted, they all had to be taken off, and we went off to a weighing shop to find out the exact weight. Then we had to return to the original shop and put them on again. I suggested she might like a gold necklace for the sake of variety, but she explained to me it would not do. If you have a dispute with your friends the first thing they do is to clutch at your neck: they might break the necklace, and they also might strangle you, whereas heavy gold fetters on your arm make it a formidable fighting weapon! So we decided to plump for bracelets. When they were at last chosen and paid for, she arranged to meet her idiot brother and her other cavalier, and have a spree before she returned to Mellawi, and of all extraordinary places she chose to take them to the Museum! probably to see the jewellery. She went off very happily. The only thing which she could not get over was your lift. She did think her last end had come when she was put in a box and lifted to the sky.

An inscription was engraved on one of the bracelets:
TO HANEM AAREF A gift of the English in recognition of her compassion towards a dying British Soldier on the 18th of March 1919.'

Then two years later:

'I know you will be interested and glad to hear that we have heard from Hanem Aaref that she is happily married and has left her old method of life!

She particularly wanted the judge to know, and thought all her English friends in Cairo would be pleased to hear about her marriage!'

Painted harlots

A well-known area of Cairo life was the infamous red light district which became familiar to Rapp as consul:

Cairo was in fact to put the finishing touches to the education in the seamy side of life which I had started in Port Said and was now illustrated by its end products. The Egyptian police had detailed one of their junior British officers, a pleasant, knowledgeable character named Tegg, to assist in investigating the cases of British subjects whose manner of life had become suspect. It was in Tegg's company that I visited the Wasaa, the squalid district behind the Ezbekia Gardens, where second and third class prostitutes of all hues, ages and contours offered their wares.

Most of the women were of the third-class category for whom Marseilles had no further use, and who would eventually be passed on to the Bombay and Far East markets, but they were still European and not yet fallen so low as to live in the one-room shacks of the Wasaa which had always been the quarter for purely native prostitution of the lowest class. Here in the Wasaa Egyptian, Nubian and Sudanese women plied their one shilling trade in conditions of abject squalor, though under Government medical control. A stroll through its narrow and crowded lanes reminded one of a zoo, with its painted harlots sitting like beasts of prey behind the iron grilles of their ground-floor brothels, while a noisy crowd of low-class natives, interspersed with soldiers in uniform and sight-seeing tourists, made their way along the narrow lanes.

The din from the cafes and their musicians, added to the cries of the stall-keepers, was strident and interminable. It was an eerie under-world with a code of its own and had until his recent arrest been ruled by a pervert king, whose sinister influence spread far beyond its bounds. He was a huge, fat Nubian named Ibrahim el–Gharbi, who could be seen every evening sitting cross-legged on a bench outside one of his houses. Dressed as a woman and veiled in white, this repulsive pervert sat like a silent, ebony idol, occasionally holding out a bejewelled hand to be kissed by some passing admirer, or giving a silent order to one of his attendant servants. This man had an amazing power in the country; his influence extended not only into the world of prostitution, but was also felt in the sphere of politics and high society. The buying and selling of women for the trade both in Cairo and the provinces was entirely in el-Gharbi's hands and no decision of his as to price was ever questioned.

Russell, the police officer, also wrote about el-Gharbi:

In 1916, when the town was packed with thousands of Dominion and Home troops, the police chief, Harvey Pasha decided to take drastic action to clear up the scores of free-lance girls and catamite boys who had sprung up outside the licensed quarters. One of his first orders under Martial Law was to establish an internment camp at Hilmiya and to throw into it any of these long-haired degenerates that we could find. In a couple of nights we rounded up about a hundred of these pests, but I noticed that the famous el-Gharbi was not among them. There was only one man in those days who could touch anyone as big as this king of the underworld, and that was my chief, Harvey Pasha, who cared nothing for beys or pashas and had a temper like a box of fireworks. Next morning in the office I asked him innocently whether el-Gharbi was to be exempted from the order, and found to my astonishment that he had never even heard of him or of his sinister reputation. He barked out an order to have him arrested at once and brought to his office, while I took cover and awaited the coming storm. Half an hour later an officer arrived, leading by the hand what looked like a huge negress, clad in white samite, her golden anklets and bracelets clinking as she minced down the corridor. I followed them into Harvey's office and for a moment feared I had imperilled the life of my choleric chief, who blew up like a landmine, demanding what the hell everyone meant by bringing that disgusting patchouli-scented sodomite into his presence, and with a bellow of rage sent him below to be stripped of his female finery, put into handcuffs and thrown into Hilmiya internment camp among his youthful imitators.

One felt some sympathy with the Australian soldiers who ran amuck in Wasa during the war and consigned a large area to the flames.

Britons adrift abroad

To complement Egyptian characters there were numerous British men and women who fetched up in Egypt, some of whom could not have done much to burnish the imperial reputation. Not from the upper administrators or officers, they were ordinary people who sometimes fell on hard times. Teaching attracted a variety of men, some dedicated, others eccentric, perhaps none more so than K.T. Frost, whom John Young strangely counted as a friend:

In July 1906 I spent my leave, accompanied by my friend K.T. Frost, travelling down the Euphrates. Frost after leaving Oxford had spent a year in the Sinai peninsula on an archaelogical expedition under Flinders Petrie, and in 1904 had joined the Department of Education as a master in the Khedivial School. His heart was more in Archaelogy than in teaching Egyptian boys and two years later he succeeded in getting the post of Lecturer in Archaelogy and Ancient History in the University of Belfast which he held until the outbreak of war in 1914 when he was killed fighting as a Lieutenant in the Cheshire Regiment. He never had any spare cash, seemed to be always poor. He dressed abominably and sometimes incongruously, wearing large boots which he called 'Nig knockers' or 'Dago dusters' and he very often lost his temper even with me and much more easily with stray people whom he met. I may add that his knowledge of Arabic was elementary. Such a man may not seem to have been the most suitable companion in a difficult and somewhat dangerous journey, but he was a very attractive character and had a keen sense of humour besides being exceedingly well informed about the countries through which we proposed to travel. When in 1914 his platoon were caught by the Germans he refused to surrender, and they were killed to a man, but the Germans were so much impressed with his behaviour that they gave him a military funeral: a very gallant end and a very typical end for this remarkable man.

Frost's behaviour throughout the voyage was in conformity with his character and he insisted for some reason on sleeping in his boots. One night when the crew were waiting for the moon to rise before starting to travel the old *rais* was chattering in a very exasperating manner to himself as much as to the crew. Frost was trying, I was pretending, to sleep. I heard Frost say in Arabic so bad that no native of Mesopotamia could understand him: '*Rais!* I want to sleep.' The *rais* continued to chatter. The demand was repeated but without effect. Suddenly Frost arose in his boots, stumbled over the cotton sacks barking his shins on the thwarts and ungainly oars, and I heard the sounds of two distinct smacks, one on each side of the cheek. The *rais* was silenced, Frost stumbled back to bed, and it was not until we were again in Cairo that he admitted to me that he had smacked the *rais* on the face.

Drink, drugs and marriage contributed to the miseries of a number of Britons who were somehow stranded in Egyptian society. Soldiers and seamen were well to the fore. Rapp witnessed this part of life as consul in Port Said after the First World War, both the tragic and amusing sides:

The British community – for the most part Egyptian Government officials, shipping agents, Canal pilots and businessmen – differed little from such British communities elsewhere, life following the usual routine of office, club, sports, dances and modest entertaining. Yet, as one would expect from Port Said's character as a transit port, there was a quota of weaker brethren, for some of whom the war was to blame. Among them a few demobilised officers, unwilling for one reason or another to return home, were becoming pathetic cases. Late one night we were informed by the police that an English major had just died at Ismailia and that there was no one to take charge of his affairs. Accompanied by Walter Purcell, our local British lawyer, I went next morning to investigate. The major, an ex-regular soldier, had taken a small house in an isolated position on the edge of the desert. There, with a Mauritian servant for sole company, he had proceeded to drink himself steadily to death. Outside the yard was stacked high with innumerable empty gin and whiskey bottles. As we examined his papers we were to find piles of unopened letters from his wife, from whom he was estranged. There was also a will in which he left everything to his Mauritian servant. This servant stayed on in Ismailia to enjoy his small fortune, but, a year later in a drunken frolic he fell into the Freshwater Canal and was drowned.

The Suez Canal pilots had an envied position in Egypt, living well when relaxing from a responsible job. Again according to Rapp:

There were some half dozen British Canal pilots, whose privileges we constantly envied. We had two particular friends, one a Scot, who once in a mood of celebration bid against me for a car I was trying to buy. When it was knocked down to him, after he had forced up the price beyond what I was prepared to pay, he surprisingly told me that he had been bidding on my behalf because he knew I wanted it. I thought it was a matter we could better discuss the next day. The second was a wild Irishman of generous disposition, whose exploits were viewed with an indulgent eye by the Canal authorities. Somehow or other they knew when he was fit to be called for duty, but once they slipped up with the consequence that a P and O mailboat did a record passage to Ismailia, in its course throwing up huge waves, causing damage to the banks and being reported by every signal station on the way. To crown the day, on arrival at Ismailia, he gathered a bouquet of flowers in the garden of the Agent Superieur and then proceeded to the front entrance to present it to the Agent's wife. It was far from being my only experience of the amused tolerance shown by the French for such extravagances.

The Cairo underworld also contained its proportion of British malefactors and dropouts:

The aftermath of war was still very much with us in other ways, often involving soldiers who had been demobilised locally with the idea of gaining their livelihood in Egypt. Among them were many who had failed to make good and some who had succumbed to Cairo's temptations. An attempt was now being made to rid Cairo of undesirable non-Egyptian elements, a process made much more difficult by the privileged position of foreigners under the Capitulations. British subjects could not be exempted from the consequences of anti-social conduct we criticised in others; hence our Consular Court made full use of its authority to deport undesirables who had become involved in Cairo's underworld, occasionally as addicts or traffickers in heroin or cocaine. One tragedy concerned a British doctor of a well-known family. He was returning from Singapore and had left his ship in Suez to seek in Cairo the drugs to which he had become addicted. He had been found sick and penniless in a sordid hovel after he had disposed of his watch and personal papers for his last shots of heroin. For heroin was coming to replace the much less harmful hashish, hitherto the traditional dope, whose import from the Lebanon was now being rigorously suppressed.

Marriages between Britons and Egyptians caused endless worry to the authorities. They were often contracted in haste with neither side knowing much of the other's life. There was inevitable disillusionment. It was related of one such marriage that the British husband soon deserted his wife and wasted his life in the casino at Monte Carlo, 'a case – it was said – of marrying in haste and repenting at les jeux.' When necessary, Rapp could rely on Sister Margaret who had once helped Hanem Aaref:

We had another helper in the person of an Anglican nun called Sister Margaret, whom I remember with much respect. She was dedicated to the welfare of British women who fell on evil times, often through no fault of their own. In some instances it was British girls who had married Egyptians, usually when they were students in England, and had found the conditions of life to which they were now exposed quite intolerable. Under Moslem law a wife had virtually no rights or protection, a fact that an Englishwoman who has differences with her husband soon discovers. We had frequent enquiries from British girls wishing to marry Egyptians. We would send them in reply a copy of the solemn and detailed warning about the risks they would incur, which had been drawn up by our legal adviser. This was not always effective, but I can think of a few marriages that turned out happily, usually when there was some equivalence to the educational and economic background. Even this, however, was not indispensable: there was always the popular Oxford town wife of a well-known Egyptian minister to prove the contrary. She had expanded enormously with the passage of time, and one day confided to my wife: 'It's not fat, my dear, but water.'

She had been an assistant in a hairdresser's shop in St Giles, Oxford, frequently visited by Egyptian students. She had an ugly Oxford accent and was quite conscious that the British society ladies did not think much of her. Equally insecure for a different reason were the many marriages of British soldiers to local girls, who were nearly always of the national and religious minorities such as Syrians, Armenians, Copts, Italians and Greeks. In some cases the parties had no common language and an interpreter between them was necessary at the Consular marriage. Too rarely was there any basis on which a permanent relationship could be built, but the necessary formalities had been completed, the permission of the soldier's commanding officer had been obtained (which he could in any case hardly refuse) and so the ten minute ceremony had to take place with all it portended.

These marriages were numerous, and I had to solemnize as many as three in one day during my time as acting Consul. On one occasion the bridegroom was missing, but he was eventually found dead drunk and incapable on a bench in the hall. He was in no fit state to be married and the marriage was obviously doomed anyhow, so I declined to carry on until I had had an apology for his conduct through his commanding officer in the hope that delay would induce reflection. But the apology was forthcoming and the marriage took place. The next I heard of this particular soldier was that he had been courtmartialled for theft and sentenced to three months in gaol, following which he was sent home and his wife, who had been a friend's nursemaid, saw him no more. Desertion of these wives seemed the rule rather than the exception, causing me to wonder how many cases of bigamy went undetected or condoned. Years later, when I returned to Cairo, I happened to enquire about the state of the Benevolent Fund I had once helped to administer. I was to learn that those most in need had been the abandoned wives and children of such soldiers. But the wives, many of whom had seemed poor enough creatures, had clung to their British passports and had often made pathetic efforts to bring up their children decently, even teaching them to regard defaulting fathers as mythical heroes.

John Young on one of his tours of the Egyptian countryside during the war came across a strange example of a mixed marriage:

One day in a village I entered the headman's house on business connected with taxes. It was a very poor village lying on the banks of the Rosetta branch of the Nile. The house was built of mud unbaked brick, the flat roof heaped up with bundles of Indian corn stalks together with piles of round cakes of buffalo dung drying for use as fuel. The room in which I waited had an earthen floor. Dust lay thick on the divan and the rest of the scanty furniture, while innumerable flies circled in every direction. Hens ran in and out of the open door pecking at what they could find and two mangy scavenger dogs snarled round each other in a corner over a bone. After I had waited for a little while a young English woman and a small English boy walked in. The woman appeared to be about twenty and the boy about eight years old. She said: 'My father-in-law will be with you in a few minutes. How is the war going? They tell me that Germany in winning but I never see an English newspaper here.'

Presently the headman came in, the young woman and the boy went out and the remainder of the visit was spent in business. When I took leave I was escorted to the village boundary by a *ghaffir* (guard) who explained the domestic situation in the *omdah's* house. The headman's *(omdah's)* son, an engineer by profession, when studying in London had married his landlady's daughter and had brought his bride out to the family home in Egypt where she had only been for two months. The little boy, he thought, was her brother who was being sent each day to the village school. When I arrived at the next village the headman there confirmed the *ghaffir's* story and remarked that he thought the engineer loved his wife and treated her well. 'But', I said, 'I hear he beats her.' It seemed to me an odd case. Here was this young English woman captivated by the charms of an Egyptian Moslem of no class, who had probably given her an utterly false description of his rank in life and of her future home and she had now found herself in the mud hovel of her father-in-law in a remote village of the Egyptian Delta leading the life of a peasant and would, if she remained there, be in a few years a wrinkled hag, for *fellahin* women are old before they are thirty. I pictured her as time went on trudging down to the river every morning, afternoon and evening, with the other village women to scoop up water for washing and drinking, an empty petroleum tin balanced on her head and her long black garment trailing behind in the dust. And her young brother! What a life for him! He was to be brought up with the other village boys and to be educated in a school where no language was taught but Arabic. Later when I returned to Cairo I reported the case to the British Consulate and also to the British Agency, when it was discovered that her marriage papers were not in order and she and her brother were sent back to England.

Rapp had to deal with the fatal result of another weird liaison:

A report had reached the Residency that an Englishman had died at Sohag in suspicious circumstances, local gossip having it that he had been poisoned by his English wife with the help of her lover, an Egyptian doctor. A considerable delay had occurred in sending on the police reports to the Consular Court and by the time they finally reached us some nine months had elapsed. Nevertheless, after further enquiries, there seemed every justification for an exhumation order, and this was made. I travelled overnight to Sohag with Dr Sydney Smith, the medico-legal expert of the Egyptian Government. In the grey light of dawn he removed the internal organs from the now mummified body. I had then to stay on to take depositions from various local witnesses and was given lunch by an Egyptian judge who, himself a strict Moslem, produced a bottle of inferior port in my honour to serve as table wine, which made doing justice to his hospitality on a hot day a greater ordeal than the exhumation. The upshot of the case was that the arsenic found to be present in the body was not sufficient to warrant proceedings. So the wild young woman who, then only twenty-two, had already buried two husbands was free to continue her career by becoming engaged to a wealthy young man in Cairo and decamping with the family jewels in preference to marrying him. No doubt he was fortunate.

The final case of Britons adrift is a pathetic one, of an unfulfilled marriage:

Some tragedy was mingled with a certain grim humour. So it was with the repatriation of some of the British inmates of the Abbassia lunatic asylum, of whom the war had caused an accumulation, a few of the unfortunates having been put ashore from ships passing through the Suez Canal. To ensure their peaceful departure it was sometimes necessary to resort to various stratagems, which I had to think up with the British doctor in charge. There was, for example, one poor woman who imagined herself to be the financée of Kitchener. Every day she washed her best intimate undergarments – which she refused to wear – against the day when Kitchener woud appear to claim her as his bride. We had arranged for her to travel to England with a nurse, but when she heard of it she refused absolutely, contending that, as Kitchener's fiancée, she was entitled to be accompanied by someone of higher social status. So I wrote her an extremely official looking letter on blue foolscap paper to explain that Lord Curzon of Kedlestone (who was then Foreign Secretary) had expressed the wish that she should return to England, where she would be suitably received, and that he had designated a lady of suitable social standing to accompany her. The lady was, of course, the nurse in ordinary clothes. The poor woman took the bait, and the last we heard of her was from Port Said, where she climbed the ship's gangway clutching our letter, which she read to all the passengers she could find.

FOUR

BRITONS AT WORK IN EGYPT

John Young: educating the élite

Cromer and Boyle were at the peak of the British administration in Egypt. Beneath them were all sorts and conditions – teachers, inspectors, permanent officials, administrators of various kinds. John Young went out as a teacher in 1899 and left in 1924 from the post of inspector of the interior. He, more than most, gained a wide and intimate knowledge of Egyptian society and departed not at all disillusioned with the period of his service. Back at home in the Cotswolds he looked to his time in Egypt with nostalgia:

I write of twenty-five years spent by an ordinary British officer under the Egyptian government, whose sympathies are with the peoples amongst whom he mixed. Egypt is seldom far from my thoughts. I hear the call of the Muezzin, the droning of the *saqia* and the *shaduf*, the rattle of the watchman's stone warning that day is at hand when no one can eat. I smell the saffron being pounded in the huge stone mortars of the bazaars: the dull acrid smoke rising from burning buffalo dung on village fires: and best of all the fresh damp cool air that blows up the Nile when the Khamsin is over. I see the blue lake of Timsah from desert hills above Ismailia, deeper in colour than any in the Mediterranean: I see the white cloud of pigeons swooping round conical cotes in the Delta, disturbed by the clamour below of the black-cloaked women going off to market and I see the grey tips of felucca sails looming out of the river mist on an early autumn morning.

Young had decided to go to Egypt as a teacher when Britons were recruited to try to raise the standards of education there. Early in his time in Egypt Cromer had appointed a dour, humourless Scotsman, Douglas Dunlop, as Director-General of Public Instruction with the daunting task of building up the educational system. Young was to work under him:

75

Dunlop had tried hard to reform the system, with scant success. Education was seen by the Egyptian boys mostly as a means of getting a good job and when they left with great expectations of employment they were often disappointed. Their discontent later welled over into resentment of the British and the whole system.

Dunlop was not entirely to blame. He was but an instrument in a system imposed on him from above and he was not strong enough to resist. Egypt had never been so efficiently administered but it was not done by Egyptians and hitherto no steps had been taken to teach them how to do it.

After the tragic happenings of 1919 when Dunlop's students headed the revolutionary demonstrations he was asked to resign by Lord Allenby and although he had for years held the rank of Advisor to the Ministry of Education he received no recognition for his work.

Dunlop trained in Board School methods, was at the time of his appointment a teacher in a mission school at Alexandria and although the choice was good in some ways, in others it was decidedly the reverse. He was an industrious organizer and a strict disciplinarian but he had little experience of the world at large. His outlook was limited and he had little sympathy with the Egyptians and their idiosyncracies while he never in his long service of some 30 years acquired even a rudimentary knowledge of the Arabic language. The result was that he was universally feared and distrusted by the Egyptians and ridiculed by many British officials who could not discriminate between the dry precise manner of this unimaginative Scotsman and the hard-working, conscientious, and sensitive character that lay beneath the somewhat correct exterior.

Dunlop had to recruit suitable young British graduates to face the unknown rigours of the Egyptian classroom:

'Dunlop's young men' – as the newcomers were called – arrived in annual batches, callow and inexperienced. It can hardly be said that they were ideal schoolmasters. They carried out their duties adequately if not always very conscientiously; they did something to teach the young Egyptian gentlemanly behaviour. They came out to Cairo full of enthusiasm, not for their work but for early escape from it.

These young teachers did not mix with Egyptians and maintained a strict segregation: 'All this was thoroughly bad policy, quite apart from bad manners.' Working in the Ministry of Public Instruction was on the whole looked down upon by those outside and was seen as a stepping stone to other ministries. A joke current in Anglo-Egyptian circles told of 'the man who concealed his employment in the Egyptian Ministry of Public Instruction because he preferred his

mother to continue thinking that he played the piano in a brothel.'
Young himself was sent to teach in the Khedivial School in Cairo:

Secondary school, polytechnic and ministry were all contained in a single
building, a picturesque palace built in the late Turkish style, approached by
a short avenue of flowering trees in which doves nested with a fountain
playing in its three sided court. The rooms were lofty and the ceilings
painted in designs common to large houses of the period. It could be
reached by tram but most teachers bicycled and my journey there was
considerably delayed one morning by the crowd coming away from a public
execution which unfortunately had taken place before I arrived on the
scene. Public executions were not stopped until some years later. The school
held about 200 boys drawn from the upper and middle classes of Egyptians,
mostly Moslems with a sprinkling of Copts. There were a few boarders but
the majority were day boys who lived with their parents or guardians. They
worked hard and gave little trouble except through their excess of zeal in
asking questions. Some of them toiled day and night to pass their
examinations and I have known at least two cases where a boy who had
failed committed suicide. On one occasion when a boy had been
unsuccessful in his mathematical examination he told his teacher that his
father in front of witnesses had declared that if he failed again he would
disinherit him and divorce his mother. The next time he passed by one
mark and he wrote to his teacher to say 'Sir I am so grateful to you that
wherever you go in the world there I will follow you. Only I will travel
second class.'

Way down in Egypt's land

After eight long years of teaching, Young decided to move to the
Survey Department as an inspector. The department was run by the
British and its main job was to measure and record holdings for land
registration. This was a sensitive matter in Egypt where bitter
disputes over land were at the centre of village life. The negotiations
were carried on in Arabic and they took the British inspector right
into the heart of the Egyptian countryside where he came face to face
with the well known wiles of the Egyptian peasant. It was an unequal
struggle. Young revelled in this work:

Wherever employed I thoroughly enjoyed it and I look back on my few
years of surveying as the happiest of all the happy years I have spent in
Egypt. Life in the provinces for a British Inspector who was suited to it was
very agreeable. There being no carriage roads outside Cairo and provincial

towns all transport to villages was by pack animals. We travelled by train, on horse, donkey or camel as occasion suited, while the servants with luggage, bedding and supplies went on ahead to a Rest House or camp of tents. Rest Houses differed considerably in quality of accommodation. Those under the Ministries of Public Works or Finance in large towns were commodious, and here would foregather officials from different Departments for several days at a time, but irrigation Rest Houses or Rest Rooms over Police Stations in remote spots were rough enough. Camp life in the summer was subject to dust storms and in the winter there was frequent rain in the Delta and after a storm the ground round the camp became a sea of liquid mud.

A few years later Young moved to the Ministry of Finance, working once more on recording land holdings:

I began in Upper Egypt in the province of Minia where I spent the greatest part of a year. Minia, like the other provinces in Upper Egypt is long and narrow. The cultivation on the west bank rarely extends further back from the Nile than ten miles while on the east bank it is often a mere strip. Many of the villages lie close to the river and can be visited from the river after a short walk or ride. I was accommodated in a Government *dehabieh*, to which was attached a steam launch, a small *felucca*. The *dehabieh* was a comfortable house boat with three sleeping cabins, a dining room and study.

At first it was moored at the town of Minia, but at times I moved to more remote spots where I really had an opportunity of appreciating the river. There was always traffic. Besides innumerable sailing boats a tourist steamer in the winter would pass almost daily, and at night the silence would sometimes be broken by its approach. The brilliantly lit up three-decked ship would appear, pass, fade into the gloom and when it had passed so great was the wash from the huge stern wheels that if I happened to be in the launch I felt for a few minutes all the sensations of a violent storm. Once one of the sailors when we heard the dinner gong on a passing Cook's steamer said to me: 'I have been a sailor on one of those ships and we were always sorry for the tourists when they went to their dinner for we had our good village bread and our onions and they had to eat white bread and bad meat from Cairo.' But more often there was intense peace at night. From the deck I could see the sailing boats steal silently out of the darkness like great white birds with no sound but the gentle ripple against their bows unless farther across the water could be heard the distant chant of boatmen at their oars, a chant that is said to be a survival of the hymn of Osiris; or out of the stillness would come the call of belated fishermen to each other as they pulled up their nets.

I used to try to inspect personally some Government land in every village which meant a visit to nearly all the villages in the province. These visits meant acquaintance with the *omdeh* (headman), drinking many cups of coffee and invitations to partake of heavy midday meals, but I hardly ever accepted, pleading doctor's orders as an excuse. It was sometimes trying when in an *omdeh's* house to have to drink the coffee necessary before commencing an inspection. But etiquette was such that coffee, tea or sherbet must be offered and could never be refused. The water was drawn from the most questionable sources and I once saw the *omdeh's ghaffir* (village policeman) with fingers green after raking buffalo manure pick out the lumps of sugar and put them in my cup. Tea or mint tea was sometimes served, always of a poor quality. Sherbets were less common, but mulberry or ground barley in hot weather were occasionally given. It was really dangerous to drink the sherbets in Egyptian villages as the water was badly filtered and never boiled.

The inspection for the day over I would walk or ride back to launch, *dehabieh* or nearest railway station. A cup of tea on arrival and then followed hard work. All the papers of the Catalogue were sent to the Inspector for his approval which necessitated long evenings of reading as well as dealing with numerous petitions written and addressed in Arabic. Frequently the petitioner himself would await me. One evening on returning to Minia I saw a richly dressed Arab mounted on a finely caparisoned horse on the bank beside the *dehabieh*. I was just going to speak to him when my attention was diverted to a Cook's steamer moored near by. The Purser looked over the side and addressed me: 'Good evening, Sir. I see you are wearing a tarbush and I suppose you are a Government official. We have had a most unfortunate day coming from Assiut. We have been delayed in a sand storm and the tourists have been unable to visit the tombs of Beni Hassan. They have had a dull afternoon and some of them want to go back to Cairo by the next train. Do you know the times of the trains? Won't you come up Sir, for a few minutes?' I dismounted, handed my horse to the waiting groom and went on deck. The ship was filled with Americans who plied me with questions. Why did I wear that little red cap? How high did the Nile rise in the autumn? Were the peasants still heavily taxed? Were the women ill-treated by their husbands? One lady said: 'I just knew you were a Government Official from your beautiful complexion.' They had been thoroughly bored and my visit was an entertainment. As I went down the gangway the richly dressed Arab, a claimant for Government land, rode up on his horse, dismounted and presenting his petition with one hand with the other seized my fingers and kissed them. Nothing could have been more opportunely staged.

When staying at Assuan I got permission to use the old Coast Guard Rest House on the slope of the desert hills overlooking the Cataract Hotel. It was very seldom occupied and Ibrahim, the old Nubian caretaker, was delighted to see me and gave me a warm welcome. When once staying there in the month of February I was much annoyed by the constant cries of a cat belonging to the premises. I complained to Ibrahim who said 'By Allah! The cat is oppressed. It is now the month of *Imsheer* when all female cats want to marry. She can smell the male cats down in the town because the wind is blowing from the north and she is too weak to go to them and no one can hear her but Allah.' I gave orders that the oppression must cease and that a male cat must be procured before sunset. In the evening peace reigned and the next morning Ibrahim said: 'I sent my little son Bayumi down to the town with a basket and he brought back a beautiful male cat. I shut both cats in the back room and now the oppression is lifted.' The cat was quiet from that day onwards and showed me particular indications of affection and gratitude.

During my time in Upper Egypt I encountered several exceptionally violent dust storms. The first experience was when I was in a camp of tents pitched on a sandy shore projecting into the Nile. We had suffered for several days from the 'Khamsin'. In the afternoon the south wind had dropped. Not a breath stirred. I was taking a siesta in my sleeping tent though fortunately I was unable to sleep, for happening to look out of my tent I saw what appeared to be a dense black wall of dust moving at great speed up the Nile valley from the north. I ran out and gave the alarm to the servants. We were just in time. The storm burst upon us with such violence that we were forced to lie flat with our faces to the ground. I was nearly suffocated, but the storm only lasted for a few minutes. I could not have endured it for much longer. When I looked up all the tents of the camp were down. The dining tent was wrecked, crockery broken and a rush mat had been swept out of the office tent and disappeared for ever. But the storm had passed up the valley leaving the air clear. The *Khamsin* was ended.

While Young was recording his lands, there was a great change in the administration of Egypt. Sir Eldon Gorst, consul-general, mild mannered, accommodating and patient, brought in after Cromer in 1907 to introduce more liberal policies, had died disillusioned after an unsuccessful time in Egypt. The British government now backtracked and once again brought in a strong figure to keep the Egyptians in their place. In came Field Marshall Lord Kitchener of Khartoum, he of the large military moustache and pointing finger. He took over in 1911 more as colonial governor than consul and according to Young:

He came with a great reputation and it was the opinion in the Turf Club that 'K' would succeed where Gorst had failed. If Gorst's endeavours ended in failure it was not through lack of capability but because he had chosen to follow the more difficult path. Kitchener's line of action was of a simpler nature. Backed by his Government at home and with determination to treat

Egypt more like a province of India than a Suzerain state of Turkey under a British military occupation, he settled down to the position of a Colonial Governor and commenced to issue orders on his own responsibility with very little consideration for the feelings of the Khedive or the Egyptian government. He toured the country almost like a Viceroy.

He was, however, quite popular amongst the peasants, proclaiming himself their friend and taking their interests to heart. He tried to rid them of their chronic indebtedness and opened for them a special kind of village savings bank:

A Cairo schoolboy in composing an essay on Economy wrote: 'First came Joseph who said, "I think there is going to be a famine so store your grain!" Then came our Lord Jesus who said: "Take on thought about tomorrow", and at last came Lord Kitchener who said: "Put all your money into village savings banks."'

Meanwhile, Young continued his surveying and registering:

Once when staying at a Rest House in the Delta my visit coincided with the annual recruiting for the Egyptian Army. Every male Egyptian was eligible for conscription unless he paid a fee of £10 or was exempted by cause of physical defect or through holding a certain religious position. Considering that the recruiting was by lottery, that the population of Egypt was over 14,000,000 and that the size of the Egyptian Army was limited to 15,000 there was a good chance that a man might never be conscripted at all. But such was the terror in which the army was held, undoubtedly a survival of the horrors of the Sudan campaigns under the Khedive Ismail, that many paid the fee, maimed the trigger finger or injured an eye rather than run the risk of being parted from their homes for three years service.

Recruits on whom the lot had fallen underwent a medical examination in the Police Station and owing to the wide field of choice the examination was of the strictest nature, only those of the most perfect physique finding themselves in the army. From the upper windows of the Rest House I watched the proceedings. The recruits awaiting examination were marshalled in the inner yard hidden from our view. Each one in turn was called in before the Medical Officer. If accepted he was retained and if rejected he was free to pass out by the front door under our eyes. In the open space outside surged a vast crowd of relatives and friends, men, women and children, all pressing to the door, feebly restrained by the police. Behind the crowd two groups of women circulated in orderly movement, the one performing the dance of joy in honour of the rejected, the other the dance of death for the accepted recruit.

Every few minutes a dull scuffling noise was heard from within, something like that of a rabbit bolting from its hole. Then a rejected candidate shot out through the door, naked to the skin, his clothes in his arms but free. Immediately there commenced the dance of joy. Then would follow a sickening pause. The news spread that the next recruit had been accepted. He had not come out and the dance of death took up its mournful refrain.

At the conclusion of the examination the new soldiers, some of them miserably clad, many of them badly nurtured and all of them dejected, were marched under escort to the railway station accompanied by their wailing relatives who behaved as though they were attending a funeral. Very different was the appearance of these men when after a few months they returned to their villages on leave, smart, well fed, clean and happy. I have been told by the Senior British Medical Recruiting Officer of the Egyptian Army that the annual recruiting medical examination was looked upon as a great event and that the villagers would not miss it for anything in the world.

During the First World War Young was asked to leave his department to take on the less enviable task of tax-collecting. The peasants were suffering from a fall in the price of cotton and as a result were more reluctant to pay their taxes. Young was called in to help. The response was not very spontaneous. In each village he gathered the defaulters together, addressed them and warned them of the consequences of not paying up. He adopted quite unorthodox methods of tax gathering:

I put the village *ghaffirs* to keep the entrance and exit of the *omdeh's* courtyard where the people were gathered and making a personal collection myself, I often raised a sum of £50 or £100 in one day, handing it over to the *Sarraf* (Tax Collector) in the presence of the *omdeh*.

He summarized all his experiences in an imaginary scene depicting one day's work:

The courtyard of the house of the village *omdeh*. There is a narrow entrance to this yard on one side and an exit on the other so that the yard is used as a high road connecting two quarters of the village. A crowd of 40 or 50 *fellahin* wrapped up in coarse black or brown garments, squats on the ground in front of the veranda of the *omdeh's* house. On the veranda the Inspector, the *omdeh* and *Sarraf* are seated, the Inspector and the *omdeh* on chairs, the *Sarraf* on the floor with his books in front of him. Immediately below the veranda stands the Sheikh of *Ghaffirs* (head village guard) full of importance. *Ghaffirs* are scattered throughout the village mustering debtors for the Agricultural Bank. The inspector has just finished making his address and everyone high and low is drinking coffee.

Omdeh (to *Sarraf*): How much have you collected to-day?

Sarraf: By Allah only 540 piastres.

Omdeh (turning to the crowd and speaking in tones of dismay): 540 piastres! The inspector says that is not nearly enough. He says he is going to stay here until more money is paid. Remember that while you are asleep the Bank is awake.

Crowd (murmer): Tomorrow if Allah wills.

Omdeh: The Inspector wants money now and he will stay here till he gets it. Have you no religion? (In a voice of despair) Who can pay? The inspector wishes the instalment today from someone who is rich and who has sold cotton.

Voice from crowd: Abd al Hadi Muhammad the Judge in the Religious Court! He can pay.

Omdeh: Of course! Bring him here. He will pay at once.

Judge: I ask leave to go to my house and I promise that in a few minutes I will bring my full instalment of £50.

Omdeh: The Inspector says a *ghaffir* must go with you.

Judge: By my honour! That would be a shame. Have I not given my word? (Turns his eyes up to heaven).

Omdeh: My brother be not afraid. You must listen to the words of the Inspector. Go with the *ghaffir*.

(Exit Judge protesting accompanied by *ghaffir*. The latter reappears).

Ghaffir: I went with the Judge to his house and he said to me at the door: One minute while I find the money. And then he entered his door and by Allah I waited outside and then I went round to the back where I found a little girl who said that the Judge had fled from the house. The Judge has fled from us!

Omdeh: The Bank is awake my brethren! Its eye is large!

Sheikh of ghaffirs: Yusef Said can pay.

Yusef Said: I am very poor. I swear by Allah the exalted I have no money neither in my pocket nor in my house nor with my friends. I have no one to help me but Allah.

His clothes are then examined. His purse is opened but nothing is found. More exhortation follows and the *Sheikh of ghaffirs* gives him a resounding thump on his back. Yusef Said now sees that the game is up. He takes off his turban and produces from it the full instalment in silver. He counts the money and murmuring: In the name of Allah the Merciful, the Compassionate, he hands it over to the *Omdeh* and sits down to see the rest of the fun.

Enter young woman in tears.

Young Woman: By Allah! I was carrying a Bank note from my house when suddenly *Sheitan* (Satan) took it from me and threw it into the village pond. It has gone from me and my house is destroyed. Allah! Allah! (beats her cheeks).

Husband of Young Woman: Silence woman! Here is the note.
(Raises stick to beat her).
Omdeh (seizing the note and puffing out his cheeks): But this is only for £5. Your instalment is £10. Where is the remainder?
Young Woman: What do you mean, *Omdeh*? When you have not paid a single piastre of your own instalment. Shame upon you *Omdeh*!
Husband of young woman: Silence woman!
Omdeh (turning pale): Silence woman!
Sheikh of ghaffirs (horrified): Silence woman! Silence!
Young woman: I will not be silent. It is shameful!
Omdeh: I take refuge in Allah.
Inspector (to *Sarraf*): Is this the case?
Sarraf: By Allah it is indeed the case.
The Omdeh looks as if he is going to faint. Then he loudly demands a glass of water which he drinks with great gulps, after which he rushes out of the veranda and returns with his instalment of £25, hands it to the *Sarraf* and makes off without bidding farewell to the Inspector.
Voices from the crowd: All is from Allah.

Sir Thomas Rapp, consul

As a consul Thomas Rapp, already quoted on several occasions, saw life from a different angle from those in the Egyptian administration. His employers were in London and remote from the problems he had to deal with and the, sometimes appalling, conditions he had to live in. There was a legendary security of tenure in the job though, however inefficient you might be. It was firmly believed 'that you only got turned out of the service for rape, arson or murder, and you must commit at least two of them.' Rapp began his service in the Middle East in 1920, after his two terms of training in Cambridge:

My own destination was to be Port Said and my position that of acting Vice Consul. Early in February 1920 I took passage in the troopship *Oratava* to Alexandria. My first impression of Egypt was the characteristic acrid smell which greets the traveller well before his ship reaches port. The second was the entire inadequacy of the Arabic with which I had been wrestling for coping with porters, cab drivers or for obtaining one's simplest wants. Alexandria did not delay me long and the following day I took the train to Port Said.

Whatever reforms were contemplated for the Consular Service, Port Said was as yet unaffected and my introduction to official life was strange and puzzling. The Consulate had never been properly manned for its heavy wartime task with consequences that were still apparent. My chief was a kindly but obviously very sick man, who had developed some amiable eccentricities. I found him without clerical assistance of any kind, so that he had himself to register the correspondence, keep the accounts and reply to all letters. As a result all was confusion and the office was bogged down with arrears of work. One of my first tasks was to take over the registration of correspondence. My chief, who suffered among other things from insomnia, was wont to prowl round the office at midnight, particularly interested in seeing whether I had registered the letters as he desired. But what he wanted above all else was that the registration number in the top right hand corner of each paper should be surrounded by a perfect circle. One morning I found the following note on my desk: 'Mr Rapp, I want you at the outset of your career to learn how to make a perfect circle. I regret to say that your predecessor, in spite of my many admonitions, never achieved this, but you will please make the necessary effort.'

The consulate had many duties in a busy port such as Port Said and consuls were often involved in court cases involving British subjects:

The Consulate at Port Said had its courtroom, where the Consul officiated as provincial judge with the Vice Consul as registrar. The judicial atmosphere gave encouragement to disputants in personal quarrels to consider the Consul as the proper repository of their confidences. It usually fell to the Vice Consul to deal with these tangled situations, which more often than not concerned the matrimonial and domestic disputes of British subjects of Mediterranean origin, or the quarrels between neighbours inhabiting houses, whose balconies lent themselves to an exchange of courtesies and dirty water. I was still too young not to feel some embarrassment when uninhibited young women began to strip to show me the bruises inflicted by their husbands (who often had corresponding teeth marks), nor could I properly appreciate the more intimate details of their marital relationships which they were sometimes anxious to expound. On the whole the justice meted out by British Consular Courts gave little cause for complaint, and the only case of actual abuse I heard of happened many years before. It concerned a consul in a remote post driven to distraction by a nagging wife. Eventually he caused her to appear before him in his official capacity and sentenced her to twenty-four hours detention in the lavatory.

One odd incident involving the Navy occurred in my early days when the Shah of Persia was passing through Port Said. My chief had instructions to go on board the P and O liner in which he was travelling to convey some friendly message from the British Government. The cruiser *Ceres* being then in port, it was arranged that the Captain should accompany him as well as myself. It was also agreed that the Captain would invite the Shah to visit the *Ceres* and preparations had consequently been made to pay him full honours. The Shah declined to budge, but the Captain then asked the

Consul and myself to accompany him back to the *Ceres* in his launch to have tea. As we approached the ship the officer of the watch mistook the Consul, who was in full dress uniform, for the Shah: and as we mounted the gangway the guard presented arms, whistles blew and the band struck up the Persian national anthem. The fury of the Captain knew no bounds and the honours came to an abrupt halt.

This must have been about the last official appearance of my first chief. Even in the unreformed service, noted as it was for its extreme tolerance, his disabilities had finally made his replacement necessary, so he retired to Eastbourne to spend his last days writing to the newspapers about the iniquities of income tax assessments.

By this time I was beginning to find my feet after my strange initiation. We were still being paid pre-war salaries in spite of the cost of living having risen threefold. My salary as a probationer was £300 per annum, whereas the far from luxurious Marina Palace Hotel, where I first stayed, was charging me exactly at that rate for simple board and lodging without any extras. Luckily, I was soon able to join the mess of the few British officers still remaining in Port Said. It was in an old, insanitary house and it was there that I had my first experience of bugs and learnt something of their habits. The first night I soon awoke to find myself covered and saw a further number in procession along the ceiling preparing to drop once they arrived immediately overhead. In time one managed to cope, though never quite successfully.

Later I was to live more comfortably with the manager of the National Bank, Sidney Bray, whose family was in England. He was an engaging character; and with two other guests we led a cheerful existence. His flat was ideal for easy living, situated as it was over the pleasant English Club and within a few hundred yards of the Consulate, Sporting Club, sea and Casino Palace Hotel. At the Sporting Club, now a dejected public garden, there was always tennis with football and hockey in winter. Cricket flourished in summer, our usual opponents being teams from the naval ships or army units. The Casino Palace Hotel was likewise a very different place from its forlorn and dilapidated present. The sea, where we bathed from April to December, still lapped the road outside its terrace, which was the chief centre of the social life of the foreign communities. Among other things I arranged a series of tea dances with a ladies' committee which carefully vetted the invitations. It was amusing to watch the French mothers, seated sedately round the room, exercise their duties as chaperons with eagle eye. The conductor of the orchestra was a rascally Englishman, whose wife trouble frequently caused to him to appear at the Consulate.

In 1922 Rapp was transferred as acting consul to Cairo which was still suffering from the post-war disturbances:

The Consul in Cairo at the time was a very able and likeable man, whose mother had endowed him with the names of Hyacinth Louis to add to that of Rabino. The combination was not ideal for the head of a British community and he never ceased to regret the handicap. His father had been governor of the Imperial Bank of Persia, and he himself had received a predominately French education, which on occasion could affect his English idiom. Rabino was beginning to put on weight, which had recently caused him some moments of extreme embarrassment, for on donning his uniform to attend a King's reception at Abdine Palace, he found that this was only possible by discarding his underclothes. To his consternation during the ceremony the seams began to split and he was forced to a hurried retreat.

The work of the consulate was generally hampered by the penny pinching of the Foreign Office in London which expected it to work on the thinnest of shoestrings:

The straits to which we were reduced can be judged from the fact that as acting Consul, I found myself obliged to receive all money and affix all stamps to documents, if irregularities were to be avoided. Later, after Rabino's return from leave, the Foreign Office agreed that the position was intolerable and authorised us to engage a British clerk locally to handle such matters. At Army headquarters we found a well-recommended Australian sergeant, who wished to be demobilised locally as he had married an Italian Cairene. He was obviously not particularly bright, but seemed honest and he was all that offered at the salary we would pay. Yet the atmosphere of Cairo had defeated us: he turned out to be the perfect example of a dual personality, at one moment a drug addict and at another a respectable family man. And to meet the expenses of his double life he robbed the till while I was on leave and ended his Egyptian career in gaol. It was hard on Rabino, who was called upon to refund the missing money at the behest of an unsympathetic inspector.

Rapp in Suez

Rapp, now married to Dorothy, continued his career at the other end of the Canal from Port Said, in Suez itself. Life did not much improve for him there:

In the summer of 1923, having served for thirty months abroad, I was entitled to four months leave in England. We took a comfortable one class Bibby boat, the *Warwickshire*, from Port Said, but my chief recollection of the voyage home is of the melancholy presence of a senior Consul-General's wife, who never ceased telling Dorothy how sorry she was not to have met her a year earlier, when she would have begged her never to contemplate marriage with a man in the Consular Service. A vice consul's wife was likely for some years to be condemned to a gipsy existence without a proper home of her own. It was rare for quarters to be provided: usually the best vice consuls could hope for was to take over their predecessor's accommodation together with his sticks of furniture at a valuation, prepared to abandon everything at short notice when after a year or so a telegram from the Foreign Office ordered a transfer to another post. The climate of many Levant posts was likewise unkind to women and children, and there were considerable health risks to be faced, typhoid and dysentery being very common. A wife had a persistent struggle to keep up appearances and to make both ends meet. One had to agree with the Consul-General's wife that life was unlikely to be a bed of roses, but for Dorothy the die had now been cast.

The change to Suez was in some ways a doubtful blessing. In Cairo we had managed to procure a small furnished flat on the edge of the desert at Heliopolis, whereas at Suez my predecessor had had to relinquish his accommodation and there was nothing else to be found. It seemed hard, when one saw the pleasant houses provided by the Canal Company and the various shipping companies for the staffs and agents, that the representative of the British Government, even if of junior rank, should not be provided with the basic necessity of living quarters. So there was nothing for it but to lodge at the Sinai Hotel at Port Tewfik, that part of Suez at the very entrance to the Canal. The hotel was a stark and comfortless place run by the French wife of a Suez Canal pilot called Carew, who had lost a leg through a Turkish bullet when piloting a ship through the Canal during the war. There Dorothy quickly fell victim to a severe attack of influenza.

The only result of an intensive search for something more permanent was the possible lease of a three-roomed wooden bungalow on the Canal front belonging to the Peninsula and Oriental Shipping Company. The bungalow, abandoned some time before by the company's agent for a comfortable flat, was in a state of considerable dilapidation; rats chased each other at night between the piles on which it was built and cockroaches, mosquitoes and flies flew in through its unscreened windows. It was a poor refuge from the heat and cold; likewise the kitchen and sanitary arrangements were primitive in the extreme. It certainly took a considerable toll of Dorothy's health, but there was no alternative as a rather shocked inspector, who later visited Suez, had reluctantly to admit.

With the office I had taken over a Cypriot clerk who for many years had attended to shipping matters and kept the accounts. There was soon to be a visit from the inspector, in anticipation of whose arrival I had received instructions to examine and report on the old accounts and shipping documents, searching for any irregularities. It was an insidious task, the more so as there seemed much requiring explanations that were not forthcoming. Obviously the clerk's conscience was troubling him and, after showing increasing signs of depression, he finally absented himself from the office on the plea of sickness. Then one morning he appeared to say that he had been offered a job at Port Sudan and wished to be released immediately. I had to reply that this was only possible after proper notice and the inspector's visit. The same evening I was sitting on the balcony of our bungalow when an unknown young man hurried up the path to say that my clerk had blown his brains out, in the same breath offering his own services as a replacement. I quickly went round to his flat to find out what had happened. It proved to be only too true. The pity of it was that although he was certainly not guiltless of malpractices, there was probably nothing that could have been brought home to him in a court of law.

Rapp's time in Suez ended on another depressingly low note, misfortunes borne with a fortitude which an uncaring Foreign Office did not deserve. In the summer of 1925 he was ordered to cross the Red Sea to Jidda, at that time a notoriously unhealthy and unkempt town, and no place for a family. He immediately sent them (now wife and daughter) home to England. He was about to leave himself when fate intervened. At an official lunch for the Japanese Emperor's son, he ate tainted crayfish – usually a delicacy from Suez Bay – which caused severe food poisoning. He was rushed to the French hospital:

I was cared for by kindly nuns but it was hardly a cheerful place. It was in the heart of Suez, shut in on all sides; and airlessness plus a shade temperature of over 100F added further discomfort to fever. The wing where I was abutted on the mortuary, whose door, clearly visible, was some twenty yards away. There had been a spate of deaths, and the ceaseless activity around it and the sound of coffins being nailed down intensified the depression of illness. My recovery being somewhat slow, the doctor decided that I would require a change to a cooler climate to throw off the effects of the poisoning. The Foreign Office agreed to my taking some sick leave at home – and I remember how good it was to feel one's strength gradually returning with the cool sea breezes as I travelled home from Port Said in the old *Malaya*. Crayfish had very definitely changed the course of my career.

Rapp later served in Morocco, Bulgaria, Moscow, and Yugoslavia where he was captured by the Gestapo. He returned to the Middle East after the Second World War.

John de Vere Loder, intelligence officer

We have already met Loder trying to fathom the mysteries of an Egyptian family. He was not in Egypt by choice. He was a serving soldier during the Great War, yet a soldier with a job which brought him into direct contact with Egyptian life. He served in military intelligence:

Cercle Mohammed Aly, Alexandria
17 November 1916

Dear Father

The Intelligence have applied for me and the Colonel has allowed me to accept. I am expecting orders at any moment, probably to join H.Q. Eastern Force which deals with the canal and operations East of it.

I am not quite sure what my duties will be. There are several branches of the Intelligence. I(A) is general Intelligence, dealing with agents, collecting and summarising reports, etc., I(B) is suspects and contre-espionage, I(C) maps and topography, I(D) wireless and ciphers, I(E) censoring and press bureau work. I am practically certain to go to either I(A) or I(B).

He wrote home again with a quite cavalier disregard for the official secrecy of the day. Did the authorities know of the proposed leaks?

Headquarters, Eastern Force, Ismailia
21 November 1916

Dear Mother,

I reported here on Saturday and find myself with the I(B) branch. It deals chiefly with contre-espionage and suspects, i.e. measures to prevent the leakage of military information, the control of all movements of civilians in the Canal Zone, the strict supervision of neutrals, enemy subjects and natives, particularly those working for Government, and the state of local feeling in various districts. Practically it is the connecting link between the Ministry of the Interior and the Military Authorities.

I shall only be here till the end of the week to learn the ropes and pick up as much information as I can from back files of the questions under discussion and the sort of cases which arise. I shall then be sent as Intelligence Officer to Port Said where of course one is more directly in touch with agents themselves. I will write and tell you more about it when I get there.

25 November 1916

By the time you get this you will have learnt that I have turned detective! I am going to Port Said (well-known as the wickedest town in the world!) tomorrow to be Intelligence Officer there. I hope I shall catch some spies. Of course you understand I don't creep round in disguise much myself but sit in an office and take reports from the people who do. There are a thousand and one different things to see to, from tracking Turks and

Germans to identifying native bargees and of course for one really interesting case there are a thousand comparatively dull ones.

Casino Palace Hotel, Port Said
3 December 1916

Dear Mother,

Life is really quite like a page out of a novel if one chooses to dress it up that way. The air vibrates with hushed whispers, the stairs leading to the office resound with the stealthy tread of stage villains, corpulent Egyptians with tarbooshes, down-at-heel Greeks, Syrian refugees, and terrified enemy aliens. Rifles, revolvers and ammunition pass in and out disguised as rations, in the office we keep invisible ink, secret drawers and insoluble ciphers. Letters arrive by special messengers enclosed in two or three envelopes covered with mystical seals, while the least member of the organisation is known by a number, and the greatest by a single letter. Meanwhile we pass to outsiders as ordinary staff officers about whose occupation the civilian may speculate, but only superficially fathom. Little do they realise that their every movement is watched, and that, as we sit in the hotel bars of an evening, we are gathering the threads of a case into our hands, which will convict the wealthy Greek contractor of undermining the integrity of the British merchant service, the erstwhile Austrian (now a Russian protected subject) of disseminating propaganda inimical to our interests, and the humble fisherman of passing information to submarines. Woe to such persons if they should fall under suspicion! Expulsion is the least of the troubles which can befall them, internment an eventuality at which they may well breathe a sigh of relief, for death is the penalty reserved for him whom our clutches grasp sufficiently firmly to allow no loophole of escape.

7 December 1916

Dear Father,

My education is progressing. I am worming my way into the confidence of the elite of the town. It is our business to know everybody and make them tell us what they think of everybody else. A drink to the manager of the Bank elucidates the fact that a man with authority to do so drew money yesterday deposited at the outbreak of war by a well-known Turkish merchant when he had occasion to fly the country. A few paltry compliments to Molle – daughter of the local dry goods king – bring to light the interesting fact that there is an unregistered Bulgarian clerk in the office whose special hobby is to keep a list of transports by which goods are shipped. During a friendly chat with the director of the Eastern Telegraph Co. one is surprised to learn that inquiries as to the state of tomato and lentil crops in Cyprus have increased 200% in the past fortnight. Thus wheels

within wheels are set going, for a space Nos. 29, 84, and 52 sleuth
noiselessly round. A series of communications, the more important
disguised as a string of figures, pass between ourselves and higher
authorities. Then suddenly the fell blow falls. Certain shining lights in the
brilliant society of the city are quietly snuffed out and the military area
knows them no more.

The intelligence officers had to work against great odds in Port Said –
vested interests, and sheer incompetence:

5 January 1917
Up till now we have been unable to obtain co-operation with anybody. The
police, upon whose organization we ought to rely, do everything in their
power to hinder. The Commandant, an Englishman, is too lazy to move a
finger except to object to any proposal we make. The sub-commandant, a
Maltese foundling, who before the war commanded the fire brigade, is a
capable and energetic man, but as he is never controlled by his chief is
constantly influenced by personal considerations. I have never met a man
quite like him. While you are with him he is perfectly charming with a
wonderfully polished manner. Yet there is scarcely a more universally
disliked man in Port Said. He exercises a sort of fascination over you in
spite of any momentary antagonism.
    Below these two there are a number of officers, English, Irish, Maltese,
Italian, Syrian and Egyptian. They are all typical Levantines, all of them
lazy, most of them venal, and a few downright blackguards. From this
priceless collection the rank and file take their cue. In one thing they are all
agreed, that nothing shall be allowed to emerge to the discredit of the force.
One and all stand by each other, and to this end any means are good. The
lower grades, besides being corrupt, are perfectly useless for European
police work. They are all illiterate. They cannot recognise a person from a
photograph. They cannot use any discrimination and cannot be allowed any
responsibility. So long as their duties are confined to controlling street traffic
or dealing with native quarrels they are all right, but as guards for a gate on
the gangway of a ship they are hopeless.

The Fred Kano-like atmosphere of intelligence work was increased
by the kind of reports Egyptian policemen were wont to send in. For
example:

Re the English speaking German Officer of your B/1/5805. of May 11th, I
have made enquiries with no further result than the following similar but
improbable stories:-
1) The coastguard watchman Assad Karim Tash (who has I regret to say
since been admitted to the asylum) relates that during the night an

extremely stout gentleman with heavy black moustaches landed on the bathing beach here from an aeroplane and placing a revolver to the *Ghaffir's* ear demanded to be shown the Commandant's house, but startled by a slight noise withdrew in his aeroplane. The *Ghaffir* instantly discharged two shots but missed both man and machine.

2) Another coastguard perceived a gentleman arrive on the beach with a little boat; this man (who was not necessarily corpulent) pulled down a basket chair out of the sky and rested in it while questioning the *Ghaffir*. He subsequently ascended with the chair into the sky. During the interval certain smugglers ran their cargo.

The movement of persons and animals in Port Said was strictly controlled during the war, in case enemy aliens or spies moved about fomenting unrest. This control badly inconvenienced ordinary Egyptians. The following petitions to be allowed to travel were received in Loder's office:

Reasons for travelling

To buy bullox for the purpose of producing milk – Approved.
To visit the sister of my mother's husband who is beaten by her husband – Refused.
To buy cans and tins and other Jewelry (from Damietta) – Approved.
To live no more dishonest (Application by a prostitute to go to Tanta) – Approved.
To look out for a wife to marry – Refused.
To accompany muttons – Approved.
Health reasons, suffering from evil souls – Approved.
To investigate the corpse of his father – Approved.
To shave the Army (at Kantara) – Refused.

Petition by Abdel Hak Rashid
asking for the release of some cattle which had
strayed and been seized

As I am a blind and have nothing to support me except what I get from the milk and butter out of these bulls, I beg that my bulls be released and be handed back to me.

Despite all the intrigues of the spy's life Loder soon began to get bored and lethargic in Port Said:

1 July 1917

It is beginning to get unpleasantly warm for work in the middle of the day now and one doesn't feel very energetic. My only amusement is to know all sorts and kinds of people and to go out to tea and have drinks with them. It doesn't sound a very high ideal but then I am getting to be quite a passable Levantine now. It is odd how the climate gradually gets hold of one. From the health point of view I have never felt better in my life, but little by little one gets slack, my memory isn't nearly as good as it used to be. Efforts become more and more difficult to make and one loses all curiosity. I can quite understand how people who live long out here get apathetic and I have quite lost all wish to stay here.

Eventually Loder was transferred to further intelligence work at Cairo GHQ:

> GHQ Savoy Hotel
> 28 November 1917

The work up here is much more interesting than at Port Said as one has a much wider out-look. The pressure however is much greater. Everybody who has a question to ask seems to send it to Intelligence: Daylight saving in Egypt, how to feed Chinese coolies, knotty points of international law besides political and espionage matters, keep pouring in. The hours are long; 8.30 to 1 in the morning. 2.30 – 4.30 and 7.00 – 8.00 in the afternoon with an occasional afternoon off. Almost the only time one has for recreation is after dinner. I shall stick to the hotel as one can get light conversation, cinema parties etc. without having to search round for company.

Despite these innocuous pursuits there was some worry amongst the high-ups that young officers of good breeding might get into trouble. Loder noted:

The last scheme for keeping young officers out of mischief has been devised by Lady Allenby. There is to be a weekly 'thé dansant' at the Continental at which prominent officer's wives, e.g. Elizabeth Dawnay, will act as hostesses. Officers get tickets for P.T.10 from the hall porter, but ladies can only get them through members of the Committee. Gallant attempt of limited and unattractive English womanhood to pulvarise the influence of the fascinating dago girl.

Loder ended the war in Cairo, working temporarily in the British agency. Although he did not stay in the Middle East, he remained in public service, was elected to Parliament and finally rose to be Governor of New South Wales and of Northern Ireland. He was later created Baron Wakehurst and died in 1970. He was thus spared the frustrations of the Arab world yet it is hard to believe that he was not permanently marked by his early experiences there.

Francis Edwards, taxman

Francis Edwards spent sixteen years in the Egyptian Civil Service, following a career quite similar to that of Young. His memoir of work as a land tax inspector, although a shade more waspish than Young's, is still full of humour and pleasant memories. He offers an engaging account of a hard day's work, when he set off by train for Kafr-el-Dib:

. . . to investigate the arrears of taxation in that village and then on to Bartila on my horse to examine the complaint of a landowner there. I collected my maps and papers, made out railway warrants for myself, horse and groom and walked down a short hill – one of the few in the whole delta – to the Light Railway Station.

The Light Railway serves the country districts lying away from the main Cairo–Alexandria line and is an enormous boon to the country folk but the trains are not remarkable for speed or conformity to a timetable. I have – I confess with shame – improved the speed of some three or four kilometres an hour over a short journey by a small donation – five piastres say, to the driver. A larger sum would be tempting Providence.

The road to the Station was crowded as it was market day. The Kafr-el-Dib train was waiting. My horse was coaxed into a truck, my syce got in with him and I climbed into my carriage. As soon as I had settled down beggars, vendors of bread, melon seeds, monkey nuts and Arabic newspapers appeared in turn at the window. Cries of 'yallah' (go on) and the blowing of a little horn announced our departure. As we rattled along a figure from time to time passed by the window followed shortly by another wearing a khaki overcoat. It was merely a ticket-less passenger who was being pursued by the ticket collector along the footboards round the train.

In those days (1921) political agitation was at its height and the sides of the 1st class carriages were usually inscribed with patriotic phrases such as 'Long live complete Independence', 'Long live the beloved leader (Zaghlul), long die Milner', 'Independence or shameful death'.

The unity of Copt and Muslim in the struggle against the 'hater usurpers' was also emphasised. I saw once a pencilled cross under which was written 'God bless the Copts'; beside it was a crescent with the words 'God bless the Muslims'. The effect was rather spoilt by the interpolation of a later hand, 'Blast both of you' signed Pte. A Crowdy 1/11th Middlesex Regt.

About noon we reached Kafr-el-Dib. The 'omdeh' was there to meet me. We walked through the village to his house, the only one built of stone and having windows and a garden. We entered the 'selamlik' – the room for male guests. The furniture consisted of heavy dust-laden plush curtains, a thread-bare Smyrna carpet strewn with cigarette ends, a table with bamboo legs, a divan, some paper flowers in a vase and a suite of deal chairs painted

white and gold. The walls were bare except for two photographs –
identically the same – of the 'omdeh', both in one frame and an inscription
hanging text-like by a ribbon and bearing in English the words 'Please do
not spit', an injunction that is apt to be disregarded.

I told the 'omdeh' that I had come to find out why there were so many
arrears of taxation in his village. I suggested that he should collect a number
of the tax-payers and allow me to question them individually. The 'omdeh'
sent out his henchmen to gather in some of the defaulters. Thirty or forty
small land-owners were marshalled in the open space before the 'omdeh's'
house. As I approached, he was delivering an impassioned speech to them –
for my benefit, no doubt. I caught the words, 'Is not the Government your
father and your mother? Is the Inspector to be worried by worthless people
such as you? If you do not pay your just taxes I shall visit you with the
greatest severity.'

I pulled out from my pocket a list of the worst offenders and the amounts
due from them. I read out the first name 'Ahmad Gharabli. Who is that?'
'It's me' said the crestfallen 'omdeh'. I had forgotten his name and anyway
he had counted on a general rather than a particular visitation. The fellah
loves a joke and the crowd grinned delightedly at his discomfiture.

Edwards then left to examine a complaint of excess taxation by a
local landowner, Ahmad bey el Fuli. He had first to find his farm:

The 'omdeh' gave me confusing directions dragging in all the points of the
compass. I thanked him and rode off trusting to find some other informant
when I was nearer the farm in question. After following a canal for some
miles I came to a fellah in charge of a camel that was turning a water wheel.
I asked him the way to the farm of Ahmad bey el Fuli. It is no easier in
Egypt than in any other country to get an answer to such a question. He
said at first that there was no such farm in the neighbourhood and with an
Irish like anxiety to please offered me the choice of some others. I pointed
out to him in the distance some buildings whose position corresponded to
that of the farm I was seeking as shown by the map. 'What is that?' I asked.
'The farm of el Cumbania,' he answered. I had to look at my papers and
found that some thirty years ago the land in question had belonged to an
Agricultural Company (el Cumbania) who, no doubt, had sold it to Ahmed
bey. I told him this and he said brightly, 'True, O Excellency the Inspector,
Ahmad bey bought it from the Company long ago and very poor land it is
too.' I knew that it would be useless to ask him why on earth he had not
told me this at first.

In a short time I reached the outskirts of the farm. Seated on a kitchen
chair in the shade of a sycamore tree was the bey, an extremely stout old
gentleman, wearing, in spite of the heat a frock-coat, yellow boots, and a
rather battered tarbush. He rose, put up a large grey parasol and came to

meet me. We walked to the land, some 200 acres, that I had to examine before his appeal for reduced taxation could be considered. It was easy to see that the land was in poor heart; snow-like patches showed that the drainage was insufficient. He had tried to reclaim it but the main drain was too far away to be of use. He was taxed at the rate of fourteen shillings an acre. 'I was taxed £200 last year, mon cher Monsieur.'

I asked him if he could show me any accounts, details of his expenditure, sales of crops. He called out to Girgis, his Coptic Secretary, who had been following us respectfully some twenty yards behind. 'Yes, Excellency' said Girgis running up. 'What was the result of the farming here last year, roughly?' the bey asked him. Girgis looked at me, then at the bey, seeking some clue. After a little thought he answered 'There was a clear profit of £300.' The bey did not turn a hair. 'No, he's not a purchaser!' Girgis appeared slightly crest-fallen at his too ready assumption that I wished to buy the estate. He brought papers and accounts and we spent the afternoon going through them and then, having obtained the necessary information, I took farewell of the bey and started for home

When I reached Kafr-el-Dib again the train was already in the station. I jumped in as the train was leaving. I had not time to make out a warrant and as I was trying to write one the ticket collector appeared at the window. I knew him well. I said to him: 'I am sorry, there was no time to write a warrant.' After a pause he said: 'There is a very strong rule in the Company that no warrants can be written while the train is in motion.' As we jolted and jerked along it seemed hardly necessary to make such a rule. 'Well, what's to be done?' I said. 'I must consider' he replied and entered the carriage and sat down to grapple with the problem. I solved it for him by paying my fare to the next station and getting out there and writing a warrant for the remainder of the journey.

The next incident is incredible but true. After going a few miles on a more or less even keel the train stopped with a jolt. I looked out of the window and saw the engine driver and the ticket collector talking angrily to a peasant. After a few minutes they all climbed into the engine and we continued on our way. I had dismissed the incident from my mind but at the next station after a halt of some ten minutes I became impatient and went along to the station master's office.

A small crowd was pressing round the doorway. The stationmaster was questioning the peasant whom I had seen earlier. Attempted train-wrecking, I thought, but I was soon enlightened. 'This man', said the stationmaster, pointing to the peasant held between the driver and the ticket collector, 'This man was walking between the rails, waving his arms wildly. The driver stopped the train quickly and then this son of a dog asked him for a match! I am now drawing up the statement.'

We then reached our destination without further mishap and I dined at the Irrigation Rest House with an irrigation officer and the Inspector of the

Interior. After dinner we sat in deckchairs on the verandah enjoying the 'heaven under heaven' of an Egyptian night. The moon's reflection shimmered in the creamy silk waters of the canal that flowed past one side of the house. Not a sound was heard except the occasional barking of pi-dogs and the rustle of the wind in the casuarina trees. From time to time a felucca with a vast lateen sail and creaking rudder slipped by. There was a scent of mimosa mingling with the smell of rich earth and – more faintly – of native cooking on the further bank.

We fell to talking of our day's experiences and discussed the Egyptian fellah – to whose advantage each one of us really worked – and we knew in our hearts that the Englishman's day of usefulness in the villages was nearly over. In such a frame of mind we knocked out our pipes and, leaving the Egyptian question still unsolved, made for bed.

FIVE

A LACK OF GRATITUDE

In the year 1919 revolt was stirring in Egypt. The British were about to face their greatest trial since they first set foot on Egyptian soil in 1882. The war was just over, a war fought for freedom and President Wilson's principles of self determination. Why, thought the Egyptians who had suffered in someone else's war, should we not now have our freedom from British occupation? Thousands of them had been conscripted into the labour corps, prices had risen, hordes of troops had descended on Cairo. The foreigner was everywhere. Resentment was simmering, ready to boil over under a popular and dynamic leader. Saad Zaghlul arose as that leader and anti-British resentment boiled over. Britons and British interests were attacked throughout the country. The army tried to offer protection but in many cases was outnumbered or not in the right place at the right time.

The great train massacre 1919

A particularly brutal attack took place near Assiut in upper Egypt. A gruelling report was compiled by the British judge, McBarrett, who had also written about Hanem Aaref:

Train No. 77 left Assiut Station at 6.50 on the morning of the 18th of March. Two British officers, Major Jarvis M.C. and another, and five British other ranks, travelled on the train from Luxor. They had had unpleasant experiences at some of the stations on the way up but nothing sufficient apparently to make them discontinue their journey. At Assiut they were joined by Alexander Pope Bey of the Prisons Service and his native Mamour who had been on inspection duty in Upper Egypt.

The first stoppage of the train was at Mungabad but nothing alarming happened until the train drew in to Beni Korra. At that Station they were

99

joined almost immediately by Train No. 74 from the north. It was crowded with roughs swarming all over the roofs and sides of the carriages and armed with naboots, pikes, knives and other weapons. They were waving flags and shouting and evidently out for mischief, crying 'Down with the English'.

As soon as the train entered the station these people swarmed all over the train from Assiut and rushed along from the third to the second class shouting, 'Where are the English?' The Mamour of Prisons Rifaat Hafiz and a train official managed to hold them in parley, and got the shutters and doors of the first class compartment closed and apparently between this station and Nazali Ganoub (the next) these officials got all the English into the first class compartment. The train started from Beni Korra but the mob went with it, hanging on all over it and crowding the corridors. Hafiz Effendi, thoroughly alarmed at the course events were taking, sent his fez to Pope Bey and asked him to wear it; he also suggested that he should wear a black cloak and pretend to be a woman, both of which offers Pope Bey declined. In the meanwhile the Mamour addressed the crowd and made efforts to persuade the mob that no English were on the train.

More roughs invaded the train at the next two stations Nazali Ganout and Sanabo, but though they made efforts the mob failed to enter the first class compartment. They seem to have attacked the windows with sticks and the Englishmen, who were wholly unarmed, defended themselves with soda water bottles and bits of luggage. Presently the train drew up at Deriout and what occurred here is best given in the words of Hafiz Effendi who was an eye-witness:

'A great crowd surrounded the train on every side. They were carrying banners and shouting just the same as the others. A party of men came to the door nearest Pope Bey's compartment. These were breaking the door with sticks; those on the platform were throwing stones on both sides and breaking the windows. I stood at the door where Pope was, I tried to convince them my wife was inside. They said "We will neither touch you nor your wife. We want the English who seized our grain and camels, our money, who orphaned our children, who killed the women and the babies in Cairo, who fired at El Azhar and the Mosque of Husein." They insisted on searching the compartment. I remonstrated. I was slapped heavily on the neck. Some wanted to beat me, dragging me by force from the door, breaking the windows and entering at last the compartment. I heard the beating of Pope Bey. I was shouting to them "This is not an Englishman, leave him, he is a Syrian who served with the Egyptian Government and who loves you". Another knock befell me and I was ordered to keep quiet. I saw them dragging Pope out of the compartment. He was saying "I have been with you thirty years." I saw him no more. Meanwhile stones were riddling the carriage and the beating still continued between the English and the mob.'

Another witness continues the story. He saw the mob enter the carriage with knives and other weapons:

'Shortly afterwards Pope Bey got out on to the platform. He cried out "I have served you thirty years. I am an Egyptian official," but he was sticked and stoned mercilessly; he therefore entered the carriage again but was thrown out on the opposite side and stoned again – he seemed very nearly dead. I picked him up and put him in the brake van. One other officer was killed outright in the first class; all the others were wounded. Another must have been killed between Deirout and Deir Moes by the seven or eight roughs who travelled in their carriage to Deir Moes.

The train was delayed over half an hour at Deirout while the tragedy was in progress. On arrival at Deir Moes at once three soldiers got down on the free line: they ran towards the engine followed by Sef Ahmed and his Deirout companions from the first class. One Englishman tripped over the line, fell, and was beaten to death there and then: another was overtaken and killed also on the free line by an Egyptian who fired two shots from a revolver. The people of Deir Moes thought this was the English shooting and they started running away down the platform. While all this was going on, the third Englishman had gained the engine and was hiding in the coal tender. There were still two others alive in the first class being continually attacked and wounded. These two now rushed out; one of them hit Ahmed Khalil, an ex-gaffir, between the eyes with a stone. They closed: Ahmed was caught by the collar of his caftan; he drew a knife from his belt and stabbed the officer in his stomach. The officer fell and was beaten to death there on the west platform. The second Englishman escaped and gained the engine: there he hid among the coals on top of the tender.

Some one cried "See, there is an Englishman on top of the coal." So the *omdeh* called out, "Bring him down", at which two men got up and struck him, the first with a fass, the second with a club and killed him on the spot. They then cried "See there is another Englishman down here." He was beaten to death on the engine. They pulled out his body, dragging it along the ground like a sack and stripped it. One man stuffed the Englishman's mouth with earth (because he was still just breathing). He was then thrown into the brake-van as were all the others, each one having been stripped and plundered.'

Another witness speaks to a hideous detail: 'One body however was kept back while a man cut off both legs at the knee and carried them away. I saw a man drinking blood from the breast of a man who had been wounded there – he was dead at the time.'

The next station of the line (Mellawi) was the scene of a peculiarly horrible orgy. On the arrival of the train, there was a huge crowd in the station carrying banners with the cross and crescent and accompanied by a brass band in uniform. The rioters on the train addressed the crowd: 'We have ended with them, you have nothing more to do.' The crowd then pressed round the van to look at the bodies – one body was dragged out of the van. The crowd proceeded to subject the naked corpse to abominable and unmentionable indignities and finally the body was carried up the platform by a howling mob yelling '1½ piastres for a pound of English meat!' while all the people laughed and cheered. The body was subsequently found buried in a local cemetery.

The train with its ghastly load eventually reached Minieh at 11.40 a.m. The crowd there though menacing was kept in check by the local authorities and after an enquiry the bodies were buried in the Greek Cemetery in that town.

John Young was in post during these riots. He was ordered to go to the small town of Wasta where more serious trouble was brewing:

At Wasta I was to get in touch with any Egyptian local authorities and report on the situation. My orders also were to wear the uniform of an Egyptian Army officer of the rank of *Bimbashi* with tarbush and badge of crown and star. It seemed a curious and somewhat unnecessary, as well as ineffective, disguise.

We left Cairo after lunch and we reached Wasta at two o'clock in the morning when I landed in complete darkness and walked in the direction of the *markaz* building. Some two hundred yards from the shore we reached the Agricultural Bank where we found Lieutenant Amor with a detachment of Punjabis. We were nearly too late. Bands of armed marauders, in the intervals of raiding shops, had from time to time charged the railings of the Bank enclosure where Amor had collected sixteen Europeans, mostly women and children. He had withstood their attacks for twenty-four hours with rifle fire, but as his ammunition was nearly expended he feared that the premises would be broken open and, all communication by rail, telegraph and telephone being cut, he was almost in despair. He had travelled from the Fayum with his men together with a Syrian Insurance Company agent and the wife of a C.M.S. doctor. On arriving at Wasta station they had been met by a wildly excited rabble armed with *naboots*, iron spikes, knives and guns, who threw open the door of their compartment. One of them entered, seized the wife of the doctor and tore off her jewellery, but managing to jump out of the opposite door she escaped with the others into an unattached guard's van, from which they made a second escape to one of the outlying offices of the station. There they were given shelter by a friendly clerk while the attention of the mob was diverted to the arrival of the slow train from Cairo, in which was travelling Mr Smith, Inspector of the local Locomotive Yard, with his wife and small son. Severe to his men and generally unpopular he had not a chance. Surging up to his service car the tumultuous crowd dragged him out brutally waylaying him with all kinds of lethal weapons, knife, pike and bludgeon. He fell under the weight of blows and still alive rolled down the railway bank into a ditch where he was at once followed by the crowd who were about to hit him again when the deed was done for them. An individual with dishevelled hair and bloodshot eyes pushed the others aside and killed him at a single stroke, cutting his head open with a *balta*. Witnesses testified to this man's remarkable costume – light vest and European underdrawers as universally worn by slaughtermen in the public abattoir. He was evidently out for active work and undoubtedly belonged to that sinister class of men, little known yet none the less extant in Egypt, who will take human life for a small fee as occasion offers. After accomplishing his task his appearance was reported once more. As Mrs Smith and her son were being escorted to safety through the threatening crowd he suddenly confronted them, his hands and scanty clothing now stained with blood, and brandishing a *singa* (long dagger) in front of Mrs Smith, he called out 'Where is the money?' He was not seen again till the next day of his arrest.

With his Indian troops Young managed to rescue those who had been trapped, send them to safety and eventually to disperse the hostile crowd:

As far as Wasta was concerned the fighting was over. We landed and on making a route march through the town found every street deserted. All was quiet. The rising had been quelled. Then, as we returned to the river, to our intense satisfaction we saw in the distance the smoke of two steamers coming from the direction of Cairo. The relief force was at hand and within an hour two hundred British and Indian troops, the forerunner of many more, had disembarked at Wasta.

On Tuesday, the 18th, the force was four thousand strong, and a few days later the numbers had reached seven thousand with their Headquarters in a large cotton ginning factory which was given the name of 'Wasta Fort'. We began a systematic search in the surrounding villages for arms and loot though with disappointing results. The villagers were too clever for us, and portions of railway carriage cushion leather and coils of telegraph wire were the principal products of long mornings' work. The arms had disappeared. From one village the *omdeh*, well known to be involved in the rising, had escaped to Cairo where he was subsequently caught. His empty house was in disorder, cupboards open, drawers pulled out and clothing lying about. All showed signs not so much of robbery as of a hurried departure.

In another village a British Officer was sitting drinking coffee with the *Omdeh* outside his house when a well dressed *effendi*, seemingly braver than others, came up to him and said: 'We demand complete independence for the whole nation. The last drop of my blood shall be spilt for the cause. I have no fear.' At that moment British troops appeared and the *effendi* collapsed on the ground screaming 'By Allah, the soldiers! The soldiers. Save me, save me!' – and the national hero remained prostrate until the troops had passed out of sight when he slipped silently away. 'He has become mad,' said the *Omdeh*, as he sipped his coffee.

Communication by rail had at length been opened to Cairo but it was not till March 27th that the first train ran to Medinet al Fayum in which I travelled, with the Colonel in Command and a small military escort, to evacuate the Europeans who had been under protection in that town. When returning with them we had difficulty at the last moment in persuading a number of the more timid to leave. One lady said she had changed her mind and considered it safer to remain where she was, and another refused to get into her compartment until she was assured that the train was provided with an efficient machine gun. Finally they were all packed safely in and sent off to Cairo. I made a second train journey to a village on the edge of the Western desert on which a bomb had been dropped as a reprisal for continuous cutting of the telegraph line. The Colonel had asked me to address the village in Arabic to warn them that they would be even more severely punished if there was a repetition of the offence. It seemed a simple plan. We were to box our horses in the train and to ride from the station accompanied by a few troops to the village about half a mile distant. But hardly had we mounted when I realised it would be a race against time. Already our movements had been perceived and from every mud hovel and narrow alley could be seen men, old and young women and children, all scuttling like rabbits. Into the standing crops they fled and when we arrived at an apparently deserted village it was only after putting a cordon round it and making a house to house search that I managed to muster a small and not very representative audience, mostly too infirm for flight, including the *Omdeh's* half-witted brother and the village barber. The sorry company gave all the attention they could in spite of interruptions caused by distracted hens and wandering goats. They expressed their opinion that the world was overturned and full of evil but that Allah was on the watch for the wicked and, as I was closing with what I thought were a few well chosen words, a youth in *tarbush* and *galabia*, taking courage in both hands, crept out of the crops and presented me with a petition for Government employment on the plea that he had obtained the Secondary School Certificate. The Colonel seemed to think the occasion inopportune for such an application, but if he had lived longer in Egypt he would not have seen in it anything unusual.

When order had largely been restored the British were bent on extracting their revenge and trials took place of those accused of fomenting the rising or committing atrocities:

The difficulty in unravelling the threads of the confused and often conflicting information obtained was very great and the preparation of the cases falling in major part to me resulted in extremely laborious work.

1. 'No more than a good walk spoiled' (Helouan spa desert golf course outside Cairo).

2. 'The multitude of treatments to which patients subjected themselves' (Helouan spa).

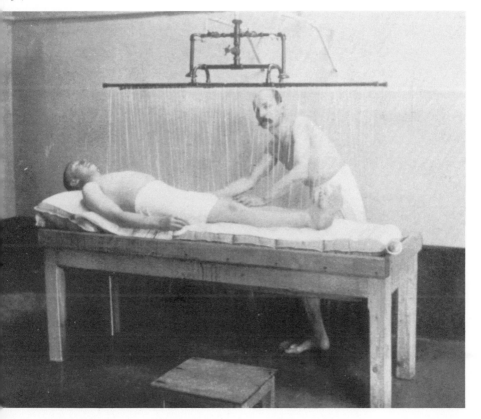

3. 'A large shaggy man with a long lugubrious face and a drooping moustache' (Harry Boyle in Cairo).

4. 'We old Cairenes cannot abide these floods of globetrotters' (picnic party at the pyramids 1903).

5. 'Lord Cromer of dominating personality' (out and about visiting Aswan). Cromer was British Agent in Cairo 1883–1907.

6. Sir Eldon and Lady Gorst in the khedive's six wheeler. Gorst was Cromer's successor in Cairo as British Agent 1907–11.

7. 'A scion of the upper class' (John de Vere Loder, captain in military intelligence who worked in Egypt during the First World War).

8. A British land inspector at work in rural Egypt 1937.

9. Thomas Russell, Commandant of Cairo Police 1918–46.

10. 'The town was burning, the sky ablaze, a pall of smoke blowing away south' (Black Saturday, Cairo January 1952).

11. General Allenby
(Commander of British forces
in the Middle East) enters
Jerusalem on foot, December
1917.

12. Allenby in Jerusalem
being shown the limits of his
new empire, December 1917

13. Pasha of Jerusalem and flock (Edward Keith-Roach, District Commissioner in Jerusalem 1937–43, with wife and various divines).

14. 'He looked a quiet grandfather; she a commanding general' (The arrival of Lord and Lady Plumer in Jerusalem, August 1925. Plumer was High Commissioner in Palestine 1925–8.)

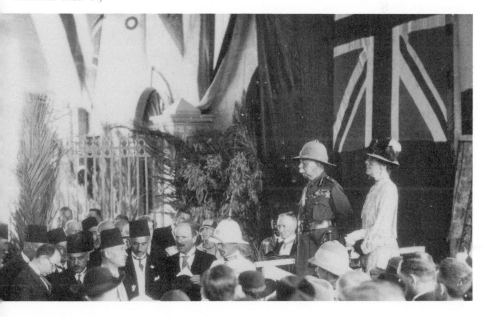

15. 'After death his Beatitude is dressed in his Easter vestments and placed in a chair' (a patriarch patiently awaiting burial in Jerusalem)

16. Sir John Chancellor 'an imposing man with greying hair' was High Commissioner in Palestine 1928–31.

17. 'The meeting of two worlds' (Sir Harold Macmichael talking to Arabs 1930s).

18. The girls of Bir Zeit school, untroubled for a while by the Arab revolt, 1938–9.

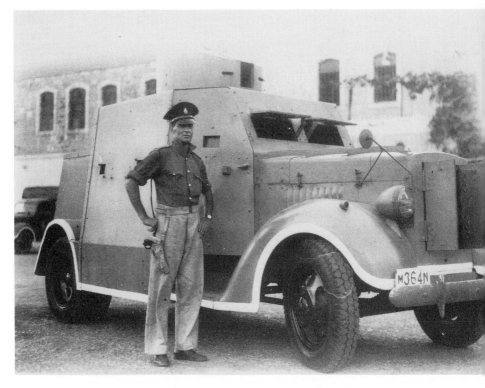

19. 'A queer sort of high-walled bullet-proof lorry' used by the British Army during the Palestinian revolt 1936–9.

20. St John Philby, 'Arabist' par excellence, who lived and worked in the Arab world 1917–55.

Witnesses had to be found and when found had to be induced to give evidence. Some gave themselves up to confinement under guards, so great was their fear and some could only be persuaded to make a statement on promise of a safe pass out of the district after the trial. The testimony of many was absolutely worthless: 'I swear by Allah that on the day of the rising, when I arose from my bed, I saw the world filled with men thick as sand; my blood changed, I fell on my back in a faint and I remembered nothing.' Others, confident at first, lost nerve on a second interrogation, hesitated and tried to recant. One witness, who had made a statement on oath that the leader of the riot was riding a white horse, when brought before the Court described the horse as 'whitish'.

Judge: What do you mean by a whitish horse?
Witness: A whitish grey horse.
Judge: What do you mean by a whitish grey horse?
Witness: A greyish black horse.
Judge: What do you mean by a greyish black horse?
Witness: A black horse.

Yet in spite of such contradictions, which had little effect on the general evidence, the trial continued on its even course. As the facts were disclosed, and all through this horrible drama, it was clear that the fellahin had been led by the principal *Omdeh* of the district, Amin al Ridi Bey, who seated upon his white horse on the railway line looked upon the scene encouraging the already excited mob to carry on their work. He it was who should most certainly have suffered the supreme penalty for it was through him that the passions of these ignorant people were aroused. But direct evidence against him was not sufficiently strong and while, of the six who were found guilty at the trial, three were condemned to death and two to long periods of hard labour, he was sentenced to imprisonment for life and was then released by the civil authorities after only serving one year.

The most astonishing part of the story is yet to come. Some eighteen months later, as I was sitting in my office in Cairo, a visitor was announced. He was Amin al Ridi Bey, the last person I should have expected to call on me. He showed neither shame nor contrition but, perfectly at ease, begged me when next at Wasta to drink coffee with him: and years later, when returning as I often did for a few months to Cairo as a winter visitor, an Egyptian fellah came up to me in the street and greeting me in the most friendly manner said: 'You don't remember me but I know you well. It was through you that I was given ten years imprisonment at Wasta. I was innocent, but thanks be to Allah I see you in good health,' and he offered me a cigarette.

The *mudir* of Minia, another acquaintance of Young's, had also participated in the riots, yet with a quite different intention. His deputy was not so loyal:

Minia was filled with British troops and the Military Court was still sitting. The town and province had had more than their share of disturbances, and it seemed that the *Mudir* had himself marched with some of the demonstrators his intention being, as was afterwards proved, not to excite but to curb them. The *Sub-Mudir* had, however, gone over to the rioters, and being thoroughly disloyal to his chief had tried to shield himself by throwing suspicion on the *Mudir*. I arrived a few days before the *Mudir* gave his evidence, and I saw him just before he entered the Court. He was very nervous but neither to me nor in the court did he say one word against his subordinate though he knew of his disloyalty and the danger which he incurred from the man. The *Mudir* left the Court thoroughly cleared. The *Sub-Mudir*, whose evidence was very contradictory, was detained and he remained a prisoner during the trial. Poor man! He came to a tragic end. He took his life by swallowing first a bottle of insect killer followed by a bottle of scent and suffered agonies attended by doctors until he died. I saw him in hospital, but no one could help. He died within a few hours of my visit. He evidently realized his guilt and probably would have been hanged.

Cairo riots 1919

In 1919 Cairo itself was also living on a knife edge. It was seething with rumours and massive trouble and violence were likely to break out at any moment. Mobs were roaming the streets, armed with any handy weapon, looking to attack and destroy foreign property and foreigners. Thomas Russell, as head of the Cairo police, had to face a number of very fraught situations which he handled with considerable skill and personal bravery. The position was worsened by the mood of the British and Australian troops. They were longing for demobilization and hated having to deal with civilian demonstrations, not knowing whether to stand by or open fire. They were maddened by rumours and reports of the massacres of their comrades elsewhere and at the least provocation could have gone on a bloody rampage in the city. Russell wrote to his father on 9 April, 1919:

Dear Father,
Today, I fear, will be known as a bloody day in Cairo, to history. The town has gone clean mad and for two days the whole city has been given over to frenzied demonstrations. I thought there was just a chance of getting through without trouble but yesterday evening things were precipitated by some British and Australian soldiers getting loose and starting a fight with some Egyptian army soldiers. Two of my mounted troop on duty got shot by stray bullets and a Fire Brigade man too. There were two bad scraps in

the night, caused by infuriated Australians getting loose, eight or ten natives got killed.

Yesterday was bad but today is far worse; the roughs of the town are out, tearing down telephone wires, barricading streets and pillaging. So far the Military have not moved though I fear they will have to. My police, of course, are unarmed and helpless.

Much of the trouble started by Armenians losing their heads and firing at the demonstrations from their houses, with the result that the mob attacked, killed the Armenians and fired or looted the houses. Some ghastly murders were perpetrated on individual British soliders caught by the mob. I also had a detective murdered – stabbed to pieces by a crowd, while others danced round his body.

The next day, Thursday, was a bad day too. The mob had barricaded streets in various parts of the town and the military were still trying to avoid unnecessary bloodshed. I had to make plans for the funeral of my two police who had been killed; the morning looked so bad that I arranged to postpone the funeral till the next day, Thursday. At 3 p.m., however, when I was just getting a bit of rest in the house my O.C. Mounted Troop rang me up from the hospital to say that the mob insisted on taking the bodies and were attacking the hospital. I dressed and dashed off in my car to the hospital at once.

When I got to Abdin police station I saw that the street ahead was barricaded with iron tree cradles. Beyond it was a howling mob of the most horrible looking roughs I've ever seen. At this moment a Fire Engine came up and tried to pass the barricade, but the mob would not let them through, so I told the engine to go back. The hospital where my men's bodies were was some thirty yards down the street beyond the barrier, so I walked over the barrier into the mob. They quickly recognised me. In fact a number of them formed a sort of body-guard round me and took me to the door of the hospital where I got a chair to stand on and tried to calm the mob down. It was almost impossible to make one's self heard and I thought it wiser to retire inside, which I did and sent a Police officer up to a window to speak to them from there. I don't think many people have ever been in the middle of such a mob. It was composed of several thousand of the roughest element of Cairo, all armed with something. Some had knives, some had spear heads, chisels, adses, tree-trunks, tree props, and those that had no weapons had great jagged bits of broken cast-iron gratings from round the street trees. The whole mob was shrieking and yelling and waving their weapons in the air. Many of the crowd no longer produced any sound from their throats, others were foaming at the mouth, and I myself saw three fall over in fits on the ground.

After some time 50 of my Mounted troop arrived with detachments of the Fire Brigade and other Police to take part in the procession, and after about an hour and a half we got the procession formed. It was headed by students on bicycles and then my mounted and dismounted Police, then the three coffins surrounded by the mourners and then deputations from the Azhar Mosque, the schools, professions, tram companies, etc., and the last few hundred yards composed of the former mob all walking in rows of eight. Before we started, I told them I would not come with them unless they laid down their arms, which they did, and during the procession through the town practically not a weapon was seen.

I naturally wanted to take the procession the shortest way to the cemetery but they would not have it, and in the end I had to give way and let them go where they wanted. You see that makes every funeral into a political demonstration, they go all round the town past the various consulates, where they stop and shout 'Long live Independence, long live Egypt the Free'.

Well I stayed with them till nearly 7 p.m. when I was dead beat and retired. The bodies actually got to the cemeteries at about 8.30 p.m. and I breathed again when I heard that everyone had got safely back, without an incident. It was all a very nasty experience.

I felt the effect of it rather on the Friday, but had a quiet afternoon, which was spent in sleep.

I had better stop this letter to give it a chance of getting posted. Best love all round.
Ever loving son
Tom

Russell's wife, Dorothea, also wrote home with a lengthy description of the Cairo happenings. She is much less laconic and put her husband's role into some perspective:

The crowd was entirely out of the control of their own leaders, students and sheikhs, who were simply terrified themselves and implored Thomas not to leave them. I am told by people who saw it all that the crowds were cheering Thomas and shouting, 'Long live Russell Bey'. People kept telephoning and writing to congratulate me on Thomas's performance and wherever I went it was the same. Egyptian Army Officers who have known this country for years say it was amazing. Two or three people have told me that they considered that he held his life in his hand all day, that it was a wonderful example of personal bravery and of handling of a fanatical crowd.

I simply can't tell you the things that people say to me about it. General Morris telephoned to me when it was all over and said, 'I cannot tell you what we think of your husband and what we owe him. He has saved a disaster.'

A separate demonstration by Egyptian women was also reported by Dorothea:

I must tell you about the Harem ladies procession. A few days ago the authorities heard that they were going to process and this could not be allowed as other people would take the opportunity of joining in and if in breaking it up any women were injured the whole place would blaze up. It was decided that Thomas's guard company were to stop it reinforced by British troops. Well the ladies were blocked in a very hot street for about three hours. Their faces were burnt scarlet, they were chaffed out of their lives by the guard co. and after having been addressed twice by Thomas and having had their legs thoroughly pulled, they were allowed to go home, Thomas having their carriages called for them. We now hear that they are all delighted with Thomas's treatment of them. It is an ill wind which blows nobody any good! It was an extraordinarily funny ending to what before hand was looked on almost as a tragedy, the Sultan, Residency and Savoy (GHQ) all being nonplussed.

Of course these Egyptian 'ladies' took the demonstration very seriously, they were playing their part with the men in the national struggle against 'the repressive acts and intimidation of the British authorities' – and it is unlikely that they were as 'delighted with Thomas's treatment' as Dorothea records. The British authorities decided enough was enough, however, and brought in General Allenby with a heavy hand to pacify the country. By the time the disturbances had been ended some 1000 Egyptians, thirty-six British and Indian soldiers and four British civilians had been killed. Many thousands of pounds worth of damage had been caused.

Black Saturday 1952

A kind of truce between the British and the Egyptians lasted some thirty years. Russell Pasha was still in Cairo, by then retired, when real trouble broke out again. A long campaign was being waged against the British by various Egyptian groups seeking true independence for the country. The British had no answer apart from force. An especially senseless action drove the Egyptians to react particularly violently. On 25 January 1952 an Egyptian police barracks on the Suez Canal was attacked when its occupants refused to surrender to British troops. In this senseless incident fifty policemen were killed, 100 injured and the building shattered. Reaction was immediate. Mobs went on the rampage in Cairo.

Russell was in hospital quite seriously ill and trying hard and to no avail to advise the authorities on how to handle the troubles – using his experience of 1919. He wrote to his son on 26 January 1952:

Dear John,

This may or may not even reach you. I've been ill for some days and Dr Moore put me into the Anglo-American Hospital yesterday. I am, it seems, thoroughly run down and have low blood pressure which is very depressing but better than high blood pressure which is dangerous. Dorothea has got bad toothache and is to have one out tomorrow. Cairo is in a state of complete anarchy since this morning. Dorothea is sleeping here and on Monday goes to the Embassy.

Quite possibly they'll burn this hospital down too! They've burnt the Anglo-Egyptian Motors, Turf Club, several cinemas, B.O.A.C. All police (except traffic) have disappeared, the Guard co. have all left their posts one's told, and have flocked up to the Azhar. No one knows what the Government are doing, the mob are doing what they like. We *hope* that someone will restore order, if it's not the Egyptian Army it must be the British, *and* quickly. We've left the house for the time being with the servants.

It's the worst possible time to be ill and especially when what one needs is peace and quiet and no worries. Dorothea is splendid and does not let herself worry at all but she's ill too, with bad colic pains at night. We sincerely hope that something definite is coming out of this: they've got all English places marked down and are setting fire as they like.

By the time you get this (if you do) things must have taken shape. It's no good jobbing backwards, but I do wish that we had sold and cleared out a year ago. I fear we are in for a bad time.

Best love to you both.

We are both too old for these stirring events!

My wretched hospital dinner is coming (6.30 p.m.).

Russell's wife described in more detail some of the events of the day that has gone down in history as Black Saturday:

Well to return to the afternoon. I went out to tea at the Spinks. By then the town was blazing, the sky a blaze, a pall of smoke blowing away south. The most awful sight and terrifying. The sky red miles high! apparently we none of us knew what was really going on and it only gradually filtered through. The next morning I rang up my dentist who described the burning of Shari Qasr el-Nil to me in detail; he had watched it all from his balcony windows and with a field glass had seen the buildings opposite burning. Mobs of men and roughs came down the street followed by a petrol lorry; quite superior looking men directed things with lists in their hands, detailing men to the back of the shops, where they set things alight. They had already prepared torches, long ones, with cotton waste or something on the end and they had bottles of petrol in their pockets. It was the most organized and prepared thing imaginable. The mob tried to set the big block of flats in which he lives afire, but the proprietor is a Moslem and went out and harangued them and they cleared off.

The trouble started in the morning with the mutiny of the Provincial Guard Company, marching up to the Azhar and incited by a most inflammatory speech from the Minister of Social Affairs. From the Opera Square to Qasr el-Nil barracks every other shop is burned. They burned the B.O.A.C. offices and Major Fanner's offices above. They burned the first floor of the great Immobilia block of flats and all the shops. The people above had the most narrow escape. While they were doing this another group was burning the Turf Club. Twelve people lost their lives there and we have four survivors here in the hospital. A young Mrs. Reed, who is terribly burned, jumped 35 feet from a window. Two *effendis* then came in from the crowd, seized her under each arm and one with a revolver marched or dragged her out through the hostile crowd and walked her to the Assistance Publique, half conscious and half asphyxiated and saved her life; she was shoeless. She is terribly ill but a little better today, face, hands, legs and buttocks terribly burned. She owed her life entirely to these two. Old D'Arcy Wetherbee had the same experience, walked out himself into the crowd and two *effendis* took him out and hid him in a shop near by. The others in the club were burned and horribly mutilated. I saw the doctor who did the p.m., one had a leg nearly hacked off, two disembowelled, one had both wrists broken. I don't know what happened to Crawford and I don't know if the bodies were identified. I was told that they were so carbonized that they were unrecognizable. Craig was found dead in a chair in an upper room, two wounds, but death had either been a heart attack or asphyxiation. Boyer, the Canadian, had one wrist broken, damaged face and one hand slightly burned after death which was probably from asphyxiation. They say the crowd threw the bodies of two who had jumped back on the flames. The tragic thing is that three had escaped early on by the back door which the secretary had unlocked for them. I suppose he locked it again thinking it would prevent the mob getting in, and the others barricaded themselves in. It was all watched by some people from the windows opposite and the Swedish Legation people saw some of it. The Ford place opposite, burnt out all their records, accounts, gone.

Barclays Bank completely burned out but strong room survived. Thirteen people killed. It is not known how many in Shepheards, but the Manager of Mena told me at least thirty-nine missing, largely servants; it was all servants and Greek tellers and accountants in Barclays. I have seen people who were at Shepheards and got away in time; they say it was too awful – the crowd attacking it but I have not seen any one who was actually in the fire. They think about fifty-nine people are missing, mainly servants who were seen screaming on the roof and the crowd telling them to jump. There were no fire precautions and no fire escapes, they say! It is the most terrible scene of ruin. If you stand with your back to the shops, Cooks, everything is burnt; then you get to the hotel which is just a great skeleton and most of it a heap of rubble fifteen feet high. The great lift shafts stand like towers above it all filled with hanging cords and wires. Continue on south, and all the shops, the Wagon Lits, all of them are burnt. Continue on towards the Opera Square and all the block is burnt right round and down Fouad el-Awal across the side street and then Cicurels stands a great ruin like Shepheards. All the restaurants, all the wine merchants, Stella beer shops, Kodak, every luxury shop – burnt. The town is wrecked.

Herbert Addision wrote a pathetic little postscript:

On Tuesday afternoon, I suppose about fifty of us went to the Protestant cemetery in Old Cairo – a desolate spot – for the funeral of the remaining Turf Club members who had died. One of these was D.S. Crawford, one of my colleagues at the university who had been outraged twice over: first he had been summarily dismissed from the government service, and then he had been murdered and mutilated.

Thus ended British rule in Egypt, in a heap of ashes and charred bodies. What would Cromer or Boyle have thought of such a finale to their life's work? Perhaps it would not have been so unexpected. Boyle had once written:

The British Official has to cultivate the painful virtue of self-restraint and philosophy enough to appreciate that it is well-nigh impossible for one nation to feel gratitude for the blessings conferred on it by another.

SIX

THE BRITISH IN THE HOLY LAND 1917–48

In 1916 war was raging in the Middle East; Turkey was fighting on the side of Germany and Austria against the British empire. An attack across the Suez Canal had been repulsed and slowly the British pushed the Turks back through Palestine, edging towards the long-coveted Holy Places.

On 10 December 1917 General Sir Edmund Allenby, supreme commander of the allied army in the Middle East, humbly entered Jerusalem on foot after having expelled its Muslim Turkish rulers. For the first time since the crusades the Holy Sepulchre and the Church of the Nativity in Bethlehem were in Christian hands. It was a triumph more symbolic than real, a glittering Christmas present offered to the British nation in the midst of a long and bloody war, to stir the imagination of those brought up on the Bible. It was remote from the mud of Flanders, a romantic event in a painful period. But far from leading to an era of Christian brotherhood, it was to herald an era of unprecedented (even for the Holy Land) bitterness.

The British were dragged into the running of the country, first as military occupiers, then as mandatory power administering on behalf of the League of Nations. The mandate contained the promise to help Jews enter the country in order to establish a national home – wherein lay the seeds of conflict. The long-established Arab inhabitants deeply resented large numbers of foreign immigrants disturbing their way of life. The Jews chafed at any restrictions being placed on their immigration and activities and, by 1939, 380,000 of them were living in Palestine. The British were trapped in the middle of a bitter conflict. During this period thousands of them worked in Palestine in a myriad of capacities from high commissioner downwards. They never settled in Palestine or developed an affectionate tolerance for the Arabs as they did for the Egyptians. They were usually in crisis, often irritated, driven to despair. They started out with the best of intentions.

John Young, agricultural expert

They began as military rulers and the army continued to play a large part in Palestinian affairs, quelling civil riots and armed rebellion. The military administration in 1918 had to find trained men to run the country, so it borrowed and stole from other countries. John Young appears again. He was then in the army and sent off to be an agricultural 'expert'. Although the idea of Jerusalem held a certain attraction, conditions there (after Cairo) were primitive. It had been a neglected provincial town under its Turkish rulers, yet nothing could impair the splendour of its Islamic buildings or the sanctity of its Christian ones. Young set off in January 1918 for his new job with some misgivings:

I left Cairo by the evening train to Kantara in the enjoyment of First Class carriage and dining car. It was the last I should see of such luxuries for a year. At Kantara a porter met me and deposited my luggage outside the station. There he left me. The comfortable conditions of Egypt abruptly terminated. A curtain fell between peace and war. Outside the lighted station all was dark. There were no conveyances of any kind and it was with the greatest difficulty I was at last able in the blackness to find someone willing to assist me with my valise and suitcase over the temporary bridge spanning the Suez Canal to the wooden hut at the railhead which constituted the Kantara Station for the Palestinian railway. 'The Milk and Honey Express,' the troop train of converted 3rd Class carriages travelled leisurely, but none too smoothly, through the night, and I reached the terminus in time for breakfast at the YMCA Canteen before motoring the long distance to Bir Salem.

It was my first visit to Palestine and very noticeable was the change from the flat irrigated rich lands of Egypt to the bare rolling down-like country, green in parts with thin early barley that opened out before me. All the way we passed Turkish prisoners marching under escort, and on either side of the deep rutted muddy track lay dead horses, dead mules and overturned gun carriages, while through the wreckage of war peeped the first scarlet anemonies with their promise of spring.

I left Bir Salem on a mild showery afternoon by car. We passed through the orange groves into Ramleh and abruptly rose through on to the grim plateau of Judea where in spite of the sharp air the little pink cyclamens were bravely showing between the rocks. We then entered the mean featureless modern suburbs of the Jaffa Road, by far the least impressive of the three approaches into Jerusalem. It was getting late and the wind after the comparative warmth of the plain blew bitterly when we drew up at Fast's hotel. Then after securing a room I reported to the Military Governor. I found him sitting in his office wearing an overcoat over his thin uniform – so unexpectedly sudden had been his appointment that he had not had the opportunity to go to Cairo for a winter outfit. He gave me details of my duties with the further information that my name had appeared in 'orders' under the title of Agricultural Expert for occupied Palestine.

The idea of giving expert advice on the agriculture of Palestine filled me with alarm. Although I had learnt something about crops and land values in my few years' experience of Government Land work in Egypt I was in no position to set up as an authority on the cultivation of olives, oranges and vines. And while I tried to console myself by remembering that if I knew little there were others who knew less it took several weeks before I could reply with any confidence to the question so frequently put to me in personal interview or down the telephone: 'Are you Captain Young the Agricultural Expert?'

Fast's hotel had been opened some years before by the German brothers Fast and was being managed during the war by two Syrians as a centre of accommodation for British Officers. Stone built and stone floored with high ceilinged rooms it seemed to me that first night one of the coldest buildings I had ever been in. The rain from outside was driving against the windows and in the main sitting-room there was such a crowd round the one wood-burning stove that I could never get near it, while in the dining-room there were no heating arrangements at all. The hotel could only cater for rationed officers, and as my rations were not forwarded from Bir Salem till the following day I was in danger of dining off oranges and Richon wine, about the only local table products then in the market, had not the Governor most generously asked me to join him at his table. Soon after dinner I went to bed with the hope, not entirely fulfilled, of getting warm, and as I walked up the long draughty passage I overheard an officer reprimanding one of the pale-faced Palestinian house boys: 'Bath water cold! Make it hot! Savez?' I could not catch the servant's reply. I think he was trying to explain that a wood-burning fire never produced really hot water but I did hear the last words of the officer as he turned into his room: 'I won't be spoken to like that by a nigger.'

Young worked hard to become acquainted with the terrible conditions of the Palestinian peasants who were suffering severe hardship because of the war. The British army was trying to ensure that they received sufficient food and that they were able to start farming again:

As the Army Authorities were anxious to know the extent of the harvest which could be expected from the country in the coming summer, I arranged a tour of all the villages under the Jerusalem Governorate and started off on horseback. I slept where I could, sometimes in villages if it was possible to find an empty room, sometimes if invited, in the camp of a hospitable assistant Military Governor, and once in the convent of a monastic order.

The conditions of the villages varied. In some more fortunate localities where the Turkish troops had not rested there might be found six or seven yokes of ploughing animals, but in the villages north of Ramalla lying on the borders of 'no man's land' things were as bad as they could be. Here I would find nearly every house damaged and the unhappy inhabitants cowering from the rain and wind behind what protection they could get. Out of their normal complement of some thirty or forty yoke of animals the number remaining would be one or two. The others, oxen, horses or donkeys had all been killed or taken away. With their ploughing animals gone, their houses no longer weather-proof and their olive trees cut down, these people seemed to have lost all hope. I spent a night in one of their villages and I noticed that their only food was maize bread dipped in oil and not too much of that. An inspection tour of this nature was strenuous work, for at night accommodation was often rough, the hours passed in the saddle were long and the villages, separated by great distances, were perched on hills difficult of access. Once when near the front line I was entertained by an Australian Officer of the Egyptian Labour Corps who offered to put me up for the night in his camp, an invitation which I gladly accepted. Before it grew dark I watched him addressing his men in limited but highly abusive Arabic, and when I remarked to him later that I was interested to hear him using such strong language, language which we in Egypt reserved for special occasions, he replied: 'Well, I just use it here every day and all day and I reckon my men would feel quite lonely without it.'

When my report on the Jerusalem villages was studied it became evident that the poorer villages were in danger of insufficient food unless they could be given the assistance of ploughing animals, and an arrangement was made for the loan of army mules for the remainder of the ploughing season. The mules, about thirty in number, arrived in Bethlehem on one of the coldest and wettest days I remember. The NCO in charge was wet through and shivering after riding the whole way from Bir Salem and had to be revived with brandy by the Assistant Military Governor, while the mules looked drenched and miserable. Then came the business of their distribution in the villages. I had thought they would be warmly welcomed, but often I was disappointed. The farmers who had most loudly called for help began to criticize. They protested that the mules, unaccustomed to peasant ways, did not suit the small wooden ploughs and that they could not make them work. But in some places the plan was a success. Two mules were sent to Nebi Samuel under a British Corporal where, being kindly treated, they remained for six weeks ploughing up many acres of land, and as often as I could I rode out with books and papers for the Corporal. On my first visit I found him quartered in one of the few uninjured rooms attached to the mosque premises. I had expected to find him lonely and longing to get back to his companions, but he said he was comfortable and contented. The next time he was sitting with the village *Imam* who told me he liked the Englishman very much and hoped he would stay for a long while. They seemed to have become great friends though the one had made no attempt to learn Arabic and the other knew no word of English. After a month I asked the Corporal if he wished to return to his unit, and to my surprise he replied that he would prefer to remain where he was. He said: 'Me and the *Imam* are such pals.'

By May 1918 the British administration was beginning to settle in, bringing with it the inevitable bureaucracy:

I was placed in the newly formed Department of Agriculture with the high sounding title of Adviser and there came an intensification of bureaucratic methods. Paper-work grew in an alarming manner. Typewriters and typists arrived, long notes were passed for comment from one office to another and as they multiplied the amount of effective work done seemed to decrease in proportion. The era of quick decisions had passed for ever.

In January 1919 Young returned to his civil life in Egypt after a year unique in British Imperial history – putting the Holy Land into order:

I had seen progress. The wasted fields were being ploughed for crops. The inhabitants of Jerusalem again looked happy and well fed. The population of Gaza were returning to their once shattered homes. Communications were open for trade. The mud track from Ramleh to Jaffa was now a metalled road and on the railway through trains were running from Jerusalem to Kantara. In Jerusalem too there had been changes. The streets were clean and the sanitary arrangements controlled. A town planning map had been projected and the Military Governor was making noble endeavours to preserve and enhance the beauty of the city.

A pasha of Jerusalem arrives

To flesh out the burgeoning Palestine administration more and more bureaucrats were summoned from home and abroad. Edward Keith-Roach was one of the first to arrive, asked to look around with a view to staying:

One oppressive afternoon in August 1919 I found myself, at the age of thirty-four, in Cairo railway station furnished with a railway warrant to Jerusalem and an official letter addressed to the Military Administrator of the Occupied Enemy Territory Administration. I was about to begin my *hegira* to the Holy Land. The last three years I had spent administering Eastern Darfur, living alone in a district of thirty thousand square miles that formed part of the huge province of Darfur in the Sudan.

I had been a month on my journey beginning with a wearisome three weeks trek by camel through sands and thorn bushes before reaching the most southerly station on the Sudan railway system, El Obeid, en route for Khartoum and the Nile. During the night we had crossed the Suez canal, traversed the desert of Sinai and in the morning light mounted the Judean hills. At Bettir, the last station before Jerusalem, the creaking, groaning train stopped for water. I let myself out on to the ground and as Arabs say: 'I sniffed the air.' It was sparkling, clear and clean. This was enough. I made an instant resolve. I would stay in Palestine!

The train moaned its way up to the Holy City and we crawled into the singularly unattractive, dirty station. I got into a broken-down rattling victoria, drawn by a couple of unkempt ponies and set out for the City and the Mount of Olives where the Administration headquarters were housed. Half an hour later we had traversed the potholes and the dust which the heels of our horses kicked up in clouds, but the soft pad of camels hardly stirred as they passed contemptuously by. We had surmounted Scopus and were approaching Olivet when the Noble Sanctuary standing on the Temple Area far below us came into view and I stopped the carriage. There she lay at my feet, without parallel, without compare, the Holy City. My resolve was strengthened I would serve her.

Jerusalem was a city where religions, cultures, nations, tongues collided in a multi-coloured confusion. Sanctity and holiness struggled to survive. Keith-Roach continues:

Early next morning I went down David Street before turning into Christian Street to make my pilgrimage to the Holy Sepulchre. As I walked down the congested, broad, cobbled steps there was an impression of too much paint crowded upon a small canvas. The steps were hemmed in on either side by vegetable shops which were aglow with colour. The route is so narrow that laden camels passing up and down cause as much disturbance as a motor coach does in passing down an English lane. Stout bowlegged Kurdish porters with huge burdens carried on packs fastened high across their bowed shoulders brushed past lemonade sellers clashing their brass saucers to call attention to their wares. Moslem townswomen, enveloped in white cotton garments that completely covered them from head to ankles and figured muslin or black veils hiding their faces passed their Arab country-women with tattoed chins and lips, wearing dresses of locally spun and embroidered stuffs surmounted with a short coloured velvet jacket heavily embroidered with gold thread.

Most of Jerusalem, Arab, Jew and European, seemed to be in that overcrowded thoroughfare talking, chaffing, expostulating, bargaining as accompanied by little Arab bucket-boys with big panniers strapped across their shoulders, they went from shop to shop, turning over, choosing or rejecting the produce. The City *effendi*, dressed in European clothes with a scarlet fez upon his head, stood beside a Russian nun draped in black, her face bound in a black veil and crowned with a high round headdress of the same colour. An Orthodox Jew with twisted sidelocks, under a black flat hat and dressed in a long coat, trousers finishing midway twixt knee and ankle, white socks and black shoes, carried a cream coloured black-fringed prayer shawl across his shoulders. A tribal sheikh with acquiline nose and piercing eye, glided by, leather straps crossed upon his chest, supporting under his loose robe of camel hair a curved ivory handled scimitar in a silver sheath. An English woman bargained with an extensive use of the sign language but with an air that shows she cherishes an idea that she is already an accomplished Arabist. She stands beside a French Sister of Charity with bat-like wings to her white headdress, who drops into her large basket vegetables that each shopkeeper gives her as she silently pleads her needs. A bearded and bunned Greek priest, black of eye and of beard beneath his black chimney-pot hat, rubs shoulders with a peasant clothed in baggy trousers, shirt and sheepskin-coat. Grey, black, brown and white robed Roman Catholic Sisters wearing a diversity of headdresses, walk alongside the rest of the shoppers and are equally jostled by the donkeys who are pushed down the steps to the shrill chirrups of donkey boys, and who in their turn are chivvied by the khaki clothed police, wearing Russian looking black lambswool headdresses. Competing with the shopkeepers were many village women squatting upon the steps, their vegetables piled high in round baskets. They appear to be having a vehement and venomous quarrel between themselves, but actually are amicably discussing some question concerning current prices. The shops in Christian Street were almost exclusively occupied by Sephardi Jewish shopkeepers, who pressed their wares upon me: amber beads, olive-wood boxes, neck-laces, rosaries, crowns of thorns, cotton shrouds and all the junk that clusters round shrines and oriental bazaars.

This then was that bewildering country, Palestine, that the British were having to administer. Any government in its right senses would have left immediately. Keith-Roach went back to Egypt the next day, determined, however, to return. He will reappear in various situations. His life was typical of many British officials in Palestine. He was successively district commissioner of northern Palestine, centred in Galilee, administrator of the Jerusalem district, and finally district commissioner of Jerusalem from 1937 to 1943 – the plum job near to the centre of power.

Humphrey Bowman: the valley of the shadow

One of the next to arrive in Palestine was Humphrey Bowman, another transfer from Egypt. He had been a humble teacher in Cairo, had spent the war period in the army, was recently married (and devoted to his young and beautiful wife Bobby), and in September 1920 invited to become the first director of education in Palestine. He kept an intimate diary of his life, full of the problems and heartaches of those who spent any period of time in Palestine. Bowman suffered more than most:

> Government House, Jerusalem 22 September 1920
> Here today and gone tomorrow is true of my flying visit: for I only arrived late on the evening of the 20th after 24 hours journey from Cairo. The journey was long but very comfortable. I was a good deal tired at the end of it. Perhaps the 200ft climb has affected my liver: anyhow I have not felt very fit since I came. This cold keen air is very healthy, but one has to get used to it! My darling has not come with me, as we thought the double journey would not be worth it. And I think we were right on the whole, but I wish she was here to help me decide on the all important question as to whether I am to accept the post of Director of Education or not.
>
> After spending the first night at the Hotel Allenby (clean but not too comfortable and a very poky room), I was invited to stay here as H.E.'s guest [Sir Herbert Samuel, High Commissioner]. I had a long talk with him and told him all my recent history and he seemed to be very anxious I should come. Then the question of pay was raised. The salary is £1200 plus £240 war bonus and £75 'leave allowance'. A house – in my case a very poor one of 4 rooms only – is provided, for which I pay £12 a month towards upkeep. Furniture is very hard to get, and living is said to be at least 20% or 30% higher than in Cairo. Financially it is not particularly good, but it is probably an interesting job. There is a lot of work to be done: Sir Herbert is very keen indeed on education. I shall discuss the whole affair with B. of course on my return. I spent some hours in Jerusalem this morning: first seeing the house allotted to the D of E which was very disappointing and which would do perhaps for a few months. It would not be big enough for us if Pamela [his baby daughter] were here and we *must* have a home where we can all live together.

Bowman returned to Cairo and after lengthy discussions with his wife they decided to move to Palestine where he became a distinguished and well liked director of education:

> Jerusalem 12 December 1920
> We arrived here on 1st November. We have now been allotted a good house

above the station in a fine position, and a magnificent view: but it is in a very bad state of repair and wants a thorough doing up. The PWD here as elsewhere are very slow. We hope it may be ready before Xmas. We are really not very comfortable, as all our belongings are still in packing cases. We are naturally most anxious to get into our own home and have our own possessions around us once more. I am gradually beginning to get into my stride here and gradually knowing a little more than I did at first.

For the next two years Bowman and his family settled into Jerusalem, he beginning to establish the foundations of an educational system, and she looking after their daughter and becoming a familiar and popular figure in Jerusalem society. They were an ideally happy family revelling in the expatriate life, despite its challenges and difficulties. They went to parties and dinners and ceremonies and the other events that Britons organized around the world. Then tragedy struck, doubly hard to bear in a foreign land:

Jerusalem 18 February 1923

How can I begin to write in this journal again? I have lost my darling – my beloved Bobby – who has been my companion, my love, my friend for the past six years. A week ago she was taken ill here at home with what seemed like influenza – high temperature and aches in the head and eyes – and pain in the limbs. Major Watson IMS came at my request after breakfast last Sunday and diagnosed flu. She had a rather bad day – but it looked like ordinary fever and cold. Then at 7 I took her temperature and it was up to 105 degrees. This frightened me, and I got hold of Watson again. He came in after dinner and found her easier and was not at all alarmed. She had a bad night and as she was no better in the a.m. we took her to the English Hospital. Watson and I took her in his Military ambulance. It was a very wet cold day, but we got her safely to hospital and put her to bed at once. I left her looking fairly comfortable, though her face was flushed and she was evidently far from well. I came again at 4 p.m. – it was pouring with rain, and I was a bit wet. We sat talking for a little, but she still looked flushed and was rather anxious about herself. Before leaving I asked the doctor if there was any cause for anxiety. He assured me there was none whatever and that she would probably be much better in the morning. I looked in again and told my darling this and it seemed to cheer her a little.

I walked home, feeling a little anxious, but reassured by the doctor's words. At 8 next morning I rang up and was told she had had a fairly good night, and as I did not hear again, did not go to the hospital till 5. I could of course easily have gone at any time but I had office in the afternoon and was lunching with Miss Ridler – so I never got a telephone message to say Bobby wanted to see me. I was of course going anyhow in the afternoon, but thought that 5 would do as well as earlier. When I got there, I found she was delirious. She had been fairly well all night up to 3.30 – talking or sleeping – then suddenly she became delirious – and later quite unconscious. I knelt by her side suddenly realizing she was very ill indeed – in fact the doctor called me and told me so. I prayed God to take her spirit to Him and to watch over our Babies and me. Her breathing was very heavy – but she had no pain then as she was quite unconscious. I stepped out of the room for a minute, but very soon I was called in again and she sank quickly with my arms on her – Darling Bobby. I do not know how I can look forward to life without you. I could not realize then that she had really gone. It was all so terribly sudden and I blamed myself for not having gone earlier, when at least I might have seen her and talked a little. And I am afraid she knew how ill she was, and I was not there, though she must have longed for me.

My darling was laid to rest in the beautiful cemetery on Ash Wednesday. There were many people there – drawn I believe from every section of the Jerusalem community. I stood by my darling's coffin as Mr Hammoud read the service. I was given wonderful strength and bore up through it all, looking occasionally at our dear house across the valley and then at the blue hills of Moab. At the end of the Service I knelt down and scattered some of the dust of Palestine on my darling's coffin – then got up and slowly walked away through the ranks of friends. I did not shed a tear though my heart was too full to speak.

Last week my darling was as well – or so she seemed – as ever in her life. On the Wednesday we dined at Government House to meet the great Professor Einstein, and as we came into the drawing room, Archer Cust said to Bobby: 'Mrs Bowman, you go in to dinner with the great man' – which made us laugh because I had been teasing her by saying she would certainly sit next to Einstein, and have to discuss 'Relativity' in German! The next night we went to a Dance at the Garrison Club. At Bobby's special request I danced right through the programme and we came away at midnight walking arm in arm, she singing with happiness.

Humphrey Bowman spent thirteen more years in Palestine as director of education until his retirement in 1936. He was to marry again in 1925, his brother's widow. Earlier in his life, on non-combattant service during the First World War, he had looked after the separation allowances for families of soldiers away on duty. He received many heartfelt letters from relatives who felt abandoned, uncared for by authority, and he kept some of the most poignant – touchingly forthright and moving:

Dear Sir, I have received no pay since my husband had gone from nowhere. Yours truly,
Dear Sir, My husband has been away at the Crystal Palace and got four days

furlong and has now gone to the Mind Sweepers. Yours respectfully,

Dear Sir, I have received your letter. I am his Grandfather and his Grandmother, he was born and brought up in this house in answer to your letter. Yours truly,

Dear Sir, I am writing these few lines from Mrs Morgan who cannot write herself. She is expecting to be confined and can do with it.

Dear Sir, Mrs Haynes has been put to bed with a little lad, wife of Peter Haynes, I am, Yours etc.,

Dear Sir, in accordance with instructions on ring paper I have given birth to a daughter on the 21st April. Yours etc.,

Dear Sir, You have changed my little boy into a little girl. Will it make any difference? Yours truly,

Dear Sir, I am expecting to be confined next month, will you please tell me what I am to do about it? Yours truly,

Dear Sir, My Bill has been put in charge of a spitoon. Shall I get any more pay? Yours truly,

Dear Sir, Will you please send my money as early as possible as I am walking about Bolton like a bloody pauper, and oblige,

Respected Sir, Dear Sir, Though I take this liberty as it leaves me at present I beg to ask if you will kindly be kind enough to let me know where my husbin though he is not my legible husbin as he as a wife though he says she is dead but I dont think he nos for surebut we are not married though I are getting my allotment regular which is no fault of mr.Loy George who would stop it if he could but if you know where he is belong to the Navy Royal Fling Corp for ever since he joined in January when he was sacked from his work for talking back at his boss which was a woman at the laundry where he worked. I have not had any money from him since he joined though he told Mrs. Harris what lives on the ground floor that he was a pretty ossifer for six shillings a week and lots of underclosing for the cold weather and I have three children whats is been the father of them though he says it was my fault. hoping you will write to me az you are quit well as it leaves me at present. I must now close hoping you are well.

The hill of evil counsel

Edward Keith-Roach kept a voluminous six hundred page diary of his life in Palestine, which he called *Pasha in Jerusalem*, and which is full of glimpses into the life of the British officials there as well as the lives of others. The high commissioners were the top men, the centre of official life and often the butt of most resentment. There were six of them during the twenty-eight years of the Mandate. For some time the high commissioner lived in unfitting premises when under Field Marshall Lord Plumer (1925–8), a veteran of the Somme and

Flanders, the decision was taken to build a splendid new government house. Keith-Roach was closely involved:

One afternoon my wife and I drove out to see the proposed site of the new Government House. A small hill top had been purchased on the west of the road leading to Bethlehem about a couple of miles outside Jerusalem overlooking, not the Holy City, but an Arab village and a Jewish industrial suburb. My wife said: 'A High Commissioner should either live in, or overlook, the capital of the country he governs; let's look for another site.' I turned up the records and found that a committee had met, examined the possible sites and rejected them all for one reason or another except this one; so the land had been purchased. We visited the rejected places in turn; south-west of the City overlooking the Western Wall was the Hill of Evil Counsel, partially occupied by the Town Incinerator. When the Committee had visited it on a windy day they had evidently been blown about and the Director of Agriculture had deplored the poorness of the soil. It was a gorgeous site, free as the air. I decided to approach the High Commissioner. Lord Plumer rejected the proposal: he said the whole question had been determined by a Committee and he could not reopen the matter.

I wrote a letter to the noble Lord and pointed out that if his decision remained, High Commissioners for centuries would look out upon an Arab village and the future industrial area. Next day, as I was sitting in my office the Field Marshal entered and said: 'K R, I thought I had given you my final decision in this matter. Do not raise the issue again.' With a kindly smile he left me. I waited some weeks and then wrote to him again and implored him to go before it was too late and inspect the two sites himself. I added that I was certain his decision was wrong. He sent for me to his office. 'How dare you' he said, 'break my orders'. 'Because,' I replied 'I am certain your decision not to reconsider the matter is wrong. It's not easy to disobey a High Commissioner or a Field Marshal.'

He recalled the Committee and we sat down at table. All agreed they had perhaps been unduly influenced by the weather the day they visited the Incinerator, and owned my choice was better. The change was made. The Incinerator was removed to the other end of the town. Government bought fifty dunams of land, some years later the area was expanded to one hundred, and planted part of it with pine trees; a forest quickly sprang up, and Austen Harrison made a design worthy of the position. Meanwhile the original site is earmarked for the Government Mental Asylum with the Fever Hospital standing below.

The new site had everything to be said for it except its historical name. Lillah McCarthy and her husband, Sir Frederick Keeble, were staying in Jerusalem together with the future poet laureate, Mr Masefield, and his wife. I took Lillah up there one perfect still night before a stone had been laid, and as a copper moon rose from behind the hills of Moab across the

Dead Sea this great English actress, creator of Masefield's *Nan* and Bernard Shaw's Margaret Knox in *Fanny's First Play*, seated upon a rock recited to me Blake's *Jerusalem*. I made her repeat the poem over and over again for nearly an hour, and the heavens seemed to glow in response to her glorious rendering. Inspired by the beauty of the moonlight, the poetry and the voice, I hoped as we drove away that the name 'Hill of Evil Counsel' had been exorcised forever.

The life of a district commissioner

Keith-Roach was totally dedicated to his work, to improving the lot of all in the country. He expected no gratitude from Arab or Jew and received little help from the British authorities who as usual were trying to run things on a shoestring. All the time Jewish immigrants were pouring in, adding to the difficulties, and there were not enough district officers to cope. Keith-Roach wrote to the high commissioner:

I wish to make it clear that the establishment of the senior officers is inadequate for this District. I am suffering from a nervous form of asthma, which is the result of overwork. My colleagues are very much below par in health. There have been several breakdowns. I consider that we are being called upon to bear a burden which is quite unjustified. This is unfair, not only to the people whose interest we cannot properly promote or safeguard, but also to ourselves.

Three months later I wrote: 'My deputy proceeds on leave next month. That will reduce my British staff to one Assistant District Commissioner and one Cadet.' In May 1935 I was informed: 'There can be no question of increasing the establishment of British officers in your District.' In November 1935 I fell seriously ill and was away for eight months; the Specialist diagnosed my illness: iritis, arising from overwork. My suffering was intense and it is due to the genius and skill of Sir John Strathearn, Ophthalmologist of the Hospital of the Order of Saint John of Jerusalem that I am not blind.

Unrest in Palestine served to compound his problems, of which not the least was the illness of his wife:

I secured a house on the slopes of Carmel and had moved into it; and all was ready to receive my wife, who was with our sons in England, when in August I received a telegram that she had had a stroke. I flew to England and found her in a coma, her left side completely paralysed from head to foot. For weeks she lay like that, but inch by inch we fought not only for her

life but for her recovery. By the time I had to return, Violet could be moved
to a chair and, with the help of daily massage, could walk again by
Christmas. Her indomitable courage undoubtedly made this possible. But
she had to live in England, a trained nurse by her side. Her illness, a son in
the Navy and another at Charterhouse, made it financially impossible for me
to live in my house; so I went to the German Hospice on Mount Carmel and
lived for the next five years with the German Sisters.

During most of the period of the Mandate the lives of British officials
who were trying to cope in difficult situations, were in danger – there
were many attacks and some fatalities. Keith-Roach narrowly
escaped on several occasions during the troubled year of 1937:

During the closing three months of the year strong military reinforcements
brought about some improvement. On the 11th of October I heard that the
police buildings which contained the telephone exchange at Jericho had
been attacked and burned out; so I went down to see about it, my car in
between two escorting cars. On our return, as I was passing the Museum,
four bombs were thrown from over the city wall; two fell just in front of my
car and two behind. The two I passed over did not explode but the other
two did. No one was damaged. A week later I arranged to leave my office at
noon to go to a meeting. I got to my car a minute too early, and as I turned
the corner a bomb was lobbed out of the window of one of the Crown
Counsel's offices below mine, and fell just where my car had been. A day or
two later a man was arrested with a loaded revolver outside the back
entrance to my house, and a few nights later an unknown person was chased
out of the garden dropping a revolver behind him.

Inevitably, other colleagues were less fortunate:

About six-thirty I was telephoned to and informed that Lewis Andrews and
his police escort, Constable McEwan, had been shot dead as they were in
the narrow passageway about to enter the Anglican Church in Nazareth.
The Galilee Superintendent of Police was in Haifa, half out of his mind with
worry. He had been recently married to one of the world's most beautiful
women, who had been painted frequently by famous artists. She had been
but two months in Palestine, was pregnant and had been stricken down with
infantile paralysis and was now hovering between life and death. I picked
him up at the hospital and we drove to the little town lying in a cup
in the hills. I saw Andrews lying upon his back on an army blanket in
the office-yard, a smile upon his lips; his dead British comrade by his
side.
    It was decided to bury him in Jerusalem and I sent his body on in the
morning. That afternoon I took an aeroplane and flew to the Holy City. The

whole of official Jerusalem was in full uniform or top hat at the Mount Zion Cemetery. As I walked by the side of Mr Battershill, the Officer Administering the Government, in my dusty khaki suit I made stern resolve. I left the funeral and went back to Battershill's house and, with the memory of that boy's smile upon his lips, I told Battershill what I really felt about the whole regime. My remarks were terse; they were not pleasant; they must have pained this officer who had only arrived from Cyprus six months before. In the heat of a sticky night I motored back to Haifa and thought about Andrews, his work, his widow and the future of his children. He was a unique character. Almost unlettered, he had come out from Australia a trooper in the Light Horse, and when I met him first he could hardly write a letter. I presented him with Roget's *Thesaurus*; but he quickly learned Arabic and Hebrew and had a sixth sense that made him one of the best intelligence officers I have ever met. He was most hardworking and was devoted to the country.

In quieter periods the work in Jerusalem was, like that of Boyle in Cairo, a continual round of trivial tasks and exotic interviews, with the additional responsibility for religious matters, however arcane:

The daily tasks are very varied. On my table one morning I pick up the following files: Report of the Committee appointed to enquire into Jewish ritual slaughter; the sittings of the Courts of Criminal Assizes, and my attendance with the Chief Justice; may an Armenian Women's Benefit Society be registered; the promotion of two Government officers; repairs in the Church of the Holy Sepulchre. I have already dealt with twenty other subjects, and as I begin to deal with this fresh pile a note is handed to me stating that the Coptic Bishop is waiting to enter my office and discuss the Coptic Pilgrimage from Egypt for Easter. I have early that morning seen the trustees of the *Nebi Musa* shrine and laid down the conditions governing their annual procession. Ten more people are to be interviewed ranging from the Mayor of Jerusalem to a visiting journalist. These completed the chief clerk enters with another score of files for decisions or signatures. I receive 30,000 letters annually.

In the case of a foreigner dying without friends I am responsible for his burial. But, on the other hand, it is my privilege to marry all British subjects and give the traditional salute to the bride. With social matters the District Commissioner has a great deal to do. They range from the lady with aspirations, who desires to be invited to an official reception, to impressing upon the head of some religious community that a schismatic member of his congregation must nevertheless be buried in the communal cemetery. Sometimes I am even asked whether an archimandrite takes precedence over an archdeacon, and should both, even if young men, be given the courtesy title of 'The Venerable'.

With three faiths competing for primacy religion was always to the fore of Keith-Roach's work. It brought its own peculiar problems:

For Moslems and Jews a day starts at sunset. For Christians at midnight. There are three days of rest weekly. Each of the three Faiths has eight official days of holiday annually when all the banks close. There are four calendars. Therefore for half the year, I never have a complete staff. The only holiday common to all communities is the birthday of His Majesty the King. Except on this day our offices are always open. Our practical and personal authority is considerable, and the officer, Palestinian or British, in charge of a sub-district probably wields a wider influence over members of the public than any other individual servant of the Palestine Government. Work may be arduous, but it is never dull. As one village wrote, either with truth or unconscious humour, on a banner hung up across the road when I was visiting it for the first time: 'Welcome to our Pasha: God help our Government'.

The years of service eventually took their toll. Climate, tension, overwork – some of the usual afflictions of the British overseas:

A decision concerning myself had to be made. Years of over-work in the Northern District had left their mark. One hot day in 1935 I was driving up from Tiberias with my secretary when suddenly I was caught at the throat by a spasm of a kind never experienced before. With difficulty I drew up the car and fought this unknown affliction. Asthma! It had me in its grasp. During my last months at Haifa I had to sit up every night in a chair: the damp, sticky climate became unbearable. After my return to Jerusalem I had had continuous attacks and I could often hardly walk up the office stairs. So it seemed in the interests of the service better to leave after my third extension of service. It was a difficult decision to make and when I had taken it I realised what a privilege had been mine to serve so long the Holy City.

He had served for thirty-four years in the East. His leaving was marked with speeches, ceremonies, gifts, and receptions. For a brief period enmities were forgotten and members of the two communities who had tried to kill him expressed a kind of sadness at his going. But it was after all the biblical features of Jerusalem and the Holy Land, not the political realities, which enchanted him and remained his last memories:

The calm and space of the Haram al-Sharif, the lamentations by the Wailing Wall, Calvary flooded with candle light, the figures which people each scene, Orthodox Jew, bearded Greek and hooded Armenian. The Muslim divine, together with the ordinary folk living in an extraordinary place.

The City fades as the sun sinks behind her crenallated walls; then turrets and towers, minarets and spires, and finally, domes of mosques, synagogues and churches, detach themselves and stand out for brief minutes like a train of camels on the skyline. The stony track wanders through scattered patches of cultivation dotted with old, old olive trees, and past a sheltered nook where fig trees grow.

The Russian Church in Gethsemane reflects the setting sun. The bells crash out and die away; others from across the valleys respond. A muezzin calls to prayer. A shepherd passes by, playing his pipe. Night falls and Jerusalem remains in the memory.

A sense of humour

The British took out with them to the empire a certain sense of humour, usually incomprehensible to others. Some jokes were good, many were racial some were relics of public school nonsense and prejudices. In Palestine the opportunities for anti-Jewish jokes were too obvious to miss and such mockery of Jewish mores was not considered improper at the time. It was said, for example, that the motto of a newly formed Jewish regiment in the British army was 'No advance without security; no charge without overcharge'.

The Dead Sea area with its Biblical notoriety was the cause of a certain amount of merriment amongst the more irreverent British troops. Its waters were believed to be particularly efficacious:

DEAD SEA SALINE or MOTHER LOT'S OLD-ESTABLISHED APERIENT
This famous beverage of the Desert Corps E.E.F. clears the system, promotes great functional activity; expedites (and even anticipates) leave.

It is far better, cheaper and easier to procure than Apenta, Runyadi Janos and other offensive enemy waters; and is wholly drawn from that bright and sparkling British body of water formerly known as das Totes Meer. It is guaranteed to clear out anything. It cleared out Sodom; also Gomorrah. Quite recently the Turk and the Hun have been effectively cleared out. Try a wine-glassful before breakfast. It will work wonders. Try it in your whisky or beer. You may not like it at first, but you will be astonished at the results! Try it on your friends. Try it in your bath; you cannot sink. Worth a guinea a bottle. Our price, 1 Piastre at the drink, bottles extra from the N.A.C.B., Jerusalem. For prices in bulk apply O.C. Dead Sea Post, E.E.F. Palestine.

Also in crystallised form. Of this preparation 'Staff Officer' writes: 'I have tried several grains when reading German and Turkish official communiques and find digestion much promoted.' 'Gunner' writes: 'Have placed it on the tails of vultures and cormorants about Jericho with great success. Have now a large ornithological colleciton.'

None but genuine bottles and packages bearing a vignette portrait of Miss Dora Lot, the Belle of Gomorrah, famous far and wide as 'Dead Sea Dora' (Registered Trade-Mark).

The area with its hot, barren salt wastes was later improbably established as a tourist resort. Keith-Roach helped to launch it:

An hotel and health resort were established at the northern end of the Dead Sea and named Kallish, the Hebrew name for potash. I was asked to inaugurate it, and having been offered and partaken of bread and salt at the threshold at the subsequent luncheon I said that undoubtedly this was the most important social event that had taken place in that region since the destruction of Sodom and Gomorrah. This remark hit the popular imagination and when they created a nine-hole golf club there they called the Club 'the Sodom and Gomorrah Golfing Society' and invited me to be the first President.

Sir Henry Gurney, chief secretary of Palestine, wrote a letter describing the activities and rules of this unique golf club, particularly applicable in times of unrest:

The Society's course is a low one, being situated at 1300 feet below sea-level on the shores of the Dead Sea and being composed entirely of sand, salt and a few stones. On this admirable links we compete every year at Christmas for a trophy known as Lot's Wife. Incidentally it must have been very annoying for this woman always to be known as someone else's wife and never to have a name of her own, but the fact is that we've never been told what her name was. She was originally a beautiful girl modelled in salt, but one year the winner took her to an unsuitable climate where her figure got so old-fashioned that she had to be rebuilt in marble, which gave rise to rumours that the British had no intention of leaving Palestine anyhow.

As the course is a bit out of the way and not without its excitements, you need an armed escort. Some of the wilder hitters carry Verey lights but on the fairway itself any sort of firearm is really enough, though one year a member did get kidnapped out of a bunker near the seventh green and was away for three days. Some people said it was because he was excavating without a permit from the Department of Antiquities.

It's surprising how a few bullets overhead help to keep your head down. Sometimes there is an aeroplane flying at 500 feet below sea level but if you start thinking about this you won't be able to concentrate. When we came to revise the rules of the Society recently we found it necessary to adopt some of the latest definitions in the Palestine glossary, such as:

Law and Order – a condition in which no more than fifty bullets pass a given point in one hour in any direction. Among the Jews the phrase is used for a state of affairs in which any number of bullets travel in any time in the direction of the Arabs. Among the Arabs the term is not widely known.

Dissidents – people over whom it is useful to be able to say you have no control.

Gurney went on from the specifics of the golf course to describe the more general situation in Palestine:

Palestine, as you know, is full of uncertainties. The first thing you have to do here in Jerusalem is to find out in which particular century anyone else is living. There are people who still think it's the Middle Ages and claim to have been living in the same house for 1700 years. To us it is 1947, but the Jews are in 5707 and the Arabs have it that it's 1366. When a witness before our United Nations Committee produced a map showing the whereabouts of the population in the year 3000 BC the Committee were visibly impressed and no official comment was offered on this piece of factual evidence. On the other hand there are several people living in the next century or two and much ahead of the facts, such as some politicians and press correspondents. So we have given up bothering very much about what year it is, and anyway many of the things that happen in Palestine would be unusual at any time.

As there are also three official languages (English, Arabic and Hebrew) a large part of the population are more or less continuously engaged in translating. But the strain of this is relieved by the existence of three holidays a week; Friday for the Moslems, Saturday for the Jews and Sunday for the others. The authorities hope that the Palestine problem will be solved before anyone else accustomed to holidays on Monday or Thursday wants to come here.

Nearly all problems have answers, but no one has yet discovered an answer for the Palestine one, and that is why there are more facts and statistics about Palestine than about any other place of its size. If all the books of statistics prepared for the nineteen commissions that have had a shot at the problem were placed on top of one another they would reach as high as the King David Hotel. You can tell from them exactly how many Jewish boys with blue eyes whose parents exported grapefruit to Syria in 1946 now attend Arab schools and vice versa. It seems a pity that from all these figures and graphs and diagrams no one has yet been able to discover what they prove.

You can get most things in Palestine if you care to pay for them: what are short are such things as tempers and accommodation for mental patients. There is also a scarcity of wives, since all the British ones were exported to make room for the Secretariat staff of commissions of inquiry and on what are known as security grounds. These grounds occur frequently and have something to do with a few malcontents variously known as terrorists (by the civil), thugs (by the Army) and Fighters for Freedom (by themselves). They are a great nuisance to everyone and get denounced from time to time.

Every now and then we have a Solution and the next few years are occupied in showing up the mistakes in it, so that by the time the next one comes you can't imagine how anybody could ever have thought of the one before. There are no prizes and nobody's decision is final. When you eat your Jaffa orange this year you will know that it comes to you with the compliments of the only official body on which Arabs and Jews consent to sit together. Arab oranges are so remarkably like Jewish ones that you can't really tell them apart. Railwaymen like the orange season because the growers arrange for fewer mines to be placed on the track than at other times of the year when the trains may be carrying less valuable traffic such as the military. Dislike of the railway often leads people to extremes – passengers have been known to get out and blow up the station. This has a most accelerating effect on the train and disposes of a lot of encumbrances like signals and station masters.

Riotous behaviour

The peace of the Holy Land was often shattered by unholy disturbances – Jew against Arab, Arab against Jew, both against the British. Rioting started early on and continued until the last days of the Mandate. Keith-Roach's baptism was instantaneous:

I was nearly killed in the riots at Eastertide (1920). Coming away from the Basilica of the Holy Sepulchre about midday on Easter Sunday I ran into some Arabs who were attacking Jews. Seeing a big Arab about to hurl a stone at a Jew I called upon an Arab policeman to help me arrest him, but the policeman faded away and I suddenly realised that I was in the midst of a hostile mob and could count on no support from the partially trained police. I seized two Arabs who were molesting a Jew, but the only reward I got was to be severely bitten on both hands by the assailants' lady friends who came to their aid. Then I saw an enormous Moslem heaving a stone, so I collared him and brought him along the domed lane towards the Damascus Gate. As we were nearing the Gate, he called lustily upon God and the Prophet to defend him and demanded aid from passers-by. One Arab gentleman took a running hit at me over the head with an iron bar which I managed to divert at the expense of a badly bruised left arm. At this stage Captain Archie Cresswell came to my assistance; I could just get one arm free to blow my whistle and some soldiers came running up rattling the bolts of their rifles. I asked them not to shoot and we managed to get our man safely into prison.

The roar of a mob when it is really out for blood produces a nasty feeling, and, although I have heard it several times, when it begins there is always the same kind of sensation in the stomach that an earthquake creates; yet it is extraordinary how quickly the brain readjusts itself to the situation. Indeed the more the situation deteriorates the cooler the brain becomes and it works far better than at any other time.

Jerome Farrell was working in the Education Department under Humphrey Bowman when further riots broke out in 1929. Once again everyone was attacking everyone else and there were some very serious incidents. The British were unprepared and enrolled all and sundry as specials and soldiers:

About half past twelve on Friday the 23rd of August 1929, as I was working in the office on Mt. Zion outside the city wall, I gradually became aware of noise and shouting at no great distance. Across the valley towards the Montefiore cottages some dozens of fellahin were prancing, yelling, waving heavy sticks and beating upon the closed doors and shutters of the houses. It did not appear that the attackers were then in a state of uncontrollable fury but rather that they were shouting to maintain their courage until worked up into a proper condition of irresponsibility.

After telling my Chief, the Director of Education, that there was a riot I went back to my room, changed into old clothes, khaki helmet, slacks and jacket, to look like uniform, took a pistol and went to the Police Headquarters where we were immediately issued with rifles, bandoleers and revolvers. This was about 4 o'clock.

The volunteers were sent off to various parts of the country on patrol and were caught in a number of incidents, attacks on both sides, and deaths:

The valleys were full of mist and we could see little of the countryside on the way out. On the return journey the weather had cleared and all seemed peaceful. Later in the day, when I was occupied elsewhere, there was fighting about the Jewish settlements on this road outside Jerusalem. Best, a Government Immigration Officer, was killed and another special was seriously wounded. The latter was a theological student from Wycliffe Hall at Oxford. The Principal of Wycliffe Hall, Graham-Brown, with about forty of his young men, was then on a holiday tour of the Holy Land and saw the beginning of the riots at noon on the Friday. He paraded his party and called for volunteers. All but one or two responded. The abstainers were conscientious pacifists. Only a young and healthy English crank could volunteer to save Jews from massacre by doing clerical work, as did one ordinand who was wearing the Amalgamation blazer of my own College. I reported him in writing to the Master. The volunteers were then marched up to the police barracks. This welcome reinforcement, which could not have been reckoned upon, almost doubled the number of special constables enrolled in the first hours of the troubles. But the utility of the Wycliffites was not merely in their numbers; they were young and nearly all had been trained to arms in their school or University OTCs. Of the other specials the majority had seen war service but lacked the fire of youth. These were British Government officers of all grades from Departmental chiefs to second-division clerks, employees of commercial firms and engineers from the Electric Light Station then under construction. There were also a few Public School boys home for the holidays.

Some of the English school boys were employed to patrol the suburb where most of the British families lived, a dull duty; but one Reptonian, aged sixteen, was allowed by an indulgent father to go everywhere and see everything. He had come straight from camp on Salisbury Plain and wore his OTC uniform. As he was of sturdy physique and a good shot, the police put no obstacle in his way. After the riots were over he was reported to the Commandant of Police by a Jewish resident in Tell Pioth for brutal language or behaviour, but he had then returned to school in England so that no disciplinary action could be taken in Palestine. The complainant was advised to write to the Headmaster of Repton. The Jews were not always very quick or reasonable in obeying police orders, and being by nature sensitive, resented the rough language which they sometimes provoked. Indeed it was said of them that they preferred to be killed courteously than be protected discourteously.

Thus was the British Empire protected by electricians, schoolboys and Anglican ordinands. The men of Wycliffe Hall did well in several engagements. The next day Farrell moved out of Jerusalem to investigate other incidents:

We moved off to the Nablus road in two touring cars. The driver of mine was just down from Cambridge. He was Campbell McInnes, son of the Anglican Bishop in Jerusalem. The car was the Bishop's and was emblazoned with mitres on the panels. In this episcopal war-chariot we proceeded slowly northwards, halting to examine everyone on the road. Not since the Crusades has the Church been so openly militant.

The regular soldiers who helped to put down the trouble were young and inexperienced in dealing with rioters. They tended to shoot first and think second. This led to some tragic mistakes, some less than tragic:

Early in the disturbances a body of troops detrained after dark at Jerusalem station and a detachment set off down the Bethlehem Road to garrison Tell Pioth, the Jewish settlement. No civil guide accompanied them. On the way they saw that a lantern was being waved in their right rear, clearly by an enemy signaller. The detachment opened fire. The bullets passed over the main body which was forming up in the open space outside the station, and the OC at once deployed into a defensive position behind an earth bank. Our Captain could not have bettered it so far. But before any casualties resulted it was found that the enemy signaller was a shunter on a railway siding.

The second incident was more tragic. When the troops first marched towards Colonia, about five miles down hill from Jerusalem, they were approaching a place where there was known to have been very recent trouble. The population was mixed, Arabs and Jews, and among the latter were armed specials whose credentials perhaps, had not been closely examined. All were in a very nervous state. Seeing the troops approach, an old Arab, who had been employed during the Turkish regime in the British Consulate, sent out his servant on to the road to wave a toy Union-Jack in welcome. He waved the flag and the soldiers at once shot him dead as an enemy signaller.

The third incident, like the first, had a happier ending. As more troops arrived from Egypt and Malta, a small motorized column was sent from Jaffa northwards and inland across the coastal plain to Tulkarm, which in earlier troubles had had a reputation for turbulence. No British civilian was found to accompany the force but the District Commissioner sent off an ex-Turkish infantry officer, Afif Atut, who was employed as Inspector of Arab Education under the Mandatory Government. He travelled in the leading car with the Commanding Officer of the Column. As they approached Tulkarm they saw a dark mass of people standing on a rise and the officer began to prepare for action. Afif told me that the column was about to deploy and open machine-gun fire. He offered to go over to the people on the rising ground and enquire their intentions. When he reached them he found that the Mayor amd Corporation with an assembly of leading citizens, had come to welcome the troops and to entertain them with roast mutton and rice.

Keith-Roach was also involved in quelling the disturbances, upbraiding the leaders, arresting gunmen and generally showing the flag:

Accompanied by the Christian Arab District Officer and a Palestinian police officer I visited the Arab village of Kalonieh which lay just off the main road to Jaffa. It was a splendid site, both for its own defence and for the inhabitants to attack Motza (a Jewish colony) where we stopped near a burning cowshed belonging to a fine old Jew, Broza; the moaning of the cows that had been without water for forty-eight hours and not been milked was piteous. As we were standing talking a shot came from the Arab village and hit the wall at our feet. I had recently read that in some International Sports a Russian lady, who rejoiced in the name of Popover, had won the high jump. She woud have had little chance against my District Officer on this occasion. Without a run he must have sprung five feet in the air and came down on his feet in a crouching position with his head against the wall. He presented such a ludicrous picture that I laughed until the tears ran. I proposed that we three walk up the hill and interview the turbulent villagers. This however was too much and they accompanied me at a very long distance behind. However, despite a few badly aimed shots, I got into the village, sent for the Mukhtar and elders and then gave them such a 'ticking off' that they delivered over to me three armed men whom I took away as hostages. We had no more trouble from that village and a military round-up next day became unnecessary.

At Ain Karem, a village where, tradition says, the Angel Gabriel appeared to the Virgin Mary, the villagers were organising looting parties. So we called there on the way back to Jerusalem with the hostages in the back of the car. While I was addressing the villagers an Arab gentleman dressed in flowing robes edged his way to the front, folded his arms and looked at me in a truculent manner. I decided it was time for action. Shifting my feet so as to get the weight well poised, I suddenly shot out and took him in the jaw and as he fell to the ground continued my harangue. He turned out to be a lawyer. Far from bearing malice we always afterwards used to shake hands warmly when we met.

SEVEN

A GALLERY OF CHARACTERS IN PALESTINE

The high commissioners

The situation in Palestine threw up a gallery of characters and situations which lightened a generally gloomy picture. Relationships among many kinds of different men were often good although the common anti-semitism of the time and other racial attitudes were never far from the surface. At the top of the pile were the six high commissioners and some of our authors give thumbnail sketches of their more informal side. First came Herbert Samuel (1920–5) chosen, as a Jew, to initiate the policy of the Jewish national home in the teeth of Arab opposition. He sought above all, however, to be fair. Keith-Roach wrote of him:

Sir Herbert could be extremely frigid as well as extremely human. At his office table and in discussion he was often icily cold and almost repelled those in front of him by the isolation of his manner. At other times, such as visiting quarters of towns and villages, when those with him thought a little special dignity and aloofness were required he would disregard both and assume an almost unnatural attitude of 'hail fellow well met' with everyone.

The hidden warmth of his character came out when he was playing with children; then he would throw aside his mask and reveal the real man. He had a fund of games and anecdotes, which children loved and my wife and children and I have spent many a merry evening with Nebi, Geoffrey and Nancy Samuel and their parents. Sir Herbert was a dark haired, fresh complexioned impressive man of soldierly bearing. In repose he had rather a moody face with a searching yet almost furtive expression, but his whole countenance lighted up when he smiled. One never went to him with a problem without coming away the gainer. He arrived to take up his appointment dressed in the tropical uniform of a Privy Counsellor or Colonial Governor, a white jacket with gold braid on collar and cuffs, and a white steel-spiked helmet upon his head. His photograph in this uniform was broadcast far and wide and was immediately bought up by the Jews all over the country. A small carpet factory had just been established in the Holy City by some oriental Jews. What better subject could be portrayed in wool than Sir Herbert Samuel? So the High Commissioner had to suffer silently in the knowledge that some scores of small mats were being woven, his helmeted head the centrepiece surrounded by a majenta and yellow background. They were popular and found a ready sale. Some years later I was in Damascus and saw hanging over the large mirror in the shop of a Moslem hair-dresser one of these mats. I was somewhat surprised to see it there and walked into the shop and asked the old Moslem if he knew whose portrait it was. He appeared to be amazed at my ignorance and said: 'What! By Allah, do you not know who that is? That is Mustapha Kamal – the Ataturk.'

After Samuel came a more military man in the form of Field Marshal Lord Plumer of Messines. As Keith-Roach reported:

Lord and Lady Plumer arrived in August. And here I must digress.

In Turkish times the foreign Consuls in Jerusalem had lived in an atmosphere of pretentious splendour. They wore uniform upon all possible occasions, and when they went officially to a religious service or to call upon the Governor they were preceded by kawasses dressed in Turkish costumes, voluminous trousers, gold-embroidered short coat and hussar jacket of blue cloth and gold thread. Each kawass was armed with a six foot silver headed staff shod with heavy iron, with which he struck the ground every second time his left foot touched the ground.

Upon the Occupation the two ex-British Consular kawasses were transferred to Government House and the same style of dress was maintained except that they were now clothed in scarlet and wore a little more gold upon their jackets.

On the day of Plumer's arrival he was met at the railway station by the principal officers of Government and by the religious and social heads of the communities. We were drawn up in line, when in came the train and down stepped the noble Lord, dressed in the khaki uniform of a Field Marshal. Behind him came Lady Plumer in a light grey satin dress of the Queen Alexandra period and perched on top of her head a large hat with high waving plumes. He looked a quiet grandfather; she a commanding general. The Chief Justice was presented and they started through the ranks to walk towards a small dais from which Lord Plumer could address the assembly, when crash went the two staves on the stone platform, the gorgeously apparrelled kawasses striking the harder in honour of the day. Two fine blows thundered down the platform and resounded under the station roof. Lady Plumer's hat quivered; her features expressed extreme surprise; the Baron met the blows more stoically but his hand went up and clasped his walrus moustache. Two steps forward and another clang shook the roof. Surprise gave way to amazement, and gradually amazement to humour, and by the time Lord and Lady Plumer reached the dais to receive those to be presented, Lady Plumer was twitching and shaking with fun so that she nearly collapsed upon her husband who was himself suffering from an acute attack of shingles.

The presentations over, the Field Marshal delivered the shortest speech yet made in Palestine. After a pleasant reference to Sir Herbert Samuel he added 'Lady Plumer and I come among you as strangers. We hope when I come to leave, we shall leave you as friends. We thank you "for your welcome".'

Plumer stayed for three years during which time he devoted himself to his job even to the point of ill health:

He displayed selfless devotion to duty, and he was ably assisted by his wife. He had given the last ounce of his strength in the service of the State. He loved playing bridge and gradually it became the custom for me [Keith-Roach] to have an hour with him every Tuesday night for 'shop' and then stay on to dinner and play bridge at a penny a hundred until half past ten. When younger people came to dine he and his wife played roulette heartily for infinitesimal stakes.

A rather pretentious system had been introduced to Palestine by an aide-de-camp of Sir Herbert Samuel, and it has since been followed by other High Commissioners. When guests are invited to dine at Government House they are lined up in the drawing-room, the doors are flung open and 'His Excellency the High Commissioner for Palestine and Lady' are announced in stentorian tones by the Aide-de-Camp, and then the High Commissioner goes solemnly round the gathering and each guest's name is called out while he shakes hands. Such pretension to vice-regal standing was unthinkable to the Plumers; when they invited people to dine with them both were to be found at the drawing-room door to receive their guests, who quickly realised that they had been invited to dine in a gentleman's house. Once a year, on the King's Birthday, Lord Plumer held a Levée and then, naturally, he was announced with due and fitting ceremony.

He was a keen supporter of cricket and every summer Sunday, after church, he went to the Sports Club to watch the local match. He told me the two things he valued most among all the honours he had received in life were the Presidency of the M.C.C. and the cricket ball presented to him after the last match he saw played at the Club.

The next to try his luck as high commissioner was John Chancellor:

Lieutenant-Colonel Sir John Robert and Lady Chancellor arrived early in

December. Governorship was no untrodden road to him. He had already had fifteen years' experience in Mauritius, Trinidad and Southern Rhodesia. He had an unpropitious start. His aide-de-camp was killed in an aeroplane accident just before he was due to leave England.

Keith-Roach reports that it was decided to hold a reception for him in a large tent at the Jaffa Gate. The occasion did not go as well as hoped, which could also be said of Chancellor's period in Palestine:

The five hundred guests were all fitted in, not only in order of precedence, but also by careful ticketting organised in communities and departments as well; a complete chessboard, but so arranged that each individual without much difficulty could be brought up and presented. I had had the canvas walls hidden by flags and oriental hangings. The day arrived with the first rains of the season; and a violent storm broke. The road from the station to the Jaffa Gate was slippery and one of the police escort horses slipped and fell in front of the carriage. Arrived at the tent Sir John and his wife were blown about and when they got inside it the rain-water trickled down on his immaculate uniform and Lady Chancellor caught a cold. I presented five hundred guests and remembered all their names, titles and distinctions without mistake, except that by an odd freak of memory I forgot the name of the American Consul and his wife, with whom I had been dining the night before!

The next morning the Government House butler, who had married Lady Plumer's maid, on stepping out of a hairdresser's shop after being shaved, fell down an unprotected area nearby and striking his head on the wall as he fell was killed instantly.

Sir John was an imposing man with graying hair and well defined regular features. He was strikingly handsome in uniform, his unwrinkled countenance giving an impression of a good-looking Shakespearean actor. He was not pleased with Palestine. He had hated the cold wind and discomfort of the tent; he disliked his temporary dwelling as well as the quarter in which it was situated; the fact that the Arabic Press because of the good rains acclaimed him as 'Green-Footed' did little to mollify his opinion.

Sir John was an experienced and first rate administrator, and his leaving after three years' service in Palestine was a loss to the country. But he was glad to go. He had been but indifferently housed most of the time and undoubtedly he missed the somewhat spacious days of his previous governorships. He had been troubled by problems of unemployment and disliked the era of constant strife. Lady Chancellor was a charming lady of slight physique and gentle grace.

Sir Arthur Wauchope and Sir Harold Macmichael, the fourth and fifth high commissioners respectively, were very different personalities, each creating their own atmosphere at Government House. Keith-Roach again gives the account:

Lieutenant-General Sir Arthur Wauchope arrived to assume the post of High Commissioner. The offer had come to him as a bolt from the blue! He had commanded the Black Watch in the War, and from 1924 to 1927 was British military representative on the Allied Commission of control to Berlin although he did not know the German language and did not acquire it. He left command of the troops in Northern Ireland as a Major-General to come to Palestine.

A tiny, wizened man with long silver hair waving in the breeze, he was continuously looking into space with his mouth open and head cocked to one side so that he bore out the popular idea of a poet. He was amazingly active and tireless for a man of fifty-seven and quite unperturbed by the difficulties and responsibilities of the post. In a short time he was to reveal an iron constitution and will and had everybody guessing by his intolerance and charm, by his bursts of temper, by his calculating shrewdness and his inconsistencies. He was what the Scots call 'fey'.

Sir Arthur was a genius at gardening, and early and late was planning the grounds at Government House. He collected roots, bulbs and seeds of every flower in Palestine, and had them planted on the hill. Most have taken root. A score of prisoners were brought up every day to hoe and plant and water. From a barren hillside in five years he made a beauty spot. Government House grounds remain a lasting memory to his determination, knowledge, judgment and taste.

And so Sir Arthur Wauchope left us a Jekyl and Hyde. Jekyl was so devoted to Palestine, her mountains, her beaches, her trees; a perfect host; so extraordinarily generous to persons in trouble; a liberal patron of the arts; such a lover of beauty, of music and of nature. Officials saw more of Mr. Hyde. Five years before he had left John Bull's Other Island to create, some said, Little Arthur's England.

With the arrival of Palestine's fifth High Commissioner, Sir Harold Macmichael, came a complete change at Government House. A poor man was replacing a rich man. Gone were the replicas of old masters from the dining-room; the arched cubby holes let into the white walls no longer held choice pieces in bronze, wood or glass, but were filled with heads of African deities carved in hard black woods. In the drawing-room maps replaced landscapes. Embroideries and carpets no longer hung down from the minstrel gallery. The bookshelves no longer housed the poets, but cheap editions of crime novels. Sir Harold found his recreation in reading every crime and mystery novel published, and in billiards and in cutting down trees. Gone were the spacious days when the goblet rang and the music of harpsichord and violin were heard and visitors flocked to and fro. 'MacMic' had been known as the outstanding civil servant in the Sudan, and after filling the post of Civil Secretary he had passed on to be the Governor of Tanganyika. A Classical scholar with a vein of shrewdness and cynicism he has never allowed his heart to rule his mind. He was as firm as a rock and a great strength at the back of his officers. He had always been a quiet, cold dignified man who liked to be left alone with his books, his writings and his corncob pipes. Marriage, two daughters and governorship had made no difference in his mode of life. Years of training had made him a stickler for form in official minute and method. He cut himself off almost altogether from contact with people, but did everything through his Chief Secretary.

His wife, Nesta, was a great hustler and became very active in every kind of social endeavour. The spinning of local wool became her battlecry until, during the war, the Red Cross claimed her.

Oh you English!

Whether such men were the correct ones to run Palestine is a moot point. They did not solve the problem but matters were probably beyond solution. The remoteness of Macmichael could not have impressed the more open and emotional Jews and Arabs. The stiff upper lip misled some into thinking that the British were all cold fish. Keith-Roach reported an occasion during the second war when the mayor and municipal council of Jerusalem came to see him:

I had given up smoking for the war, but with difficulty had surmounted the urge to smoke a cigarette that morning as I walked about my office thinking of the many things it would be necessary to do. Then Their Worships were announced. So we sat down and I gave them the traditional coffee and cigarettes and mentioned the measures that might have to be taken as regards supplies and rationing because of the probability of the Mediterranean being closed. They were perturbed. Suddenly the Mayor, Mustapha Bey, jumped up, held his hands clenched to the side of his head and almost screamed in his intensity of emotion: 'Oh you English! Why don't you show some emotion? England is left alone to fight and you show nothing.' Little did he realize the depth of my feelings!

The last chief secretary of Palestine, Sir Henry Gurney, had the appearance of imperturbability to the n-th degree. He served at the end of the Mandate and his calm infuriated the Jews, particularly that earlier iron lady Golda Meir. She was once discussing Gurney's coolness with another British official:

'Yes', she said 'that was why we hated him. No one in that position had any right to be unruffled. He ought to have been pacing his room day and night, trying to find a solution to the Jewish problem. It was our objective to ruffle people but we could not make any impression on him.'

Some Jews and some Arabs

There was Mr Ussishkin of the Jewish National Fund whom Keith-Roach writes about:

Stolid, unimaginative, Menachem Ussishkin was more accustomed to everyday clothes than to evening dress. In Palestine, like elsewhere on the Continent, a dinner jacket is called: "a smoking". On a visit to England Menachem and his wife were invited to dinner at the Trocadero with some representative body of Jews. As his wife and he reached the top of the stairs leading to the private room where the dinner was to be given he was confronted by a notice: "No smoking". So, in the belief that this applied to his recently acquired dinner jacket he took his wife back to his hotel and changed.

Two mysterious Jews in Haifa were causing some disquiet in 1944 by reports of their activities. Sir Patrick Coghill, head of British security in Syria, relates the following:

These stories were vaguely sinister – but quite impalpable. You could not put your finger on anything and yet they left a feeling of doubt and suspicion. Arthur Giles, the head of the C.I.D. in Palestine, had heard these stories and off he went to Haifa to investigate. The trail led to two Jews of Dutch origin about whom the police had no records of any sort and as such could be assumed in normal circumstances to be blameless citizens – so Giles decided on a friendly call to test the ground. The pair were pleasant to meet and showed no trace of anxiety, so Giles said quite bluntly that he had come to see them as he had heard odd stories about their activities. These, he said, were probably quite harmless, but in War he could take no risks and he must ask them to tell him what their commercial or other activities were.
They replied, 'We are chemists.'
Giles then said, 'What sort of Chemists? Analytical? Consultant? Manufacturing? Cash?'
'We are manufacturing chemists.'
'Well, what do you make? A manufacturing chemist can make all sorts of dangerous things and there is a war on.'
'It is extraordinarily difficult to explain what we make.'
'I'm sorry – but you must explain.'
'But we want to explain, but it really is terribly difficult to explain.'

'Look here – I have been extremely lenient and easy with you so far and most informal. If you don't come clean and explain what you are up to, you will force me to become most official and turn the heat on.'

'But we *do* want to explain . . . But perhaps this will explain . . . You know big stores like Marks and Spencer where there is always a department for cheap leather goods – or so-called leather – most imitation – But all through that department there is a beautiful scent of the best morocco leather. You know that, please?'

'Yes, of course I know it. But I don't see . . .'

'Please, we make the smell!'

Keith-Roach, rather uncharacteristically once tried to embarrass an Arab major by staging an early version of Clochemerle:

We help Municipal bodies in varying ways, from criticising their budgets to arranging receptions. I had induced the Municipal Council to construct a public lavatory for men and women near Zion Square in the centre of the New City to meet what provincial papers describe as 'a long felt want'. It had cost some four thousand pounds and was fitted up according to Shanks' best specifications. The Council, as it neared completion, was justly proud of the latest addition to civic utilities. The new Mayor, a Moslem, came to see me about the opening. He felt a little diffident about it, yet thought such mark of progress should not pass unheralded. His Worship caught me when I was in a frivolous mood and although I had had little experience of similar events I remembered once having seen in a French comic paper a drawing of a local Mayor, assisted by the members of the town council and accompanied by the town brass band and a handful of spectators, performing a like ceremony. All that could be seen of the Mayor were His Worship's legs from the feet to the knees and his head and top hat. So, speaking in Arabic I gravely drew His Worship's attention to the precedent set in France, and hinted that that appeared to be the accepted ceremonial. Shocked, and frightened that he might be called upon to perform a similar rite, His Worship beat a hasty retreat: for once a public building was opened without speeches.

Keith-Roach also tells of a Muslim cleric who had been trained in Cairo:

After the British occupation he obtained the job of 'Khatib' (preacher) in the town of his birth at a small monthly stipend. My friend the 'Khatib,' finding the job of reading in the Mosque and exhorting the pious not sufficiently lucrative, attached himself to the Mufti as his 'echo' and for many years his rascally old head, adorned with a tarbush wound round with many yards of beautiful white cloth, was always seen in the Mufti's company. The Mufti was gathered to his forefathers, and his satellite hoped to attain the vacant post.

So he asked me to obtain for him the post of Mufti. It was impossible to accede to his request and for five years I did not see him. On my return as Commissioner in 1931 I met the old reprobate. By this time he had become a person of some affluence. At least he had married a second wife; his family consisted now of thirteen persons; the small one-storied house that he had inherited from his father had grown until it consisted of four more storeys. Did I forget to mention that he had been made trustee of funds for some pious foundations? And, after all, man's first duties are towards his family! I went and had tea with him one day.

While I was sitting in state, surrounded by red plush divans, sipping tea, two naked children, the twin offspring of the recently acquired second wife, were carrying out the calls of nature but a few feet away while various ladies of the household peeped through the door. I noticed an enlarged photograph, more than life size, of the old man hanging on the wall and surrounded by a most flamboyant and gaudy frame. He informed me that the frame had cost him £P.3; but, alas, the photograph had cost him five! I told him how well these small sums had been invested. He replied that a couple of years before he had gone to the passport office to get a passport to go to Egypt, first paying two shillings to a nearby shopkeeper to have his photograph taken for the passport; he thought no more about it. Some months later he was interviewed by some influential Moslems who demanded of him whether he knew that there was a coloured portrait of himself in a shop window, surrounded top, sides and bottom by portraits of Jewish women in very decolleté dress? Horrified at this exposure of his undoubted weakness he rushed to the shop and found the story was all too true. He demanded of the Jewish proprietor that he should immediately remove his photograph from the window. The Jew however refused and said that he had enlarged the portrait; he had had it coloured; it was a good advertisement, and the only condition on which he would remove it was that the holy man should purchase it for five pounds. Weeks went by; public opinion in his own circle raged against him; his wives visited the window; the Jew remained firm and he was bound to give way, and hence the purchase. For after all 'business is business' and many are the ways in which money is made in the Holy Land.

A wreath of funerals

More surprisingly funerals provided considerable comic relief. The large number of sects in Palestine meant that many different traditions of burial and mourning were followed. Financial considerations played yet again a not inconsiderable part. Keith-Roach revelled in funerals:

While many of us in Palestine eschew banks and still bury money in the ground, we do not believe in leaving it hidden there permanently. Therefore, although we take funerals seriously, those who use coffins do not believe in throwing too much good money into the ground without hope of return. We bury our dead within twenty-four hours, so that there is none of that gloating for days over what is known as 'funeral furniture' in many parts of Europe. Burial follows death so swiftly that there is no time for elaborate measurements. In other words, to coin an expression from the cheap tailors, we buy our coffins off the peg on which they are hung up in the shops. Coffins are simply constructed. Not for us the elegant casket nor the polished oak. We are more frugal and so utilise any type of wood that is available, clothing its imperfections underneath cotton materials.

The non-Palestinian spectator obviously gets a surprise the first time he sees a little funeral procession wandering along the narrow streets; choir boys, robed in black and red, carry a couple of wobbly candle lamps fixed to the end of poles; a cross is borne between; an odour of incense is detected; the priest robed and vested follows; and then, if the deceased be a member of a Church that believes in the open coffin, a couple of young men precede the corpse carrying the coffin lid bolt upright. The front may be covered with pink and tinsel but as the lid passes by one notices stencilled in the inside across the old box boards from which it has been frugally made up such captions as: 'Buy Jaffa Oranges,' 'Huntley and Palmers Biscuits,' 'Use best solar oil,' 'Glass with care,' 'Bottled in Liverpool,' 'Keep in a cool place' or on occasion: 'Stow away from boilers'. The ashen face of the loved one may be brightened up with a circlet of flowers. My small sons were particularly heartened once at seeing the head surrounded by a chaplet of golden marigolds with a large one popped in the mouth.

The most distressing funeral I attended was during the riots of 1938, when a distinguished young Semitic scholar was murdered as he was entering his office. The whole of Jerusalem was stirred, as he was a lovable character. Owing to constant succession of speeches in the courtyard of the hospital, we left the Holy City for the Mount of Olives two hours late. The body carried in a litter was borne ahead by four unshaven, unkempt men, and finally dumped beside the grave. The grave itself was a deepish hole about a metre in circumference with a small cave dug out of the side near the bottom. Scrambling without ceremony across the adjoining graves a motley crowd of lookers-on mingled with the mourners and pressed up towards the open hole. The parents were leaning upon my arm, the broken mother alternating between prayer and invectives against the murderer. Arguments ensued between the bearers and the grave digger as to whether the dimensions of the resting place were sufficiently large for the dead man who was generously built. The body was measured with a walking stick, a mattock was produced, and while the curious crowd peered and pushed and the mother was exhorted to stop her cries and made to sip brandy and eau de cologne alternately, the sides of the hole were dug out and the little cave enlarged. At length all were satisfied and my friend was lifted up, dumped feet first into the hole, doubled over and then the head thrust into the cave and immediately there was a rattle of stones, thrown upon that part of the body which remained visible. Meanwhile the old father was hoisted up to the head of the grave and in trembling tones intoned the Kaddish for his much beloved son. The leader of the bearers, dressed in a long greasy striped coat buttoned up close to the neck, decided that the stones were not being sufficiently well rammed down; so he hopped into the grave and holding his arms down to his sides jumped rapidly up and down turning round like a teetotum upon the grave and what it contained.

When I lived in the Old City funerals of every type passed our door almost daily and our two sons used to be highly diverted and interested in the processions: in fact they became almost authorities on the subject. But the Orthodox Greek Patriarch's funeral ceremony is almost unique because he is buried sitting in a Chair. After death His Beatitude is dressed in his Easter vestments, gorgeous robes of white silk and silver, and placed in a chair before rigor mortis has set in, and carried for burial on Mount Zion. Now it is very difficult to maintain even a semblance of dignity for the dead man, as the Chair is carried from the convent down a steep lane and up the Hill of Zion; for, despite a band around his throat, his head will flop from side to side, and his crown is in constant danger of being laid in the dust. As no one in the Orient has any idea of keeping a line and many desire 'to touch but the hem of his garment,' by the time the grave is eventually reached his condition may best be described as part worn.

But the best story to do with a coffin took place in the year of grace 1942. Our buses are singularly like the carriers' carts that used to visit the villages in England in the last century. When the bus is full inside 'jump up on the roof' is the general custom. Near Lejjun, on the Haifa–Jerusalem road, a young peasant signalled the bus and asked to be given a lift. After much argument, he paid the fare asked, but there was room for him only on the roof, as the bus was full up inside. Mounting the roof, he found a shiny new coffin being taken to Jerusalem and got inside for shelter from the rain. Some distance further on, two other villagers halted the bus and the large-hearted driver, for a consideration, agreed to take them if they sat on top. Clambering up, they muffled themselves in their abayas, and the vehicle rolled merrily on. Suddenly a strange thing occurred. The lid of the coffin began to rise before the horrified eyes of the outside passengers. A hand came forth gropingly and made gestures to feel if it were still raining. Shocked to the cores of their beings, the two villagers edged away, howling: 'The dead has come to life! Allahu Akbar! Save us!' And without waiting for the bus to stop, they took flying leaps to the roadside. Fortunately, they were only slightly bruised and, picking up their skirts, they rushed into the hills.

EIGHT

KEEPING THE PEACE:
PALESTINE IN REVOLT 1936–9

Soldiers of the king

The British army had a terrible time in Palestine, never really fighting, constantly engaged in riot control, stoned and shot at by all and sundry. Mostly they coped very well, taking resort in humour or spit and polish, but sometimes misbehaving disgracefully. Soldiers do not like to act as policemen. They followed a tradition of bemused service, rarely knowing who the real enemy was. During the 1936–9 Arab uprising army forces and patience were tested to the limits.

The Arabs were making a concerted effort to try to force the British government to put an end to Jewish immigration. They attacked Jewish immigrants and settlers and fought the British army whenever possible – they hid in villages and in the hills when being chased. It was virtually a national uprising and meagre British resources were stretched to a limit. Soldiers engaged in continual searches, kept roads open, chased suspected rebels.

Miss H. M. Wilson, a young British teacher, spent the year 1938–9 in Palestine in the Arab school of Bir Zeit (now a university on the West Bank) and kept a charming and detailed diary of her stay. She was in a unique position. She got to know the Arab villagers well, often meeting the rebels, and on her frequent sixteen-mile trips into Jerusalem was given lifts in British army vehicles when she heard the soldiers' side. She had an amused consciousness of belonging to both sides. Before Arab buses stopped running from Jerusalem because of the danger of attack, Miss Wilson regularly took one to Bir Zeit. On the journey passengers were usually searched for arms:

We were stopped on Mount Scopus for the usual police routine of turning out all the male passengers and searching them for arms. A British

policeman on this job had confided to me on one occasion that he regarded
it as a useless performance unless the women were searched too. The men
simply slipped their 'stuff' to the ladies, and he had seen one bulky dame
who he was sure was sitting on a machine gun! I had some proof of this
(fortunately it was not arms or ammunition, or I don't know what I should
have done) when, as the men rose to get out, a hairy brown hand came over
my shoulder from behind and dropped a roll of pound notes into my lap. I
stuffed them into the front of my dress and looked up to see which
passsenger it was who was honouring me in this way, but I couldn't be sure.
So when they had all got in again I held my hand with the notes in it
backwards over my shoulder, and hoped there wouldn't be a fight. It was all
right. I felt a single hand take them quietly.

When the buses stopped the only way to travel was to hitch lifts in a
military vehicle:

Going into Jerusalem, I got a lift one Friday in mid-November from a
detachment of the West Yorks Regiment, in a queer sort of high-walled
bullet-proof lorry. It was acting as convoy to some Jewish trucks from the
camp at kilo 41, whose drivers were in a hurry to get home in time for the
Sabbath at sunset. I had walked more than half-way to Ramallah before they
overtook me. The lorry slowed down and a soldier stuck his head out,
eyeing me as if I was an unclassifiable specimen altogether. Then he called out
'Are you English?' I shouted 'Yes', and he jumped down and saluted. A couple
of infantine-looking lads inside the steel box of a vehicle helped me to scramble
in over the back. I squatted down on a tiny wooden stool beside them.
''Ow far've you walked, Miss?' asked one.
'Four miles'.
'Cripes! just like our route marches at 'ome.'
     They went on to inform me that they were aged sixteen and seventeen. I
didn't believe it, but they certainly looked no older. I told them that I was
teaching boys of that age in an Arab school. They stared, and one of them
remarked cheerfully 'I killed a couple of Arabs yesterday.' Perhaps the
fathers of some of our children at school, I reflected. Storms of indignation
have been provoked by the rebel terrorists' method of employing Arab boys
under eighteen to shoot and kill, because under that age they are exempt
from the death penalty if they are caught. I couldn't help wondering
whether there was so much difference in employing these English lads out
here for killing.
     About the end of November I decided on a permanent technique for
getting lifts back after the week-end. This was to go and wait at the northern
boundary of Jerusalem, where a police pill-box had been set up and where
all traffic was stopped for permits to be examined. Accordingly I turned up
at the pill-box one chilly Tuesday morning at 7 a.m. and found an Irish
policeman in charge. He was sympathetic, and on my assuring him that I

didn't care a hoot what I rode in, open lorry or dust-cart, he said, 'Right you are, Miss, we'll squeeze you into something,' and brought me out a chair from the pill-box.

There came a procession of military lorries bound for Ramallah. They fitted me into the now familiar front seat with the canvas door and lent me a fine thick khaki overcoat for a wrap, as everything was open and the wind was piercing. At Ramallah there were two soldiers on traffic inspection duty at the roadside. I told them I wanted a lift on, and one of them ran ahead to a convoy of vehicles drawn up a little way in front, waiting to start for the north. He halted and saluted outside the smartest car; an Oxford accent was borne to my ears, and he came back to say 'The General will take you Miss!' I went up to the car and beheld two magnificent military personages, one of them equipped with a thoroughly intimidating monocle. He invited me to get into the front seat, and after we had started he became delightfully human and remarked that he had had to cadge lifts himself down near Sarafand. He went on to talk about safety on the roads and how hard it was to keep military movements from leaking out. A battalion set out recently to search a certain village for arms. It was all supposed to have been kept a dead secret. When they arrived they found chalked on the wall of the first house, 'Welcome the 2nd Battalion the — Regiment!'

These British soldiers, friendly enough to individuals, acquired a reputation for appalling behaviour during their searches of villages where rebels were suspected to be hiding:

Driving with the troops in this way and listening to their talk, I came to realise what probably accounted for such bad behaviour as there really was on the part of our men in villages, when due allowance has been made for rumour and exaggeration. The men were bored stiff. At lonely military outposts such as kilo 41, and even at Ramallah, there was no cinema, no recreation, and going to search a village was their one excitement. Soldiers are traditionally careless of other people's property. In houses which the troops had searched, there were signs of partial burning and wanton destruction; mattresses partly burnt, also olives, oil upset, maize half burnt and trodden into the ground. Some rooms looked as if lighted paper or matches had been thrown about. The people were not specially indignant, taking it rather as part of life's general unpleasantness. 'Turkish soldiers before 1918,' they said, 'English soldiers now. All soldiers are alike.'

Spring term 1939

British soldiers often visited the Bir Zeit village and school at night and roused teachers and villagers alike seeking suspected Arab 'rebels'. This is Miss Wilson's account again:

It was ten o'clock. I was in bed, listening to my crystal wireless set, my ears completely filled with music. Suddenly a tremendous hammering on the door penetrated even the headphones.

'Wilson! There are soldiers at the door saying they must come in. Come and see what you can do!'

It was Mary, Miss Naser's [the headmistress] sister. I jumped out of bed, scrambled into a dressing gown, and ran into the adjoining dormitory. Most of the occupants of the two long rows of white beds were sitting up, goggle-eyed. I ran on downstairs to the big barred front door. As I was lifting the first iron bar, I espied a bayonet point sticking through the crack between the two halves of the door. Next moment my attention was distracted by Latify, the school cook, who came flying across the hall with her black embroidered dress pulled on anyhow, and threw her arms round me.

'Miss Wilson! what are you doing? In Heaven's name, don't open!'

'Don't be afraid,' I said. 'It's better. They are English and I am English.' I opened the door, with Latify still clinging to me. There stood five soldiers, one of them a corporal.

'We want to search the building.'

'For rebels?'

'For any men'.

'There are none here.' I hoped to goodness there weren't. I gave my speech about Arab ideas on girls' schools and added how frightened the people were. Latify gave visible proof of that. She was shaking.

'Very good, Miss. Goodnight.' Off they went.

I wondered whether I should encamp permanently in the hall. I hung about for a few minutes, but the stone floor was chilly and recollections of bed were enticing. I went up, and was leaning out of my bedroom window trying to make out what was going on in the village, when there came hurrying footsteps once more through the dormitory and Sitt Naomi's voice at my door.

'They have taken Jayyusi and Sayid!' (two of the masters who slept down in the village). 'Come and see what you can do!'

'Where have they taken them?' I looked hurriedly round for some clothes and my electric torch.

'In their lorries – we don't know where.'

The business seemed to demand haste. I drew the line at running after lorries all the way to Ramallah. Bundling a sheepskin coat on top of my dressing-gown, I left my hair loose as it was and with my feet in bedroom slippers scampered down to the front door, out and through the gate into the road. There was a faint rumbling and I could see the tail light of a lorry disappearing. As I stood there, Sitt Naomi joined me, with her black hair also loose and wearing a thick coat covering – I didn't enquire what.

Soldiers and lorries were everywhere. The men of the village, most of them wearing the peasant's long robe and headcloth, were being marshalled in single file. One by one they were led forward and halted in a strong beam of light projected from an armoured car. A soldier pulled back the man's headcloth and held his head from behind so that the beam shone full in his face, while another standing by the car with a paper in his hand shouted 'What's your name?' The man's answer was compared with the paper, and a whispered conversation followed with the most important actor in the drama, a well-guarded personage invisible inside the armoured car. This was an Arab spy.

After the villager had been reported on by the spy he was passed on into the ranks of those who had already been 'done' and who were lined up in rows on the far side of the open ground, guarded by soldiers and shouted at if they spoke or moved. We wondered whether the masters from the school were mixed up in all this. I asked the nearest group of soldiers if I could speak to the officer in charge. They pointed me to a magnificent figure standing by one of the lorries; a six-foot Colonel wearing a khaki greatcoat with a fine sheepskin collar. Still, my coat was all sheepskin, so I didn't hesitate to go up and ask him whether he had got any of our masters and if so what was likely to happen to them. He replied, not unnaturally, that he didn't know precisely who he had got, but that if there was nothing against them they would all be let go in half an hour or so. I talked to a party of 'other ranks'. Some of them said they knew me and had given me lifts on the road. One of them asked 'Is your 'usband 'ere, mum?' indicating the crowd of villagers. When I said no, he didn't exist they began to make sniffy comments about the Arabs and asked if I wouldn't rather be in England. I said I quite definitely wouldn't at the moment, this being an experience I should never get at home. 'Eh though, Miss, these Arabs!' they went on, 'Two Englishmen could lick a hundred of them.'

Sitt Naomi was standing within earshot, and I began to fear an explosion. So we hastily started to plan a single combat, to be staged at Bir Zeit, between the Mufti and a selected champion from the British Army. At about eleven o'clock the remainder of their transport came along the road from Ramallah, and they said the show was over. Verey lights were sent up as a summons to any troops who might still be in the village. The lorries began to load up; the villagers were dismissed and streamed away along the road in ghostly white groups in the moonlight, all but seventeen of them, who were put into an empty bus to be taken to prison at Ramallah.

On this occasion the soldiers had apparently behaved well enough. On others they did not:

The chief topic of conversation at school so far this term had been the looting by our troops in villages. Everyone, staff and children, had come from the holidays full of stories. Jayyusi, one of the masters who lived at Tulkarem, told how all the people of Tulkarem had been turned out of the houses and the town left empty for the troops to search. He said 'nearly everybody' had missed something. He himself had lost money. They had complained to the Colonel in charge, but nothing had been done owing to lack of proof.

The girls used to talk about it during afternoon walks. I asked what kind of things the soldiers took, and they said silver ornaments, or spoons and forks, embroidered cloths, and men's underclothes. Sara, one of the top class whom I taught English, asked me sadly 'Why are all soldiers thieves?'

We were very soon to have an instance of it at Bir Zeit. Soldiers had come to search the village again and villagers, school people and military were jostling each other in the village square. I was hailed from the gate. Miss Naser and Sitt Naomi were standing there with a woman who was crying and pouring out some story.

'What's the matter?' I called.

'This woman says the soldiers who were searching her house have stolen twenty pounds!'

This was the worst moment yet. On reflection, it seemed best to take her at once to the officers to give evidence, before the troops left the village. Once they had gone it would be useless to do anything. Miss Naser knew the woman and said she was not likely to have invented the story. The party of eight soldiers who had been doing the searching had just marched past on their way to the Government school and to their transport. Sitt Naomi and I hurried after them. Fortunately the woman's husband, old Abu Daoud, had acted smartly. He had already, by means of the troops' interpreter, reported the theft to the adjutant. When we arrived we found the party of soldiers who had come from searching the village lined up and prevented from mixing with the others. The adjutant came to meet us, bringing the interpreter, and heard the woman's account of events, while her ten-year-old daughter, Najla, a bright looking child, was pushed forward by neighbours and declared that she knew which soldier it was: he had a pimple under one eye! The adjutant gave orders for the eight men to be taken inside the Government school and searched by their corporal. We settled down on rocks at the roadside to wait.

Next moment a soldier came towards us and shouted for Abu Daoud. We watched the old man being led up to the eight where they stood in line, a couple of hundred yards away. Evidently he was being asked to pick out his man. Then he was sent to one side and his wife was called for, and lastly the girl Najla. She was smitten with shyness and hid her face in her arms crying 'I don't want to!' I took her hand and went along with her for part of the way while she recovered confidence. She appeared to play her part all right, and after a couple of minutes the adjutant came towards us. He saluted me and began 'Well, officer!', going on to say that eighteen pound notes had been found on one of the men. The money would have to be taken to Jerusalem to be shown at the military court which would be held there, probably within a week. Abu Daoud would be summoned to attend, and would get it back then. I passed this on to Sitt Naomi, who translated to the old man. He nodded with slow dignity, and told her to ask the adjutant not to have the soldier punished. The crowd broke into exclamations of relief. Sitt Naomi cried dramatically to the world in general, 'British justice is maintained!' And so back to work, for what was left of the morning.

Miss Wilson was even nearer the action one March morning in Jerusalem:

I was on my way as usual to the pill-box at the northern boundary where I hoped to get a lift. As I was going along St George's Road, about thirty yards ahead of me an Arab was standing, leaning against the wall at the side of the pavement. I was not taking any particular notice of him, when suddenly he crouched forward and fired four shots at a man who was crossing the road a little way in front of him. As soon as he had fired he darted into a house. The man who was shot did not fall but staggered about the roadway, screaming.

My first reaction was, 'I shall either faint or be sick.' Next moment I knew I should not do either and I wondered, who has been shot? I did not dare chase the Arab, in case he still had some shots left, so I ran up to the man in the road. He was dressed in khaki and looked like a policeman going off duty, unarmed. He was very dark, with a little moustache, and I could not be sure whether he was a Jew or an Arab. There was a pool of blood in the road. I got him to lie down and put my haversack under his head, and looked round at a completely deserted street. I had an impression of a normal number of passers-by before the shooting, but now it might have been the middle of the Sahara. For what seemed like whole minutes there was nothing in the world but bright sunlight, and the smell of the asphalted road, and the man struggling. At last a bus appeared with its police escort – two Jews and an Arab. I waved: it stopped, the police jumped out and lifted the wounded man inside. The Arab policeman drove on with him, while the two Jews, who had rifles, stood in the roadway exclaiming excitedly in Hebrew and looking about for somebody to arrest. I pointed to the house into which the terrorist had disappeared. They ran up to it and fired a couple of shots.

When the bus and the police came along, people had begun to reappear, out of gardens, from behind walls, in a comically cautious manner. At this further shooting they promptly vanished again. I remember noticing one stout gentleman trying to conceal himself behind a particularly thin tree. I went through a gate into the back garden of a house which appeared to be unoccupied, and met a little British policeman emerging with a white face. He said he had only just escaped being shot by the Jewish police at the front! Of the terrorist there was no sign. More British police were quickly on the scene, and one of them took my name and address and asked me a lot of questions.

During the next few days a message came from Ramallah to say that the police wanted me again about this affair. An elderly, fatherly Arab inspector wrote down the story of the shooting as I told it to him, asking advice about the spelling of words such as 'disappear'. At the end he asked if I would kindly correct the English of the three pages before I signed them. I assured him truthfully that it was a wonderful piece of composition, much better than the kind of thing I had to correct every week. From force of habit I nearly put marks out of ten at the bottom instead of signing my name. He told me that the man who had been shot was a Jewish supernumerary policeman; he was only slightly wounded and would be out of hospital probably the next day. I was allowed to read the inspector's own statement of the affair, which of course I found enormously interesting. I was tickled to see that he had described the Arab assailant as tall whereas I had said he was short! Anyhow, short or tall, he had not been caught.

The Wilson diary ends in July 1939 when she left for home, by which time the Arab revolt had more or less come to an end.

Doctor Foster

Elliot Foster was working as a doctor in St Luke's hospital in Hebron during the thirties and he, as a medical man, both treated wounded rebel soldiers (to the anger of the British army) and reported on cases of British violence against the Arabs. He kept a diary where he recorded his revulsion, feeling only '5% loyal to the British Raj, at any rate as exhibited in Palestine'. He had to deal with casualties caused during the British army 'sweep' on the town of Hebron in 1938:

From the small hours of Saturday morning, I received at this hospital a series of casualties inflicted by the British, presumably on curfew breakers. A great number of broken crowns were treated during the day at the PHD and at this hospital. These were either inflicted by 'brigands' the night before, or by the British engaged with conducting the search. Of those who were treated by us, each declared that he had been beaten by an Inklesi (Englishman) in the morning, not by a brigand in the night. All declare they were shot in daylight – and all are convinced they were shot by the English. Myself in the early morning sunlight I walked out on to the hospital balcony for a breather. I heard the crack of a rifle – there was sporadic firing all the morning – and I saw a man walking along a field path in Wadi Tuffah fall over. There was a keening of women, and I saw a small party run out and pull him into a hut in the same field. I never saw this man at closer quarters, but I am informed that he died later the same morning. The body of a man was brought up to the mortuary at about the same time, recently killed by a single bullet that had torn through the muscles and great vessels of his neck. It would be difficult to argue that these casualties were inflicted on dangerous enemies or their allies. Of those I saw in life, two were old men, three were children, and the only youth, if his story be true, was shot from a distance, inside his own house. Another corpse brought up was later identified as a deaf and dumb man, seventy years of age.

Less tragic in effect, but equally so as an index of the criminal futility of such retaliatory proceedings, was the looting and wanton destruction of shops in the market. I give here examples that have impressed me for various reasons.

A neighbour of mine, Haj Rajab el Dwaik, owns a store that has been burned out – nothing remains of the stock. He is a man well liked and trusted by the Hebronites, especially the poorer classes, and he kept a 'safe deposit' in which such folk left sums of money of which they were in no immediate need, but which they feared to keep under the crowded conditions of their own lives. All the money in the shop was gone.

There is a boy at present in one of my wards suffering from enteric fever. His father, Abdallah Abu Ghazaleh, is an epileptic, and desperately poor. He is kept with his family by the charity of neighbours. This man's household goods, poor enough in all conscience, and consisting almost solely of straw mats, were all destroyed by fire.

Evidence of Daud Abu Shukur of Hebron, aged 50 years:
Soon after sunrise on the 20th inst. I was sleeping in my little open shop opposite Haj Rajab's shop. I was woken up by an English Soldier who searched me. Then he went over to the shop of Haj Rajab and broke the padlock with an iron bar and forced open the shop door. He took out some packets of cigarettes and called to his companions, two of whom then appeared in the street, and gave them some packets. Then he went back into the shop and sprinkled kerosene from a drum over the shop and set it alight.

Verdict of Coroner 7 September 1938:
I find on the evidence that the deceased, *Fathi Hashid Abu Shakhdam*, male aged 15 years, of Hebron, died during the night of the 20–21 August 1938 of gunshot wounds sustained by him on the morning of the 20 August. Among the acts of wanton and reckless barbarity perpetrated by English members of the Military and/or Police Forces on that morning the killing of this child of 15 years stands out by itself.

The deceased and a cousin of 19 years of age were first of all severely beaten, inside the yard of their house at about 7 a.m. by a party of English soldiers or police.

Re Khalil Hamameh and his neighbours:

Khalil Hamameh is a railway employee living in the Manshia with his mother, his wife and his baby daughter aged two years. He was awakened at about two a.m. by banging on his street door and demands for admission. Suspecting it was the Police or military search he got his identity papers and went down and opened the door. Three Englishmen in plain clothes demanded that he take them into the house of Ali Dabbagh. He took them a few yards along the alley to Ali Dabbagh's house, being beaten and kicked all the while. When he failed to open the door the three Englishmen beat him mercilessly and he ran back to his house. His mother seeing him streaming with blood and cuts in his head, tried to lock him indoors and bolt the street door, whereupon the Englishmen fired through the door wounding her in the hand and wounding the two-year-old baby girl in the thigh, fracturing it.

Meanwhile the occupants of the flat upstairs, alarmed by the shouts and lamentations, came down to enquire. This is the statement of old Haj A. Rahman, the head of the family:

I am seventy-five years of age. When I came downstairs, attracted by Khalil's cries, I saw three Englishmen in mufti. One was a tall man wearing a dark suit. He and one of the shorter men carried revolvers, the third carrying a stick. One of the smaller men immediately assaulted me, boxing my ears and face and kicking me. The other smaller man searched me and took LP 5 notes and 40 piastres in silver and also my watch. They then went upstairs to our flat, and assaulted my son and my grandson. They went into my grandson's bedroom where he had been sleeping with his wife and searched his coat which was lying on the bed. From the pocket of his coat they took LP 115 in notes, which he had just obtained in connection with a deal in sheep.

Then they marshalled all the women and girls in a line, nine of them all together, and questioned them in Arabic asking them their names and saying, 'How much today?' God knows what they meant. They then made indecent gestures with their revolvers and sticks. Finally they broke all the windows and glass and lamps etc. I am an old man and I lived under the Turkish regime. The Turks were unjust and cruel and I hated them. During the war I hoped the English would win, for they were famed for their greatness and justness. But never in my experience of the Turks have I witnessed such a scene. The Turks, brutes though they were, were angels compared to you English. Why don't you massacre all the inhabitants of Palestine and have done with it. You rob and insult and beat and kill us – why not have one massacre, and get it over?

The old man said this quietly, and without anger, although his face was contused, and swollen from the punishment he had received. I visited his house, and saw the wreckage and took a photograph. There was not one single window pane or cupboard pane or lampglass or lamp oil container intact. Every thing that could be smashed had been smashed.

This British contempt for the Palestinian spilled over on one infamous occasion to the football field – as reported by Dr Foster:

3rd April 1939
I read in the local rag today of a soccer match in Jerusalem between police and some military team, in which the soldiers had an argument with the referee, and four of them left the field as a 'protest', the rest of the game being of course a complete farce. It recalls a similar incident that happened here a short time ago, which was much more unfortunate in that the opposing team were Arabs, the Boys School, in fact. Here a team of the Worcesters appeared without officers, and systematically fouled throughout the game. One of my Arab friends appeared the next day with one of the richest black eyes I have ever seen. Some happy warrior had simply hauled him off and busted him one. Naturally this incident created a bit of a stir, as well as genuine surprise for though the English might be slipping lower and lower in Hebron's opinion, they were surely still to be relied upon to be 'sportinje' (grand old Arabic word!) A written apology was sent to the Headmaster, and a return game requested. It is to Hebron's credit that they accepted the offer, though the temptation to refuse must have been very strong, and a properly refereed game was played.

Spit and polish

It is characteristic of the British that, while trying to cope with rebellions and riots and running amok, they still managed to be bureaucratic, inefficient and obsessed with spit and polish. Bureaucracy run wild and happily exemplified by the following ordinance:

In connection with preventing trade in animal manure a bill was recently published stating – inter alia – ownership of all animal droppings on any land shall be vested in the High Commissioner.

A telling instance of inefficiency coupled with bureaucracy was described by Keith-Roach:

Efficiency was the order of the day. The story of the Safad table was typical. Furniture of any sort was scarce in 1921. The District Officer of Safad wanted an office table and wrote to the Chief Secretary that he had found an old one in the town and could he be authorised to purchase it for one pound and a half Egyptian. An ex RASC Officer, Colonel Solomon, had lately been appointed Director of Commerce and Industry, and he was interested in standardization on approved Army lines. TABLE, WRITING, TWO DRAWER, OFFICERS, FOR THE USE OF. But centralization was his hobby. Despite the difficulties of getting wood transported 2,700 feet up to Jerusalem from the coast, he had succeeded in getting a carpenter to make what he termed a 'standard-pattern office table' with an appropriate number of drawers. So when I asked him to authorise the District Officer to purchase the existing second-hand table he wrote back that no money from his vote could be expended on second-hand furniture, but that he would supply a standard table. A table was duly finished and despatched. It was invoiced out to the District Administration at three pounds plus transport expenses. It was transported by porter from the factory to Jerusalem Railway Station. Thence it went to Lydda and was sent on by standard-gauge to Haifa, where it was reloaded and despatched by narrow-gauge to Samakh Station, near the southern end of the Sea of Galilee. A porter took it on a donkey from there to the Sea of Galilee and deposited it in a sailing boat, whence it sailed to Tabgha at the northern end. There it was taken in a cart owned by Jewish settlers to Rosh Pino, and then sent on camel back along a stony track up the steep hill to Safad, a journey of five hours. It was three weeks on its journey. Eventually the long-suffering District Officer acknowledged the receipt of 'a damaged table top containing one drawer only and no legs'. He added that the second-hand table he had wanted to purchase was now sold and asked what he was to do. I made no further reference to our efficiency zealot, but instructed the District Officer to spend up to £P3 from his Contingency vote and buy anything he could find.

The Palestine police in addition to coping with riots had to satisfy their inspector-general in their military appearance. Policemen were not used to parading as guards officers and often let the side down at public functions:

SUPERIOR POLICE OFFICERS CIRCULAR NO 17
Subject: Boots – Superior Officers, of.
Since I have had the honour to command this Force over a period of four years, I have done my best to teach officers that long riding boots unless properly cut, properly put on and properly adjusted are nothing more or less than an eye sore and make officers who wear them the laughing stock of people who know what long boots should look like.

The boots of superior Police Officers at the Garden Party yesterday did very little credit to this Force. Some officers had all four tags of their boots showing above the boot. More than one officer had no top boot garters at all. Other officers had boot garters on but had not got the buckle in a dead straight line below the knee and had the overstrap of the garter flapping and

loose. I have said it before, and I say it again, I shall be most grateful if officers who are not in a position to provide themselves with a properly cut pair of English boots would wear puttees (Inspectors' pattern). The only alternative to this is for them to absent themselves from functions at which officers of the Fighting Services are present since the Officers' boots, and incidentally the breeches, of the Palestine Police Officers as at present worn, in my opinion, give this Force a name for ignorance and slovenliness.
Inspector-General

SUPERIOR OFFICERS CIRCULAR NO 18

It is considered desirable to smarten up and make more distinctive the summer full dress and full undress of Superior Police Officers, and to this end the Inspector-General orders that the blue cummerbund now worn by mounted other ranks will in future be worn by Superior Police Officers on ceremonial occasions when summer full dress or undress is worn.

It is however necessary with the wearing of the cummerbund to adopt a specially long skirted jacket and Superior Police Officers should if possible now provide themselves with such. The bottom of the jacket should coincide with the bottom of the fringe of the cummerbund. Officers of 5 foot 9 inches and under will however find that to coincide the bottom of the jacket with that of the cummerbund will mean a jacket excessively long, the flash of the cummerbund should therefore be proportionately reduced but in no case more than one and a half inches.

TO CLEAN SCARLET COAT

Unless a scarlet coat is very dirty, it is perhaps better not to wet it at all, but leave it to dry in a warm room all night. Brush it well in the morning, just washing the inside of the tails and applying the red coat solution. When dry press with hot iron using a damp cloth, afterwards clean the buttons with plate powder and ammonia. When finished hang in a wardrobe.

Thus attired the superior police officer was surely better ready to crush any crowd of rioting Arabs.

Every sign of sentiment dulled

By 1948 the British had been 'running' Palestine for thirty years. They had tried in vain to find a solution to an intractable problem – reports, committees, plans, commissions. Neither Jews nor Arabs wanted a solution on anything other than their own terms, and the British had nothing left to offer. They decided to hand everything over to the United Nations which sent officials to Jerusalem to take over when the British left: 14 May was announced as evacuation day.

As British forces withdrew both Jews and Arabs sought to gain as much advantage as possible, ready for the final struggle. By 15 March there were just two months left – two months to run down a complex administration, two months of increasing violence.

The irony of the situation became starker as the two sides waged a violent struggle for the 'city of peace'. Churches, mosques and synagogues were used as strategic points and little charity was in evidence. During this time the British were gradually decreasing in numbers, trying to leave in an orderly fashion, while the United Nations was vainly trying to supervise a truce. Sir Henry Gurney kept an ice-cool diary of his feelings and of events during the last two months, a monument to the end of his famous unflappability.

15 March

On this wet and cheerless day in Jerusalem – it was snowing this morning – all is quiet, because in this weather both sides prefer to remain indoors. But the nightly battle begins regularly about 8 o'clock and continues sporadically till dawn. Two nights ago our windows were blown in by some monstrous explosions when some more Arab houses just outside the zone were destroyed by Jews. The sky on these occasions is criss-crossed with tracers, yellow for the Arabs, red for the Jews. There is little sleep to be had, and one remembers that Jerusalem cocks have started crowing at 10.30 ever since the time of Peter.

Two more British police deserted with 13 Sten guns last night. It is a tragedy that these men should forfeit their whole future for a handful of gold (though prices and pay are high) and at the same time make things much more difficult for the loyal members of the Force. But out of 3500 British police there have been only 16 possible cases of desertion in the last six months, and the temptations are great. No one envies them their task.

18 March

This afternoon representatives of our Arab government officers came to see me about their abolition terms and the situation that was facing them. The interview was conducted in a tone of great moderation and politeness for an hour. I am afraid it must be said that we appreciate their point of view and they ours. It must be heartbreaking to face this disruption of all the work you have done for your own people as well as complete uncertainty as to what is going to happen to yourself. The UN Commission's staff have run out of food. The Police Sergeant who was shopping for them in the Arab markets has been threatened. Eggs in the Jewish markets are about six times the Arab price, because Jewish hens are much more expensive, and eggs and bombs don't mix well. However, the United Nations must obviously be fed. They are not as fed up with Palestine as the British. UN has not had Palestine for a year yet.

The snow has gone, and today is glorious with a quarter-moon, in which every sniper and bomber in the place should be out. But there has been only sporadic shooting all day, and even the Bishop got only some machine gun bullets in his bedroom. But this is premature.

20 March

Today has been our first glorious spring day; the air itself almost coruscating in the brilliant sunlight in which every stone and tree becomes a jewel – Jerusalem the golden; or, as Josephus put it, a golden bowl full of scorpions.

21 March

An afternoon of battle and bullets, and the Army playing football among them. Another lovely day.

24 March

Arab bomb in Yemen Moshe yesterday evening broke several of our office windows. I had gone at about 6.15, half an hour before the explosion. The Arabs loaded a three ton truck with explosive, locked the steering, fixed the throttle full on and drove it, unmanned, at the outer defence of this slum quarter facing Zion. It brought down the upper framework of my window, and Dobbs, who was in his office a few yards away, was showered with glass. There were no casualties.

A good joke is going the rounds. 'When Arthur Balfour visited Palestine for the only time in 1925 he was asked by the Customs on entry, "And have you anything else to declare Mr Balfour?" '

27 March

The Good Friday services seem to have gone off all right. Last night between 3.00 and 5.00 in the morning there was a battle in which a number of new machine gun posts around here joined in. Mortars and bullets made it impossible to sleep.

28 March

Easter Sunday and a glorious morning. Went to a choral communion service at St. George's to the sound of battle beyond Bethlehem.

1 April

A lovely spring afternoon, in which the Russian tower on the Mount of Olives stood sharp against a soft blue sky and the Mountains of Moab were etched with delicate, distant shadows. I was looking at the garden which is now almost at its best.

8 April

A mukhtar of an Arab village near Gaza was responsible for a good story recently. A British military convoy was attacked by Arabs near his village, who mistook them for Jews. The mukhtar, on learning of their error, was most apologetic and invited the whole military party to breakfast and added: 'Please bring some ammunition with you, as we have wasted about 200 rounds on you.'

11 April

On this second Sunday after Easter, the day broke with a hail of bullets going in all directions around the house. Firing had been going on all night, and sleep was impossible. There is now much more of this in and around Jerusalem than anywhere else in Palestine; we have now had it, on and off, for four months and its stupidity becomes more and more evident. Yet the Administration is still functioning and limping along, with every man at his post. The Director of Education told me yesterday that he can now communicate with his District Inspector of Schools in Galilee only through Police wireless, but the schools are all carrying on and both Arabs and Jews are determined to continue them.

12 April

For the third night running there was practically no sleep, owing to heavy firing all around the house. The Lebanese Vice-Consul just down the road was shot on his verandah; the donkey that brings the Belgian Consulate's milk was shot outside his door; two Arabs were killed and four wounded last night.

15 April

The Belgian Consul-General's milk donkey is still lying outside his door, and no one can move it for Jewish snipers. A Police armoured car is going to have a shot tomorrow. Meanwhile it is by no means so pleasant a donkey as it was.

At last the time came for most Britons to leave. The area they controlled had slowly contracted and those leaving had to be escorted to the airport:

28 April

Got up at 5.45 and went to see the convoy off from the King David at 6.30. About 100 British, including many heads of Departments. It was quite a bit of history, though it didn't look like it. Air passengers in old mackintoshes are not a stirring sight. But this party represented the main body of the Government leaving Jerusalem, the Holy City, in the early light of a grey morning; policemen in blue in their green armoured cars; the parting of many friends and the finish, in some cases, of a life's work. The Press and the photographers missed it, and it all went off soberly and quietly, with handshakes and some rather studiously casual waves, hiding all kinds of thoughts and emotions. None of us would have had it otherwise; every sign of sentiment had been magnificently dulled.

Earth's proud empires pass away

A skeleton staff was now 'running' the country:

29 April

I called a meeting of the office staff – only some 70 remain – and talked to them about their difficulties and ours. The importance of the typist and stenographer only becomes clear when they are not there. Many of them are loyally putting up with all sorts of dangers and troubles, and are really trying very hard. Others have just gone. It is a fact that the Government of Palestine cannot now do very much. The Courts have stopped, and so has the Post Office except for urgent and official telegrams; nearly all our prisoners have escaped, and the prisons are not functioning either.

11 May

The Army have been practising with guns and mortars around the outskirts of Jerusalem today. This is a bit unfortunate as it spoils the psychological effect of the cease-fire. Otherwise a quiet day, and we played tennis this afternoon. If anyone had told me three months ago that we should be playing tennis within three days of the end of the Mandate, I should have laughed at him. But in fact we have run out of work.

This morning we assembled all the Secretariat staff remaining and I gave them a short speech of thanks and said goodbye to them. Several were on the edge of tears, and all were genuinely sad. I said that they could be proud of belonging to the best administration Palestine had ever had – which is true – and that we should not forget them. All of them – Jews, Arabs, Greeks and Armenians – who have served us loyally and in many cases devotedly.

To leave Gurney for a moment we find that the same kinds of leave-taking were happening all over Palestine – on small occasions or large. William Fuller was district commissioner in Jaffa and presided sadly over the disintegration of British authority. Offices closed, water supplies were interrupted and looting was rife. Everything was grinding to a halt. He tried to keep up appearances, driving around his district unprotected, especially in a no-man's land between Jaffa and Tel Aviv:

I went alone in my car, though it was a harrowing experience driving alone through a deserted area. Knowing that there were expert unseen gunmen all round, I just looked straight ahead trying to appear as nonchalant as I could. Both sides – Arab and Jewish – honoured the trust I placed in them.

Lowering the Flag

The 13th May was my last day in Jaffa as I had to be in Sarafand on the 14th to enable me to be with the Army in their withdrawal south to Egypt on 15th May. General Murray, Flanagan, the Superintendent of Police and I formally drove out of Jaffa on the morning of the 14th May as the last three representatives of the Mandatory power to leave.

On the afternoon of 13th May the Army arranged a special ceremony for the lowering of the Union Jack at my office. It was pathetic in so far as there were no members of the public present to witness such an historic ceremony – but it was very touching to me. At 6 p.m. that night I walked up alone to the flagstaff over my house, saluted the flag, and hauled it down for the last time.

One of the most poignant stories of trying to cope in an impossible situation comes from Sir Arthur Kirby who was general manager of Palestine Railways. The railways were a favourite target for saboteurs – twenty incidents were reported in March 1948 alone, ranging from 'pointsman shot and killed at post' to 'passenger train derailed by sabotage'. Kirby directed the railways from Haifa which quickly became the scene of continuous fighting and shelling. British military and police protection was gradually withdrawn from the town, and to Kirby's particular chagrin from his headquarters as well. These were then captured first by the Iraqi army and soon afterwards by the Jewish Haganah. All the records of railway staff were lost in the fighting. Kirby was desperate. He was worried that his faithful staff would lose their pension and other benefits. He wrote a bitter report to Gurney, tersely entitled 'Termination of the Mandate – Railway Headquarters.' Its final paragraph was definitely not of the stiff upper lip variety expected:

The foregoing is a sorry story, but the situation in which we now find ourselves would not have been anything like so bad if only I could have been given a warning to evacuate essential documents, etc. from the Headquarters offices. I was angry when I heard that the police security had been withdrawn from the building without notice, but I was not astonished. I accepted it as just another security problem I would have to tackle – just another example of my being expected to make bricks without straw – but I was stunned with incredulity when I realised the situation on Wednesday morning. The Railway Headquarters were left isolated in the frontier area between Arab and Jewish forces. I do not challenge the strategic necessity for this move since that is something beyond my province, but some warning could and should have been given to me. It is unbelievable to me that while on the one hand the District Commissioner was given 24 hours notice of the move and so was able to salve something from his offices, I was left completely unaware of any immediate necessity to vacate my Headquarters. I have been expected to carry on the railway and ports under almost impossible conditions; I have taken upon myself risks and responsibilities which have seldom, if ever fallen upon the General Manager of a Colonial Railway; I have achieved more than could have been hoped for – yet I am not, apparently, thought to be sufficiently responsible or worthy of confidence to be informed of operations which were so vitally to affect the work of my Department and the welfare of the thousands of people who have given their services loyally to the railways for many years. It is a fitting culmination to the disillusionment which I have suffered during my recent years of service in Palestine – but I never expected the final disillusionment to be so catastrophic or severe – nor did I expect such harsh confirmation of the bitterly disappointing realisation that I can expect no more from the Colonial Service and that, for my self respect, I must seek retirement, and enter a new field of endeavour.

And so back to Gurney:

13 May

Everything is now ready for departure at 6.30 tomorrow morning. This 'goodbye' business has a depressing and upsetting effect on everyone. Yesterday I called on the Armenian Patriarch, one of our best friends, and had a long talk with him in which he deplored our going. We sat at one end of his vast green reception room and discussed Jerusalem. How illogical it was, he said, to fight for a city because it is sacred and to destroy it in so doing.

The offices where so much work has been done now stand bare and empty; the boxes and cupboards have gone and the rooms begin to look once more as though they might belong to a hotel. The Police locked up their stores (worth over £1m) and brought the keys to the United Nations, who refused to receive them. I had to point out that the United Nations would be responsible for the administration of Palestine in a few hours' time and that we should leave the keys on their doorstep whether they accepted them or not; which we did.

14 May

Practically no sleep last night, since soon after midnight firing started and went on in the usual stupid way until about 4.00. As the sun came up over the Mount of Olives, the shooting stopped and we got up and dressed for the last journey. We moved off at 6.45 from outside the King David, four police armoured cars and 17 civilians in two cars and a 'bus'. The BBC and press photographers were there in force. In Allenby Square and along the route were tanks and troops, obviously out in strength and happy to be going. At this early hour only a few Arabs were about, and they waved us cheerfully on.

At 8.00 the High Commissioner inspected the HLI guard-of-honour at Government House, and left a few minutes later, the Red Cross having taken the place of the Union Jack. At the Kalandia airstrip he said goodbye to us, and flew off to Haifa for the last ceremonies there. We then entered our Dakotas and flew to Ramat David, where our York picked us up and flew off at 11.00 for Malta and Heathrow. We landed at Heathrow on a perfect summer night at 11.30. As we drove into London, the clocks struck midnight and the Mandate was ended.

NINE

HERE AND THERE IN THE MIDDLE EAST

Britain had a number of other interests in the Middle East in addition to her main worries in Egypt and Palestine. In the Sudan large areas were administered by a single British officer. In the Gulf the British 'advised' the local rulers. In remote spots British officials beavered away representing the mother country, often in woefully insalubrious conditions. Members of the Levant Consular Service were sent all over the area. Diaries and letters give glimpses of life in some of these posts.

Persia: oil in their lamps 1892

The British had long had an interest in Persia, trying to exploit the country economically and also trying to ensure that Russian interests in the area were kept at bay. Britain had established a legation in Tehran where relations were maintained with the ruling monarch, the shah. Herbert Richards had first gone to the Middle East in 1880 to work for a trading firm in Iraq. He was a pioneer in many ways, being the first European to reside in two towns in Persia, Ahwaz and Shuster. In the latter, a place of deep religious faith, his presence was looked upon as a great insult to Islam. Religious leaders preached against him in the mosques urging the faithful to kill him. On one occasion a mob surrounded his house and he was only saved by the intervention of Persian soldiers. He nevertheless stayed there, living as he wrote in 'intense heat and the foulest smelling place ever known'. In 1901 he decided to leave trade, joined the Levant Consular Service and was posted to Tehran. The Persian royal court at this time was very conscious of its dignity and the European diplomats in Tehran equally anxious to impress with pomp and power:

At the turn of the Century, the Legations used to pay their respects to the Shah twice a year, on New Year's Day, and on the Shah's Birthday. They went in all their pomp, show and vanity, well bedecked with gold lace, brass buttons, cocked hats and swords. The officials of the British Legation rode on well groomed Arab horses, all of chestnut colour, escorted by outriders of the Guides Cavalry Regiment from India in their striking uniforms with gay penants flying from their lances. These were all mounted also on chestnut coloured horses, dressed in red hunting coats, white breeches, black knee boots, everything spick and span and every bit of metal shining like silver or gold. This was a fine and imposing cavalcade as we clattered down the streets to the Palace to the admiring gaze of the population who turned out to see the Show.

The Russians came next in their parade with fine, well equipped Russian Cossacks, but not quite so smartly turned out as we were.

The Germans were also excellent but much smaller in number. Their six or eight men were handsome in dark blue and silver.

It was a fine array of Diplomats from all countries in the world – gold lace and decorations galore with the one outstanding figure in the person of the United States Minister in sombre black evening dress, which is not a becoming attire for daylight state functions.

We all gathered in one of the big rooms in the Palace where some of the Crown regalia was displayed, prominent among them being the Globe of the World with each country marked out in different precious jewels.

After time had been given for all to assemble and exchange greetings with each other, notice would come in that the Shah was about to enter. The Ministers would arrange themselves in order of precedence according to the date of their appointment. The smaller fry would stand behind the respective Minister. Cocked hats would be put on, as it is an insult to appear before the Shah with head uncovered, although one could have one's shoes off if one liked.

The Shah would enter accompanied by his Prime Minister and Minister for Foreign Affairs and two or three others of note. We would all bow. He would be dressed in black with his Persian Astrakhan hat on, which was adorned with the famous Peacock feathers and crown jewel; he might also have one or two jewels of enormous size and value pinned to his breast. He would exchange a few words with all the Ministers then retire. Cocked hats would come off and any Minister who wished to have a private audience with the Shah would remain, the others would disperse after exchanging greeting with the Persian Ministers. All would be over. The throng would clatter back to the various Legations.

A year or two earlier, when living in Shuster, Richards had, by his own account, played a role in a discovery of tremendous significance for Persia. He claimed to be the first European to find oil in the country – the locals had known of its existence for centuries:

I had noticed in Shuster that the natives were burning a kind of crude oil in their lamps, apparently obtained locally. By cautious enquiries (for the secret was jealously guarded) I ascertained that it came from the hills some twenty to twenty-five miles away from Shuster, but in what direction lay the deposits nobody would disclose.

It was apparent that the Sayyids had established a monopoly in oil for domestic lamps, which they worked to some profit, though in a most primitive way; and that they had no intention of permitting intrusion on the part of inquisitive outsiders. Every effort made to ascertain the exact location of the oil supply was thwarted. I started out in several directions to prospect, but was always led astray.

You can do everything, however, with money. Eventually a man was discovered who came from the very district, and knew all about the where, and the how, the Sayyids collected their oil. A shooting trip was projected (as often before) with this man as guide. An entirely opposite direction was proposed to that which led to the actual goal. The man was kept as a close guest in my house till the day of departure.

We set out on the appointed day early in the morning; and going out by a certain gate of the city, which might least attract attention to our movements, we made a wide detour before we headed for the supposed oil district. In about an hour and a half the next morning we came to a little creek, which was trickling down a winding passage amongst the hills.

We followed its course and, just near the plain, we found an artificial basin, made of mud, which received most of the oil and a little water, which later was let out by a plug underneath. When the basin got full, the oil overflowed into another basin. When collected, the oil was put into properly prepared goatskins which were conveyed to their destinations on donkeys' backs.

So the mystery, simple enough, was solved; and the means used were merely the crude result of the knowledge that oil floats on water, and that both run downhill.

Richards had made the excursion out of sheer curiosity and made no attempt to exploit his discovery. This was left to the Anglo-Iranian Oil Company a few years later. He soon left Persia and finished his career as consul-general in Chicago. In 1951 Britain was fiercely contesting the Persian attempt to nationalize the oil company and an interesting article on the subject appeared in the *Evening News* headlined 'He discovered Iran's oil':

While Britain and Iran haggle fiercely for control of Iran's fabulous oil treasure, the man who claims to have started it all watches pensively from the quiet of the English countryside.

He is Herbert A. Richards, 85-year-old retired consular official, who today emerged from obscurity as the man whose exploration on horseback into the desolate Iranian hills in 1892 brought the first real confirmation of unlimited Iranian oil resources.

Richards, who might today have been one of the richest men in the world, had no thought of getting a concession.

In his modest cottage at Bexhill, Kent County, Richards follows the Anglo-Iranian squabble with interest, but shows a complete lack of concern about the millions of dollars involved.

Said Richards: 'I made the trip without any thought of concessions. If others reaped where I sowed, good luck to them. I am quite content.'

An Anglo-Iranian Oil Company spokesman in London said: 'If Richards had exploited his knowledge in 1892 it is quite possible that he could have been the founder of one of the richest oil empires in the world.'

Keeping an eye on the Russians 1943

Once oil had been discovered Persia became of even greater interest to Britain, who tried to maintain paramount influence in the country. This was much resented and by the outbreak of the Second World War there was a lot of pro-German feeling which moved Britain and Russia to occupy the country in 1941 – there were oil supplies to guard and the allies wanted to use Persia as a supply route to the Russians. Sir Thomas Rapp, recently released from internment by the Gestapo, was given the consulate of Tabriz in the far north-west of the country, almost on the Russian frontier, with the task of maintaining a British presence up there:

In August 1943 a telegram informed me that I was to be appointed Consul-General in Tabriz, whose remoteness and isolation, not to mention its occupation by the Russians, seemed almost to indicate a further term of internment.

With his family he travelled by ship to Port Said and then across the desert by bus to Iraq. Before the next stage of his long journey to Tabriz, and with discouraging accounts of life there already in his mind, he had the misfortune to eat the wrong food once again:

Baghdad, apart from the comfort of our Embassy, I have never liked and this time less than ever, the cause being the tainted food at the hotel overlooking the Tigris that laid me low with a sharp attack of dysentery. So the journey by train to Basra, the car ride to the railhead at Ahwaz and the day's journey thence to Tehran in an unlighted train (for the electric bulbs had been stolen) were particularly joyless. It was hard too for Dorothy and Margaret [his wife and daughter] since, unlike me, they were not condemned to a starvation diet; and there was no food or drink to be had on the Persian train. Only a few biscuits, kindly provided by an American serviceman, were to allay their more pressing pangs of hunger.

There were depressing accounts of the denuded state of the Consular residence at Tabriz. While some of the missing essentials could be made good from our heavy baggage when it arrived, that pleasing event might well be months ahead, if ever. Local purchases were almost out of the question because of the scarcity and prices inflated ten or twenty times for what remained. But good friends lent us our minimum requirements of plate and linen to see us through until, three months later, the Office of Works replaced it with an odd assortment of requisitioned articles in varying condition, including some linen from the Pump Room Hotel at Bath. About the same time our own baggage arrived, less what had been stolen on the way.

Then there was the problem of a secretary. Of the last two women sent to Tabriz, one had precipitately fled and the other had suffered a nervous breakdown. There would be no further volunteers, life being quite impossible for a woman on her own. As Margaret had had some secretarial training, it was suggested that regulations could for once be waived and that she should undertake this duty.

When Tabriz was reached, we were met by Frank Ogden, the Vice Consul, and the invaluable Munshi Farbudi. Our new home and office proved to be a one-storeyed house of pleasant appearance surrounded by about half an acre of walled garden giving entire privacy. Within, it was, as we feared, completely denuded apart from a few beds, tables and chairs which had been lent to my predecessor by the local American missionaries. Yet there was one unexpected windfall: we inherited two horses belonging to the Government which had survived as an anachronism from pre-motor times.

In one way or another we quickly coped with our domestic problems. And we were able to reflect that we were better off than Major General Glinski, the newly arrived Soviet general, who on taking over the former French consulate found that the previous tenant, a Polish Jew, had removed the bath and lavatory, though he had left the electric bells as what he termed a gesture of friendship to the Russians. The garden, notwithstanding its ineradicable mole crickets, supplied us with most vegetables and a lot of fruit; and every fortnight N.A.A.F.I. stores would arrive with the mail brought by an Embassy lorry from Tehran. So, with Army supplies to fall back on in case of need, we lacked nothing for our daily sustenance. Comparing our lot with that of the local inhabitants, we were indeed well-favoured.

Tabriz as a town fell lamentably short of the beauty one had been led to associate with Persian towns like Ispahan and Shiraz. It was in fact filthy, its general appearance forlorn and its essential services functioning haphazardly, part of the reason being that the wages and salaries of all municipal personnel were in arrears and corruption of every kind rife.

One practical matter of concern to us was our water supply. This was privately owned and ran in open channels through the streets before being diverted into our house and garden. Our contract with the owners was for a twice weekly one hour supply in the middle of the day. But when I investigated the upper reaches of the channel the fact stood revealed that it was being used by riparian households for washing clothes and sundry other ablutions, which rendered it aesthetically unpleasant and hygienically still less desirable. It was therefore arranged that the large storage tank for household purposes should in future be filled at midnight, when a purer supply could be hoped for. Once in the tank it was treated to a generous dosage of salt and chloride of lime. Our drinking water was obtained from a spring at the prison some distance away and was brought by our water-boy in skins that could hardly have met with the approval of any public health inspector, had such existed.

A certain mystique still surrounded a Consul, although there were no longer any Consular guards or capitulatory privileges, nor were there spectacular progresses through the district with a considerable retinue and the huge tents that we found in a state of decay in the cellars. In the eyes of the inhabitants of Tabriz the presence of a British Consul and, in a lesser degree, of other consuls was evidence that there were countries other than Soviet Russia which were interested in their lot and were not prepared to stand on one side while Persian Azerbaijan, of which Tabriz was the principal town, was quietly absorbed into the Soviet Union.

The town was thus primarily an observation post: as a corollary there was a welcome degree of independence and an absence of routine work. Communications with the outside world largely depended on the fortnightly Public Relations van from Tehran, which brought our mail and supplies. The Persian post and telegraph service was slow and insecure, and hence usually avoided. Some telegraphic delays, it was suggested, were due to the office being surrounded by brothels. Particularly in summer the younger clerks were wont to spend an undue time watching the inmates disporting themselves naked on adjacent roofs to the accompaniment of music. Two petitions from the senior staff requesting the authorities to abate the nuisance were without result, police connivance having been purchased by the owners of the bawdy houses.

The Persian Governor-General at Tabriz was a pleasant, cultured man, yet now at the age of seventy less than ever an energetic character. It is no use, he once said to me when speaking of Soviet interference in every department of life, trying to withstand a river in flood: that can only result in being swept away, so one must wait for it to subside. The Persians considered him 'all hat', meaning that there was nothing underneath and joked about his somnolence. I had one experience of it myself on being bidden to a dinner at which he was to be the principal guest. We waited two hours for him to arrive before our host sent his son to find out what had delayed him. He returned to tell us that he had long since retired to bed.

Non-official life was simple and friendly, though our resources were few. British and Indian convoy and staging post officers were almost daily visitors. We exchanged tennis teas with the bank manager's wife, a Scotswoman who somehow produced the most marvellous cakes. A frequent visitor to these tennis parties was an English Seventh Day Adventist missionary doctor – a first rate oculist, to whom patients flocked in large numbers – who always had to leave us quickly towards sundown on the eve of the Sabbath. We had hopes of our circle being enlarged when we heard that the American Consul's English wife was to join him, but two days in Tabriz were enough for her and she mysteriously vanished never to reappear.

Soon Rapp was ordered to leave Tabriz, posted to Salonica which was at the time still occupied by the Germans. There he spent two years and eventually moved far out of the Levant to serve in Mexico. He finished his career, in the Middle East once again, in 1953.

Turkey: grievous bodily harm 1885–91

To the north of Iraq lies Turkey, a country which before the First World War was the centre of the Levant Consular Service. To be in the capital city Constantinople, in Ottoman times, appointed to the court of Sultan Abdulhamid, was the plum job. Andrew Ryan and Reader Bullard were both there as junior officials and vastly enjoyed the pomp and ceremonial. But as consul one could easily be sent to much more remote areas of Anatolia. Colonel Sir William Everett was sent out in 1879 as vice-consul in Erzerum, a town in the far east of Turkey where he had responsibility for Kurdistan. There, in 1885, began a tragic saga which ended reasonably satisfactorily only in July 1892. His sufferings for the empire were extreme. Colonel Everett described what happened. He was awoken by his wife at 2 a.m. on the morning of 13 April 1885 as one of their children was sick. He went downstairs and saw an outside door swinging on its hinges:

On opening the door, I saw, by the light of a small lamp hanging in a corridor a man whom I recognized as my groom, struggling with another man whose back was turned towards me. The groom was supporting himself against the wall of the corridor and I observed that he was bleeding profusely from a deep gash in his throat. The other man was armed with a sword and when I came out was trying to draw it across the throat of the groom. I endeavoured to separate them. The man with the sword then attacked me violently and inflicted several wounds on my head. Being more powerful than myself, I was unable either to throw or disarm him. The groom appeared too weak to offer me any assistance. Mrs Everett came out to see what was the matter. I called to her to bring my revolver which was hanging loaded by the bedside. Her first impulse was to join in the conflict, but after a minute or two she went for the pistol. Just as she was bringing it to me I managed to throw the man and we fell together. By this time I had received, in addition to a wound on the shoulder and cuts on the hands, six severe wounds on the head and face, my left ear being nearly cut off.

Mrs Everett then handed me the revolver but, the man begging for mercy, I did not discharge it at him. I relaxed my hold of him and he made a cut at my right hand, knocking the pistol out of it, cutting off the top of my forefinger and the whole of the flesh from the left side of the hand and nearly severing the thumb. I was getting very weak and Mrs Everett and I retreated into the bedroom.

We interrupt the story at this point to add a few lines written by Everett's granddaughter in 1983, over one hundred years after the attack which was embedded deep in family history:

It was still winter when this attack occurred and deep snow. My poor grandmother walked out in bare feet to call the Turkish guard. She had tried to ward off the attack with her bare hands and kept saying to her husband 'Will, use your sword' but he said 'No, I can only use that on active service.' That was apparently the rule in those days. Perhaps it still is?

To return to Colonel Everett:

I decided to get a second pistol which I kept in my study. I was determined to shoot the man if I found him. On reaching the end of the corridor where the light was very uncertain, I saw a man on the staircase with something gleaming in his hand and I fired at him. As he did not fall, I was preparing to fire again when my pistol jammed, and I returned to the light to clear it. I came back to the corridor and now saw the man clearly. I again fired, but the pistol appeared to have turned in my hand which was bleeding profusely as I pulled the trigger. A sharp knock in my leg showed me that I had shot myself, as I could not stand, and the bone of my leg was broken. In the meantime Mrs Everett had warned the guard but by the time they got to the consulate the man had decamped. He was shortly afterwards captured.

My recovery was slow and it was not until October 1886, a year and a half later, that I was able to walk without the aid of a stick and then only for very short distances.

The assailant was discovered to be an Armenian, one Mesrob, but the real motive for the attack was not made clear. At the trial he was convicted of illegally wounding with intent to kill, but the charge of intruded robbery failed for want of proof. The Everett family had its own colourful theory that 'grandfather had discovered a Russian plot and that the Russian Consulate had hired the Armenian to kill him.' The court sentenced Mesrob to fifteen years penal servitude.

Justice was done to the criminal. Was justice done to the victim? Colonel Everett had to leave the Consular Service and became Professor of Military Topography at Sandhurst. But having fought off his attacker, he had to wage a far greater struggle against the British bureaucracy to obtain compensation. It all began in December 1887 and finished in July 1892. The following letters (only a selection) sent by and to Everett give a revealing picture of Victorian bureaucracy at the top:

Everett to Lord Salisbury (Foreign Secretary)   29.12.87
My Lord,
In having the honour to place in your hands my resignation of the post of Consul for Kurdistan, I would respectfully beg to be allowed to make to your Lordship some observations having reference to the consequences of the attack which was made upon me at Erzerum in April 1885.

The injury I suffered is, in any line of life, a great inconvenience, but in my profession it amounts to a calamity and will preclude any promotion to the higher ranks of the army.

The pecuniary losses that I have incurred are also great. I address these few words to you with the request that if it be possible some compensation may be made me for the injuries which I have received while in the service of the Foreign Office.
I have etc.
William Everett, Lt. Colonel

War Office to Under-secretary of State for Foreign Affairs   19.1.88
Sir,
I am directed to acknowledge the receipt of your letter of the 5th instant, forwarding copy of a letter from Lieut-Colonel Everett, in which he submits for consideration his claim to compensation . . .

Under the circumstances it appears that Everett may expect to be treated by the Foreign Office not less liberally than if he had been wounded in action . . . Mr Secretary Stanhope (of the War Office) would suggest that the Lieutenant-Colonel's rate of Wounds Pension, viz: £300 a year, might be allowed.
I have, etc.
W.St John Broderick

To Foreign Office   Treasury Chambers
                                                    21 February 1888

Sir,

I have laid before the Lords Commissioners of H.M. Treasury Colonel
Everett's claim to compensation . . . it would appear that the attack on
Colonel Everett was devised for the sole purpose of robbery, and that the
injuries cannot be regarded as specifically attributable to the nature of his
official duties.

In these circumstances My Lords regret that they cannot award any
compassionate allowance.

Lord Salisbury asked Everett for his comments on this rejection and
he replied that he was sure that the attack was on his life and that the
Turkish court had deliberately made no effort to obtain a confession
from Mesrob. In fact the Turkish judge had said 'We could have
found out the motive if we had wished, but *we did not wish*, and
dropped the examination as soon as the man had acknowledged he
was the assailant.'

To Foreign Office   Treasury Chambers
                                                    5 July 1888

Sir,

My Lords have carefully considered the additional statements now
submitted by Colonel Everett and they regret that they are still unable to
regard the injury inflicted as one which would justify the grant of a
compassionate allowance.

Lord Salisbury must be aware of the extreme jealousy shown by the
House of Commons with regard to the increase of the non-effective Votes.
In view of that My Lords are bound to watch all such claims with peculiar
strictness.

A friend of the Everetts then brought Henry Campbell-Bannerman
into play. He thought the Treasury response 'not very consistent or
convincing' and the reference to the Commons 'particularly absurd'.
He advised Everett to approach personally a high official in the
Foreign Office, Mr Goschen, rather than petition parliament. Everett
jumped at this advice and wrote to an acquaintance of his wife,
Sir Michael Biddulph, Groom-in-Waiting to the Queen, asking for
his mediation:

                                                    Windsor Castle
                                                    3rd March 1889

My Dear Colonel Everett,

Any help I can give must be purely private. I think you should write me

such a letter as I can forward, you naming the person or leaving it to me . . . I think you must have some very strong argument to move them.
Yours truly
M.A. Biddulph

Sir Michael was as good as his word and passed the matter on to Sir Edward Hamley, an MP:

> Palace Chambers
> 5 June 1889

My dear Everett,
I spoke to Mr Goschen about your affair some days ago and impressed on him that it was not a case to be lightly set aside. He received what I had to say in a cordial spirit and promised to give fresh consideration to the matter.
Yours sincerely
Edward Hamley

> House of Commons
> 25 June 1889

My dear Everett,
I have just touched up Mr Goschen again . . . He promised to read the case in a favourable light.
Yours sincerely
Edward Hamley

Mr Goschen kept his promise and in August 1899 Everett heard that the Treasury was now 'prepared to reconsider their former decision and to accept the view that the attack was probably not merely for purposes of robbery'. Things went from good to better and on 25 September Everett was sent by the Foreign Office a superannuation form to complete for referral to the Treasury. Nearly five months had passed when Hamley wrote again:

> Athenaeum Club, Pall Mall
> 14 February 1890

My dear Everett,
I grieve to say that matters have assumed a new aspect. The War Office tells the Treasury, that when you were Consul, your time was still counting at the W.O. towards *pension*! – and that, therefore, you could not be considered as in the Civil Service – and being only in temporary pay of the Foreign Office giving no claim to Civil Pension, they have no ground on which to award you compensation for the injuries.

On the other hand the W.O. says *it* has no power to award compensation for any wounds except those received in action.

In the face of this bureaucratic impasse Hamley suggested that Everett should beard the lion and go to the Treasury to explain the impossibility of his situation. He replied bravely that 'The news contained in your letter of the 14th are certainly disheartening but nevertheless I do not yet despair.'

Everett went in March to see a Treasury official and with Hamley's and Goschen's help things seemed to get moving again. Hamley told him on 23 April that the War Office 'had taken the responsibility of recommending you as an officer in military employ'. Hamley's pressure had its effect and finally in June 1890 Everett heard that 'the Treasury had assented to my receiving a pension of £150 a year on the responsibility of the Secretary of State for War.' In July this was confirmed officially with arrears to 1888 and everyone breathed a sigh of relief that justice had been done. However, more was to come:

Army and Navy Gazette

11 April 1891

Report on Lieutenant-Colonel Everett
The Auditor-General reports I deem it my duty to report the correctness of the charge upon Army funds (of the Everett pension) has not been established.

War Office
23 September 1891
Dear Colonel Everett,
I am so sorry to say that the War Office has no alternative but to stop any further issues (of your pension) in consequence of the decision of the Public Accounts Committee, pending Treasury instructions. These instructions owing to the Parliamentary recess and the absence of the Chancellor of the Exchequer have not been forthcoming and are not likely to be, I fear, for some time.
Yours very truly
H.D. De la Bère

War Office
31 March 1892
Sir,
I am directed to inform you that no further grant of pension can be made to you, in consequence of the decision of the Public Accounts Committee. I am, however, to say to you that your case has been specially considered by the Lords Commissioners of H.M. Treasury in conjunction with this office and the Foreign Office, and that their Lordships propose to grant the

further sum of £1500 in full compensation for the injuries.
I have the honour to be,
Sir,
Your obedient Servant
H.W. Cave

Foreign Office
5 May 1892

Dear Colonel Everett,
We have just heard from the Treasury that the question of compensation is
at last settled.
Yours truly
H. Percy Anderson

War Office
24 May 1892

Dear Colonel Everett,
I have written to the Foreign Office about your question. Looking at the
progress of business in the House I should rather doubt whether the vote
could be taken this side of Whitsuntide. I am only sorry that the good
intentions of the War Office have been frustrated.
Yours very truly
H.D. De le Bère

16 Charing Cross
2 July 1892

Messrs Cox & Co. present their compliments to Colonel Everett and beg to
acknowledge the receipt of a remittance amounting to £1500.

War Office
4 July 1892

Dear Colonel Everett,
I can assure you that it has been a real pleasure to me to contribute in my
humble way to the overthrow of technicalities which stood in the way of a
course which I think was universally admitted to be just and right.
Believe me
Yours very truly
H.D. De la Bère

Exile in Diarbekir 1906

To the south of Erzerum in Turkey and nearer to Syria lies the
smallish town of Diarbekir. The British felt the need for a consul

there too and in 1906 Richard Graves, brother of poet Robert, was sent on a temporary posting. It was remote and unattractive and it is difficult to see now why a British consul was needed at all. Graves went with great misgivings:

I was in Salonica when I learned that I was to relieve Shipley in Diarbekir for the winter. I did not look forward to the prospect of solitary confinement in a dreary distant fortress on the banks of the Tigris, notorious for the prevalence of a corrosive sort of boil, known as the Aleppo button or the Baghdad date.

It took the best part of twenty-four hours to reach Aleppo. The Shipleys had not yet arrived so I had to possess my soul in patience. At that time the British Consul in Aleppo was Henry Zohrab Longworth, a burly, bearded man with a stentorian voice and a life-long experience of the Levant. He obviously sought to pass as a typical bluff Englishman. One of his predecessors had been a certain Henderson, an efficient and good looking man, who after occupying the post for several years grew an 'Aleppo button' on his face which left a deep scar, greatly marring his beauty. His disfigurement got on his nerves and he grew to hate Aleppo and all its works. He applied in vain for a transfer and finally after a desperate and unsuccessful personal appeal to the Under-Secretary of State when on leave, he blew out his brains in a corridor of the Foreign Office. While this horrid boil was doubtless the basic cause of poor Henderson's suicide, I can well imagine that long residence in that evil-looking place was in itself enough to reduce a civilised man to the lowest depths of pessimism.

At last Shipley arrived with his wife, who had driven in a flat two horsed vehicle called a fourgon. He had with him two horses, a groom and the usual escort of two mounted policemen. I bought the two horses, a bay and a black. He was glad to be leaving Diarbekir of which he had little good to say. He gave me the dope about my new post, though this did not amount to much and commended the consular dragoman, the Rev. Thomas Effendi Meguerditchian, to my good graces adding that any curiosities of English which Thomas Effendi allowed himself were not to be ascribed to him, but to Wilkie Young, a former occupant of the post who had encouraged him to employ various amusing distortions, such as watercloset (with a long O) for raincoat.

After several days riding Graves arrived at the black walled city of Diarbekir:

The aspect of the town from outside was grim and forbidding, nor was the interior more attractive, though I was agreeably surprised to find that the consulate was a fair-sized house with a reasonable supply of furniture and a large courtyard. I was soon to learn that it was said of Diarbekir: 'Its stones are black, its dogs are black and the hearts of the people are black.' The surrounding country was bleak, stony and unattractive except for the wooded slopes running down to the Tigris below the city.

It was in these areas that some of the infamous Armenian massacres had taken place in the nineteenth century and not surprisingly any Armenians still left were exceedingly wary. Graves continues:

My dragoman, the Rev. Thomas was a charming, considerate person of about forty, who spoke English fluently with his endearing mistakes. As an Armenian who had lived through more than one pogram, he kept his ear close to the ground and was always ready to report rumours of anti-Armenian tendencies. He confirmed that though there were no British subjects in the district the presence of a British consular officer was in itself a good safeguard against the persecution of the Armenians. It was pleasant to feel that one was passively protecting the security of an ill-used race, but I confess I should have been happier if this role would have been combined with a routine of positive duties.

An extract from a letter from Graves to his stepmother portrays the emptiness of his days, largely sleeping at HMG's expense:

30 December 1906

Here I manage to pass the time pretty well, though of course I have too much of my own society. To obviate this I spend a great deal of time asleep – not, of course, during the day time. My general programme is 12.15 midnight to bed. 9.30–10.00 a.m. get up. Breakfast of coffee, porridge and bread and jam. No butter to be had for love or money and eggs at present all bad. After breakfast my dragoman comes and tells me the news, which usually does not amount to much and I am active or passive according. Then, most days, an hour and a half at law or Turkish history until lunch at 1.30. Afterwards either a ride, a walk or a shoot. There are a lot of woodcock in the plantations around the town and it's great fun stalking them. After that tea and, three days a week, a Turkish lesson lasting two hours. Then dinner about 8 and three hours miscellaneous reading or letter-writing before going to bed.

Graves spent four months in Diarbekir until he was finally released without having caught the dreaded boil:

The French say, or used to say, *il s'écoute* of a man, who is always thinking he has some disease and I must say I worried a good deal about the button, whose ravages among the Diarbekirlis I knew were painfully evident. Thomas Effendi had had one, but the scar lay hidden in a fold of his beard.

The small lump caused by a mosquito bite put me in a flutter until, an hour after I had noticed it I perceived it was no longer there.

Arabia 1917: Philby and his friend beyond price

Westward from Persia we reach the vast desert peninsula of Arabia whose harsh and arid conditions mesmerized many a Briton, both traveller and resident. It attracted a certain kind of independent adventurous man – Lawrence, Philby, Doughty, Glubb Pasha, Burton. Several spent most of their lives there and all published detailed accounts. The close British political connection began during the First World War when Lawrence became intimately involved in the Arab revolt against the Turks in western Arabia. Further north in Mesopotamia the British were desperately fighting the Turkish armies and being pinned down in the famous siege of Kut el Amara.

The greatest eccentric of all, Harry St John Philby, had come from Indian service and was sent on a mission to Najd in central Arabia to seek the support of the future ruler of Saudi Arabia – Abdul Aziz Ibn Saud. He was so fascinated by the man and the country that he spent the rest of his life there. A short extract from his voluminous writings gives the flavour of their meeting in the days when Riyadh was little more than a mud brick village:

30 November 1917

At the top of the ridge we halted to enjoy the view of Riyadh – scarcely impressive. Three horsemen rode up and after exchange of greetings we all remounted and proceeded down the slope to Riyadh. It being Friday and all the world being at prayer we sat down by the wayside until such time as the Ruler of Najd would be at liberty to receive us. We waited for close on two hours eating dates and exchanging news with Hamilton [Colonel R.E.A. Hamilton, British political agent in Kuwait], who in his beard and Arab kit looks the picture of a Bedouin. In due course there was a stir announcing the end of the Friday prayers and of our wait and so we remounted and trotted on between walled gardens to the city walls and through the street to the palace where there was a tremendous concourse of Arabs. We entered the palace gate and were conducted through waiting crowds up labyrinthine stairs and passages into a large room where we were introduced to Abdul Rahman, the father of the reigning Ibn Saud.

We had almost taken our seats when by signs we were made aware of the presence of a stately figure at the other side of the room, Abdul Aziz himself, to whom we were introduced. He then returned to his seat while we gathered round his father in the seats of honour.

Philby was to pass several days in Riyadh lodged with Abdul Aziz:

Our apartments are in the palace itself and apparently form part of the women's quarters to judge by the sound of female and children's voices on the other side of a door. The rooms are on the first floor up a flight of steps leading up from a small courtyard which adjoins the pillared courtyard of the main palace building. The walls are of white polished plaster, the rooms simple, furnished with mats and carpets, a few comfortable and less comfortable chairs and one or two lampstands but no table.

The only other parts of the palace which I have visited are the main courtyard generally filled with a concourse of motley people of dour sour appearance and silent as statues, and the rooms where audiences take place, very comfortably furnished and always redolent with the scent of incense, a clock sounding Big Ben chimes and a door leading direct to Ibn Saud's private apartments.

These are occupied by his favourite wife, the other wives residing in apartments in other parts of the palace. All wives who bear children whether subsequently cast off or not are provided with houses to themselves, barren women being handed to other husbands. Ibn Saud is said to have got through some 80 wives in his time. When in camp he sends out people to choose him some pretty girl, whom he marries for the time being, returning her to her parents in due course.

Philby's mission was to get to know Ibn Saud and to report back on him and on his attitudes to the British government. The two men forged a bond of friendship and Philby loved talking to the King. This enjoyment was evident from the beginning:

During these interviews we have discussed many subjects besides the main business of the mission – religion, history, the ways of the Bedouin of Najd and his views of the future development of the country, European politics and methods.

Philby left, enchanted with his host and tried his best to keep Ibn Saud as an ally of the British – but rather sadly, as he wrote: 'My life a lonely and depressing one made endurable only by the steady friendship of Ibn Saud itself.'

Philby did return to Arabia and settled there, running a business importing Ford cars and exploring the desert. His friendship with the King lasted until the latter's death in 1953.

Harold Dickson, Arabist 1918

Whether they wanted it or not, the British became involved in administering the areas from which they expelled the Turks – Mesopotamia/Iraq, Jordan and of course Palestine. Arabia itself they left mostly to the Arabs. Harold Dickson is a prime example of a British 'Arabist' – one of those many devoted Britons who gave their life to the Arab world. He is remembered for his detailed and meticulous work on the Arabs of Kuwait. He immersed himself in their life and his books are standard on the topic. In addition he helped to establish the oil industry in Kuwait.

He had first gone to the area as a soldier and straightaway felt at home. His appointment was as district officer in Nasriyeh, a small town in a tribal area in southern Iraq. He described his life and feelings in letters to his mother:

Nasriyeh, 6 April 1918

My darling Mother,

I am glad to say I have quite recovered from my Baghdad boils; I have got eleven fine scars now which I expect I shall bear for life, a nice little remembrance of Mesopotamia. When I think of the time I went through I shall never I believe forget them. You see I elected to go on working all the time I had them on me, a period of two months.

Since I last wrote I have accomplished the ambition of my heart. I have been to Shatra and all over the wild district of the river Gharraf where hitherto no British officer has been. You know this had been my ambition for a long time don't you?

Well by dint of worrying I eventually received GHQ's permission to proceed at my own risk and with my own Arab escort. You bet I was off like a shot. I received my permission to go in the evening and before sun was up next day I was in the saddle and away. The country I went through was quite unknown and as wild as could be. None of the Arabs had ever seen an Englishman and their curiosity and that of the women especially was strange to behold. My escort consisted of 70 mounted men of the corps I am raising, these were all Arabs taken from the wildest tribes I can find, the wilder the better. They are a great crowd and I am already in love with my lambs.

Outside Shatra we were met by Khayun al Obeid – he is the famous sheik and outlaw of that part of the world, a rogue of course of the deepest dyed villains but I must say I did not expect him to give me the welcome he did. For four days and nights he feasted me and my little force, and it was with regret that I left again on the fifth day.

After forty miles riding I came to Abdulla Ibn Faleh Pasha's camp. He is paramount sheik of all the Muntafik tribes. He is a wonderful personage. I got a rare insight into the true Bedouin aristocrat's camp manners and customs. He gave me a private tent and entertained me for two days and nights. I couldn't have received a nicer or more gentlemanly reception in the west end of London. Our food was mostly rice, sheep, sweetmeats and camel milk. This latter was delicious and morning noon and night at any time one was brought a bowl of fresh milk.

13 May 1918

The hot weather is now on us in earnest at last. Things are stoking up daily but we shall all find the heat more bearable as electric fans have been issued out everywhere to us. That is in the more settled towns. Nasriyeh has got them as has also my house. Since last writing I have been away into the wilds for 15 days. Exploring again into country hitherto unvisited by British officials.

I took no tents or food but simply lived on the hospitality of the Arabs. Their hospitality is truly wonderful. Except in one or two odd spots they couldn't do enough for us. It was a series of feasts by day and night. Privacy on these occasions is what one misses as wherever one goes in camp you have some prying eyes on you, usually those of a fair damzel or so.

1 September 1918

I am posted to Kowait as Political Agent. Orders further say that there is a probability of my being sent to relieve Captain Philby in Najd, central Arabia after the situation in Koweit is put on a proper basis. Affairs in central Arabia are in an upset and your young son Harold R.P. is probably going to have to try and put them aright. The possibilities of the show are great, mother, and the field of Arabic still greater and from all accounts it is a great step upwards for me. In spite of all I am dreading the move. I love my Muntafik tribes and their bad ways and to you I will say it, though I dare not to anyone else – 'I am the only white man who at the present can manage the Muntafik.' Do you think me horribly self-opinionated and conceited mother? I have got a wonderful hold of these fellows, and I fear as soon as I go they will begin to cause trouble. I have to leave the Muntafik and Nasriyeh which I have regenerated and rendered a decent country from a howling wilderness of Anarchy.

Now I must close. This time next year I expect you will find me at Hail in central Arabia, leading a revolution and marrying the Amir of Najd's daughter!! Shades of Burton and Doughty.
Ever your loving son
Harold

Dickson in Bahrain 1919

Dickson moved first to Bahrain where his official title was consul and political agent, Bahrain islands and the mainland. Bahrain had had treaty relations with Britain for some 100 years and the ruler took British advice in foreign and defence matters. It was the kind of treaty by which Britain controlled the affairs of most of the Gulf countries – an unofficial empire:

Bahrain, Persian Gulf, 22.11.19

The islands of Bahrain are sweetly pretty, the towns are vilely dirty, the shaikh and his sons are magnificent creatures and dress in much gold etc. etc., and I think I shall get on well with them.

My house is a beautiful one though rather old and the furniture is first rate – all government stuff including every single thing I want. I am now happily settled in and though I feel lonely and regretful at leaving the Muntafik, I am looking forward to what the future will bring me. I have my three horses, two government animals, plenty of servants, a guard of 20 Indian Infantrymen.

In Bahrain there is only one other white man in business – while a little way off there live an American missionary doctor, his wife and two lady helps. So the total white population is two men and three ladies.

I have a motor launch and sailing boat and a ship visits Bahrain every 14 days – we have no telegraph line but a special wireless has been erected for the Political Agent's use.

18.12.19

I wish to send you and all dear friends and relations my very best wishes for Xmas and New Year. Pray drink my health all of you and think of the lonely member of the family all by himself in Bahrain, or as I hope by the time this reaches you some way on the mainland. Myself I shall spend my Xmas visiting the centre of Bahrain Islands in company with three Arab Shaikhs. I have planned a five days tour with them. I shall live and eat with them à la Arab.

Early in spring I hope to visit Ibn Saud himself in Hassa, that is three days journey by camel into the interior – about 100 miles inland. He has asked me to go and meet him in the spring. Personally I am hoping to be able to return with him to Nejd. It would be the greatest joy of my heart if I would go and live in the heart of Nejd for a good long time.

At present I am settling down rapidly in these islands of Bahrain. I wish you could see my house. It is such a nice place and quite wasted on a bachelor. A lovely drawing room, dining room and three beautifully furnished bedrooms upstairs not to speak of bathrooms, pantries etc. Though at the end of the world, I have been done well by a benign government.

The following year Dickson achieved his heart's wish of meeting the great Ibn Saud but he did not stay in Nejd. He returned for some time to Iraq and then from 1929 until his death in 1959 he devoted his life to the service of Kuwait. He died at 'home' in Kuwait where he was greatly missed, and his widow, Violet, stayed on to a great age. Each morning as the ruler of the state passed her house in his car he would salute her.

With Young in Jidda 1916

On the other coast of Arabia lay Jidda, home of the Hashemite family who were the allies of Britain during the First World War and who led the Arab revolt (together with Lawrence) against the Turks. The head of the family was Sherif Husain, an awkward, ambitious and devious man little liked by the British. When the Turks were expelled from Jidda the Hashemites set up government there and Britain immediately sent a resident, Colonel Wilson, as their link with Husain. The ubiquitous John Young was appointed his assistant. Life in Jidda was not easy in those days:

I left Cairo seated with the armed guard in a special carriage at the end of the train reserved for the monthly instalment of gold for Jidda (a British gift to Husain to keep him in the war), and which was packed in fourteen wooden iron bound boxes. At Jidda I reported to Colonel Wilson whom I found in shirt sleeves deciphering code telegrams on board the cruiser H.M.S. *Fox*. The damp hot climate of the Red Sea was certainly a great change from the dry heat of Egypt. In after years by comparison with the hothouse warmth of Jidda, I used to find the burning dry wind of Upper Egypt positively bracing.

It was not till a few days after my arrival that the British Consulate could be made ready for our accommodation, and we finally left our hospitable hosts in '*Fox*' to take up our quarters on shore. The walled town of Jidda lying upon the shallow lagoon could only be reached by boats of light draft and, as the launch which carried us approached over the sunken coral reefs, the many storeyed houses with their wooden latticed windows shining golden brown in the hot morning sunlight rose in an irregular silhouette above the small jetty, while here and there a white minaret stood out against a cruel cloudless sky. We landed to find the streets, narrow and crooked, covered with a final coral dust of ages in which the feet sank and made no sound. Filth was everywhere, and now and then the splash of slops could be heard, thrown down from overhanging eaves on the just and the unjust alike. We walked through the bazaar where this mixed race the Jidda people were buying and selling. They all seemed silent like their footsteps, tired and ill – a marked contrast to the noisy robust and healthy Egyptian. Great black slabs lay about on the meat stalls which proved to be lumps of red and bloody meat when the butchers from time to time drove off the flies, and mangy scavenger dogs fought viciously for scraps. There was something about this town which hung heavy on the soul.

We all felt it. Subsequent visitors to Jidda felt it too. They were delighted with it at first. On the second day they anxiously enquired about the next ship and for the rest of the visit they counted the days till their departure.

We emerged from the heavy atmosphere of the bazaar through more silent lanes until we entered the residential quarter near the Medina gate, a quarter comprising the houses of the richer Jidda merchants and the Consulates of Great Britain, Italy and France. The British Consulate which was to be our home, a typical Jidda house built of rough coral covered with plaster, rose some four storeys above the entrance door with large airy rooms, their bay windows generously overhanging the main street and the narrow alleys on either side, the windows unglazed but filled with latticed *mushrabia* (criss-cross open woodwork) and the window recess wide enough to hold a bed. A well proportioned and beautiful house, but almost commonplace when compared with the many other noble examples of Jidda domestic architecture, houses with two leaved elaborately carved thick teak doors with heavy iron hinges and fine wrought-iron ring knockers; houses with protruding windows rising tier upon tier to the fifth storey forming almost a continuous facade of *mushrabia* unlike any in Egypt and strangely reminiscent of something farther east. In this complete self-contained walled town of Jidda, the magnificent houses were its chief feature together with the city gates.

Outside the gates the bare desert stretched to Mecca broken only near the Medina gate by two or three small detached buildings, the town condenser, Jidda's only water supply and the Military Barracks with its hospital. And here a line of trenches marked the last stand of 1,500 Turkish soldiers until they surrendered in June to the Arabs after enduring ten days gun-fire from British warships. But nearer the lagoon there was one other remarkable building outside the wall: the long, low, white, barrel roofed structure terminating in a dome, the resort of superstitious pilgrims, Eve's tomb: the resting place of the Mother of the World.

As the Turks were being relentlessly driven out of the Arabian peninsula numbers of their soldiers were captured and brought back to Jidda. Young remembers one group:

A week later prisoners began to arrive in Jidda and 800 of them were immediately shipped to Suez including Ghalib Pasha, the Turkish governor of the Hejaz who was overcome with joy when he heard he was going to Cairo, for the Arabs had told him he was to be sent to a dungeon at Suakin. Of the prisoners who remained in Jidda the men were placed in the old hospital attached to the barracks outside the walls, while the Officers and

their families occupied a large house inside the town. The Director-General
of Public Security, who was always concerned with other people's business
and indeed with every business except the security of Jidda, complained to
me that he thought the prisoners were starving. Suleiman Qabil, he said,
took nearly all their rations for himself leaving each prisoner with only a
small dish of rice sufficient to last for 24 hours while all their possessions of
any value had been looted. 'And,' he added with a sickly smile, 'I feel very
unhappy about the hundred and forty Turkish Officers and their wives who
are now all living together in one house, so terribly crowded together and
confined. I cannot help fearing that many grave mistakes must sometimes
take place in the obscurity.'

A French Military and Civil Mission under Colonel Brémond was
expected at Jidda in the third week of September and preparations were
made for their reception. The Sherif gave orders that the mission were to be
entertained to dinner on the first night by Muhammad Nassif in his house,
and on the second night by Suleiman Qabil at the Municipality. Thirty
guests were to be present on each occasion.

The date of the arrival was fixed for the 19th but the warship *Destries* was
delayed at sea and the dinners were postponed. Suleiman Qabil became very
anxious. He told us he had already spent large sums on the food and he was
afraid it would not keep. Late in the evening of the 20th *Destries* was
sighted, but it was too late for the Mission to land and the dinners, which
were postponed again, were now arranged for the 21st and 22nd. Suleiman
Qabil grew still more anxious. Once or twice he telephoned to Mecca for
instructions and each time received no reply. But now indeed had come a
reply. The Sherif had commanded him to prepare for no less than eighty
guests and possibly many more. The hospitality was to be in the finest style.
No expense was to be spared and the command ended with the sinister
remark that his future depended upon the success of the entertainment. The
poor man at once sent us a verbal message begging our assistance in
crockery, silver, servants; in anything possible. He apologised for not
writing, but his hand shook so much he was unable to hold a pen.

The first dinner took place in Muhammad Nassif's house the next
evening. Except for the French Officers who were in uniform, ourselves and
the Italian and Dutch Consuls, who had by this time returned to Jidda, all
the eighty guests were in many-coloured oriental dress and presented a gay
spectacle. After what seemed hours of waiting we sat down at last at two
long tables. Though the spectacle was gay the dinner was depressing in the
extreme, interminably drawn out and badly served. The room was lit by
candles in large chandeliers hanging from the ceiling, covered with flies
which from time to time flew drowsily round the guests and fell onto the
food. The Postmaster General, turbanned and corpulent, who sat opposite
me, gobbled without speaking. An intelligent pale Algerian who talked
fluent French remarked: 'La chaleur est tout à fait insupportable.' A dark

skinned native of Senegal, overcome by shyness, remained silent, swallowing food and flies together. At length the dismal costly meal drew to a close, a meal which would have broken the heart of any London hostess, and we departed.

On the following evening we attended Suleiman Qabil's dinner. Exactly the same party of eighty guests met at sunset and nearly two hours later we sat down to an equally protracted and tedious repast. This time, however, the tables were laid on the roof of the Municipal Buildings and the whole place looked quite smart, spread out with borrowed rugs and decorated with French, British and Sherifian flags. To give an appearance of coolness to the still and stifling air a large block of ice had been placed on a table in the middle of the roof, regardless of the damage done by the dripping water on the rugs below. Suleiman Qabil appeared radiantly happy in spite of the heavy expenditure involved. He seemed to think that his future was secured but Sherif Muhsen, who sat in a conspicuous position, refused all dishes. It was rumoured that he suspected poison. On the completion of the dinner, as with feelings of immense relief we moved to the other side of a temporary screen, the swarm of servants made an attack on the remaining food and the block of ice fell down with a loud crash.

Hope-Gill in Jidda 1930–33

In 1925 King Abdul Aziz Ibn Saud of the Saudis finally expelled the Hashemites from Jidda and established the Kingdom of Saudi Arabia. Sherif Husain was abandoned by the British as a weak vessel and he ended his days bitterly in exile. The British were quick to recognize the new rulers and established a legation in Jidda. Sir Andrew Ryan of the Levant Consular Service was head of mission there in 1931 when Cecil Hope-Gill was sent to join him as vice-consul:

Lawrence of Arabia had entered by sea. As I stood on deck as we dropped anchor outside the coral reefs I could say in the opening words of his *Revolt in the Desert*: 'The heat of Arabia came out like a drawn sword and struck us speechless.' The heat in the town when I landed on the June day was 110 degrees F in the shade with 90% humidity, not the dry heat of the desert all round. One wore only a hat, a South Sea Islands cotton shirt, cotton duck trousers and white canvas shoes. The Ryans lived in a ramshackle old Turkish building of three floors and a flat roof. They very kindly housed me there all the time I was in Jidda, and I paid for my messing with them, a great boon for a bachelor. All the houses of Jidda were built of 'Coral Rag', great blocks of it hewn from the Red Sea reefs. All the woodwork was fashioned and carved by hand out of teak from India, and had weathered grey and ageless, covered with dust. There was no glass; just creaking shutters on native hinges, all dust-laden. It was all very primitive for a Legation Residence.

The Ryans gave me a top room leading on to a flat roof on which I could lie naked at night on my canvas camp bed under the stars. For baths, we only had those shallow circular contraptions with a side-spout. Before changing yet again into something fresh, one could sponge down in Condenser Water, try to dry and be all sweaty again at once. I often used to wonder what it would feel like to have a dry skin instead of hands that slid wetly over each other.

Before dinner in the evening we indulged in just one cocktail. We had a different one every night from a long list to ensure variety. It was about our only foible in the austere atmosphere, for we were accredited as diplomats to the world's austerest monarch, Ibn Saud, King of ultra-Puritan Saudi Arabia, where alcohol was anathema, and diplomats by ancient privilege could import it for personal use only. Entertaining our friends was of course a personal matter, so we were very popular with our less fortunate European commercial colleages. Ruth Ryan was our Hostess-in-Chief and kept the cocktail roster.

The floors of all our buildings were of sand and lime laid upon planks supported by palm-tree trunks. They were ageless but not eternal. No sooner had Andrew and Ruth gone off to their Summer leave after I arrived, than half the roof of the four-storey Chancery building collapsed and took with it to the ground all the intervening floors. By a miracle, no-one was even injured. I had just called in the archivist from the next room and he was standing in front of me at my desk, when the rest of my room and all of his disappeared downward behind him in a cloud of dust, leaving a smoking chasm. The negro motor-boy who was tending the lighting plant on the ground floor emerged a very scared nigger, as white as plaster, only his rolling eyeballs showing. He had side-stepped just in time.

The British in Arabia tried to take their sports with them. Sailing and swimming in the Red Sea were a delight; cricket could not be played on the stoney desert, golf was just about possible:

In Jidda, we whites among the browns – a couple of dozen or so including the staffs of our Legation, the French and the Dutch Ministers and the Netherlands Bank – took our exercise in the relative cool of the evenings. Our predecessor 'Billy' Bond had started a golf club which used the dried white thigh-bones of camels as 'flags' at the holes, flower pots for the holes themselves sunk in circular 'Greens' or rathers browns and made by spreading used engine oil on the sand. We teed up on dried-out camel droppings, just the thing. We swam and fished in the tepid water, and used a flat-bottomed punt affair with a glass bottom let into it, which allowed us to admire at our ease and under an awning the gloriously coloured corals and seaweeds and tropical fish of the Red Sea.

I myself had been given an Arab stallion by Prince Faisal, so I was able to ride out into the surrounding desert with John Gilpin [his dog] at heel. He and I, with a couple of loaned Salukis, would make for the small patches of desert scrub. There John Gilpin would work in busily, eyes shut, nose to the ground, while the two Salukis would stalk around, heads up, all eyes, until a gazelle would break from cover and flit away across the desert, in graceful bounds hardly seeming to touch the ground, and displaying its upturned white scut. The Salukis would give immediate chase, but never caught up. Gilpin, however, his mind in his nose, saw nothing until he heard my 'Gone away'. Then he would set out after them like a railway engine, throwing up clouds of dust behind him with his great paws, pounding after the others. The Salukis would soon tire and lie down, but Gilpin ploughed on, and I galloped after him. In the end he would lose sight of the quarry, give up and come back to heel, panting a bit. Dalmations have big barrels for their lungs. But we never caught anything.

I was sorry to leave Jidda in the end and so good a Chief. It had been a good experience climatically. Never again, wherever I might be sent in my career should I have to live in a worse climate. So, sorry to leave but looking forward to our next post, Gilpin and I left Jidda on 15 March 1933.

Besieged in Baghdad 1941

We move now to Iraq to find a situation which the British rarely encountered in the Middle East – siege. The British were in an anomalous position. They had ostensibly given Iraq independence in 1930 and yet in 1941 they were still there in some force – ruling the country as many Iraqis believed behind the façade of a pro-British government. In that year a group of Iraqi officers concluded that Britain was going to lose the war and staged a pro-Nazi coup. This was successful for a while and many British residents fled to the Embassy to seek asylum. Hope-Gill was there at the time:

At 2 a.m. word went out to all British subjects in Iraq to gather at the pre-arranged places. In Baghdad that meant bringing all women and children, with two suitcases for each family, to the Embassy. There the men, with another suitcase each, could remain, while their families went off in R.A.F. buses over the desert to Habbaniya, to be flown out to Basra, and shipped to safety in India.

I had come to the Embassy very early that morning and soon had to ring my wife with the bitter news, evacuation. I gave her four hours to pack and shut up the house, putting all the furniture into the big drawing-room, and telling our servant Fadhil to barricade the door, but not to let him or the boys out of her sight. But Fadhil kept disappearing into the garden. 'But, Memsahib, it's my tummy!' he explained shamefacedly. It was a cruel time for her going through our possessions and trying to decide what to save and what to lose.

Then in the early afternoon came the parting. It was a horrible leave-taking. We bade each other a hurried farewell. One hundred and thirty-two women and ninety-nine children crowded into two big R.A.F. buses; they were driven off out into the desert to Habbaniya. We men besieged in the Embassy, together with a few who had made their way into its safety with wives and children after the exodus to Habbaniya, numbered three hundred and sixty-six in all. We 'guests' of the Ambassador and his wife were faced with household plumbing, for ten! Our first concern was to dig latrines and waste-water sumps in the grounds for the men and to make indoor arrangements for the women and children left behind.

My Public Relations department was transformed now into a Morale and Amusements Committee, to keep our enforced inmates happy. It was soon reinforced by the late arrival in our midst of Freya Stark, the famous Middle Eastern traveller and writer. She had been in Persia and hurried back to rejoin us. With her fluent local Arabic and her aplomb and bonhomie, she became our most useful contact at our gates with the Iraqi police posted there, and helped us to buy fresh meat and vegetables to leaven our Spartan fare.

It was terribly hot. The register rose from 95 degrees to 114 degrees F in the shade. The beer began to have to be strictly rationed, like everything else, as our siege progressed. We men stripped to the buff but for our shorts. The women were naturally more modest, but I recall that I deservedly incurred Freya's wrath (which she took out on me later by leaving me out of her own account of those days which she published), when I let slip the mild observation one exceptionally hot day that I was now beginning to realize the full import of the phrase 'stark naked'.

We busied ourselves with helping to look after everybody and everything. Pastimes and entertainment had to be arranged. Dr Sinderson, twenty years in Iraq, was invaluable with his 'Pep' talks. The Arabs, meanwhile, were looting or destroying everything in his house, had he but known it. Padre Roach conducted services. Dr Miles, a New Zealander, who lost a lifetime's collection of microscope slides and specimens in his gutted house, was with us. All lost everything that they had not brought with them into the safety of the Embassy. Their homes were systematically looted, and then defiled with excrement. The mobs milled around the Embassy walls, too, day after day, shouting obscene slogans at us. The police guards and our tall walls, however, kept them at bay.

My Morale and Amusements Committee met twice daily. We smelled out any whiff of disaffection or weakening – for the strain on all with the heat and worry about wives and children was intense – and we did our best to deal with it and to keep everyone busy and useful. We also collected all available talent. We drew up programmes for every afternoon and evening. Lectures were discovered for the most unlikely subjects. All we lacked was a clown and animals for the children.

Towards the end of May our radios told us that 'Glubb's Girls', Glubb Pasha's pig-tailed Bedouin Arab Legion from Transjordan, together with a Company of the Essex Regiment were on their way across the desert to our relief. Also that the Indian Army was landing in strength at Basra, and preparing to fight its way to us up the Tigris. The Iraqi Army disintegrated. An Armistice was arranged with the British Military Command, which took effect at 4 a.m. on May 31st, just over a month since our siege had begun. At 5 a.m. two British Officers drove up alone in a jeep to the Embassy gate, ending our siege undramatically.

The old government then came back to power and maintained fairly good relations with the British until 1958 when another army coup brought in new rulers and a new era which this time the British were powerless to obstruct.

Tale-end of empire

A siege ended – an attempt to rock British power had failed. We have seen other attempts at other times, in Egypt, in Palestine, and still the British desperately hung on. The idea of empire persisted even after the Second World War in which British resources were stretched to the limit and beyond. But the imperial will to rule was challenged, collapsed and faded away. Young vigorous nationalists took over and eventually Britain's moment was past.

Empires are not wrapped up tidily. The British empire in the Middle East was no exception. The end was often bloody, as in Aden in 1967, in Palestine in 1948 or during the Suez invasion of 1956. Occasionally it was dignified and orderly, as in the Gulf states and Sudan. It was often obscured by absurd debates over bases, pacts and rights to return. It left unemployed many British men and women, sitting in their villa in Tunbridge Wells or their cottage in the Cotswolds assessing the achievements of their life's work. Despite the general untidiness, one can sense a certain ironic symmetry in the final ringing down of the curtain. The successors of the people who left those grey London nights in the nineteenth century, full of hope and expectation, returned many years later to that same London, carrying in their baggage the shattered dreams of empire.